SOCIETY AND ECONOMY IN MEXICO

Statistical Abstract of Latin America
Supplement Series
Supplement 10
James W. Wilkie, Series Editor

SOCIETY AND ECONOMY IN MEXICO

Edited by
JAMES W. WILKIE

Foreword by
Jeffrey Bortz

UCLA LATIN AMERICAN CENTER PUBLICATIONS
University of California, Los Angeles
Los Angeles, California

UCLA Latin American Center Publications
University of California
Los Angeles, California 90024

The preparation of this volume was supported by a grant from
The William and Flora Hewlett Foundation.

Library of Congress Cataloging-in-Publication Data

Society and economy in Mexico / edited by James W. Wilkie ; foreword
  by Jeffrey Bortz.
        p.   cm. — (Statistical abstract of Latin America. Supplement
  series ; suppl. 10)
   Includes bibliographical references.
   ISBN 0-87903-250-2
   1. Mexico—Economic conditions—1918-   2. Mexico—Social
conditions. I. Wilkie, James Wallace. II. Series.
HC 135.S625   1990
330.972'08—dc20   89-13205
                                                          CIP

To the coeditors of the *Statistical Abstract of Latin America,*
who have contributed greatly to the development of
the UCLA Research Project on Statistical Measurement of Change
in Latin America

Stephen Haber, 1980–83
David E. Lorey, 1986–87
Enrique Ochoa, 1987–
Adam Perkal, 1983–86
Peter L. Reich, 1977–80
Paul Turovsky, 1976–77

Eje Central, Mexico City

Photo by James W. Wilkie

Contents

Foreword

The Development of Historical Statistics on Mexico and Latin America

JEFFREY BORTZ

Thirty years ago scholars of modern Mexico tended to avoid utilizing quantitative data. While some may have lacked the necessary skills, others simply felt that the readily available sources were weak and unreliable. This led to an overabundance of political studies and biographies, and an under-representation of social and economic histories that would have required more sophisticated quantitative measurements.

During the 1960s social scientists began to look more favorably at the potential value of quantification. Through a series of seminal studies, a few pioneering scholars began to use quantitative data in new and creative ways. James W. Wilkie's *The Mexican Revolution: Federal Expenditure and Social Change*, first published in 1967, was one of the first attempts to construct new time series in order to understand long-term change in Mexico. In his pathbreaking analysis, Wilkie analyzed the ideology and performance of the Mexican Revolution by constructing statistical series that reflected government social policy. He also developed new series to measure relative regional poverty. Like others before him, Wilkie employed primarily published sources, the same ones that had often been criticized as being unreliable. Unlike previous authors, however, he did not limit himself to merely reproducing the published data. Instead, he went a step further and used internal annual reports by government ministries and archival data to generate new series on a number of important variables.

The use of a wider variety of sources does not represent the book's major methodological contribution, however. This lies in the way Wilkie constructed his series. Each year the Mexican government publishes its budget according to current categories. Wilkie classified the hundreds of categories that had been employed over the years into new categories, in this case, economic, social, or administrative spend-ing, generating completely new historical series for the years 1910 to 1963. In the Mexican translation (1978) he carried forward the data to 1976.

In a similar fashion, the Wilkie Poverty Index sorted previously published census data (and categories) into new variables designed to reflect the author's conception of poverty. The information reclassification that underlies Wilkie's series can only move in one direction, from narrower definitions to broader ones. Nonetheless, by using the data in a new way, Wilkie provided us with a different, more critical view of the Mexican Revolution.

Following the publication of *The Mexican Revolution: Federal Expenditure and Social Change*, an entirely new field of quantitative studies on modern Mexico emerged. The year 1970 was particularly important, with the appearance of Clark Reynolds's *The Mexican Economy* and Leopoldo Solís's *La economía mexicana*. In a curious way, the two books were quite similar in structure and intent. Both attempted to be the definitive statement on Mexico's economic growth. Both assembled most of the existing secondary quantitative sources, while making use of many primary sources. In their way, the two books represented a virtually new collection of quantitative studies on modern Mexico. In scope, neither has been equaled to date. Furthermore, by bringing together the available data, they opened the field to the more specific, yet in-depth, studies that were to follow.

Six years later the field saw a further advance with René Villarreal's *El desequilibrio externo de la industrialización en México (1929–1975)*. Villarreal was one of the first writers to employ an input-output model of the Mexican economy to construct new time series. He also used the model to argue for a change in economic policy, defending export substitution against the traditional import substitution model. In an interesting footnote, Mexico's 1982 economic crisis forced the government to implement an export-oriented strategy much like that proposed by Villarreal.

Villarreal's work was soon followed by Jesús Reyes Heroles González Garza's *Política macroeconómica y bienestar en México* (1983) and Juan Castaingts Teillery's *Dinero, valor y precios: un análisis estructural cuantitativo sobre México*, both of which also made extensive use of input-output models. Reyes Heroles used a rather traditional model to show that government spending in Mexico was not neutral in its distributive effects. He also employed sophisticated quantitative techniques to infer missing data from the existing data sets, something that most of the input-output authors have ignored. In this, his book owes as much to Wilkie as to Villarreal. Castaingts used his model in quite a different fashion, indicating the relevance of Marx's analysis of profits for understanding Mexico's economic evolution, at the same time pointing to the inadequacy of Marxist monetary theory.

Not all quantitative studies depended on input-output models. Enrique Hernández Laos published two innovative studies on industrial productivity in Mexico. *Evolución de la productividad de los factores en México* (1973) and *La productividad y el desarrollo industrial en México* (1985) not only increased our knowledge of productivity in Mexico, but also our capacity to use census data for new measurements. Hernández Laos developed time series on Mexican industrial productivity for the postwar period, using productivity models to go beyond the published sources.

In addition to the Mexican and U.S. scholars, European scholars also began to produce important quantitative studies on Mexico. Menno Vellinga used survey techniques in *Industrialización, burguesía y clase obrera en México* (1979), while Wouter van Ginneken applied Gini and Theil coefficients to income distribution data in *Socioeconomic Groups and Income Distribution in Mexico* (1980).

Meanwhile, in the United States several works appeared. Peter Smith published *Labyrinths of Power: Political Recruitment in 20th Century Mexico* in 1979. Roderic Camp published *Mexico's Leaders: Their Education and Recruitment* in 1980. Both studies extended sophisticated quantitative analysis to politics and political history.

The use of quantitative sources also had an impact on labor studies. After the Mexican Revolution, authors like Rosendo Salazar studied labor by discussing unions and leaders, and this tradition has continued. In 1951 Juan F. Noyola Vázquez and Diego G. López Rosado published "Los salarios reales en México, 1939–1950." They went beyond union studies by asking whether workers had actually improved their standard of living since the Revolution. Using published sources, they concluded that many workers had not bettered their lives. In 1967 Mike Everett used the same sources as López and Noyola in his dissertation, "The Role of Mexican Trade Unions, 1950–1963." However, he employed new quantitative techniques to modify the data, resulting in significant, new conclusions on industrial wages. He argued that a period of declining real wages was followed by a period of rising real wages. In 1985 Raúl Urban and I applied some of Everett's econometric techniques to new data in order to analyze wage dispersion (in "Los salarios y la estructura ocupacional en el sector industrial"), thus taking the field into some new areas. In 1988 I employed unpublished price and wage data from government archives to permit a revised look at the wage question (*Los salarios industriales en la Ciudad de México, 1939–1975*). This was among the first extensive uses of archival data to construct long-term wage series, an alternative to Wilkie's approach of redefining categories, or Villarreal's input-output estimations.

In the field of Latin American studies, the application of quantitative methodologies has not been limited to Mexico. After *The Mexican Revolution*, Wilkie himself began to develop and implement quantitative methods in the broader field of Latin American studies. In 1969 he published *The Bolivian Revolution and U.S. Aid since 1952*, an original attempt to measure the impact of U.S. aid on the development process. In 1974 he published *Measuring Land Reform: Bolivia, Venezuela, and Latin America*, which defined and tested the results of land title redistribution. He also wrote, *Statistics and National Policy* (SNP), further developing theory and method for measuring change in state policy. In SNP Wilkie identified the new trend of central governments to recentralize governmental power, seeking to overcome the excessive decentralization of power into autonomous agencies that had taken place following the Uruguayan model of José Batlle y Ordóñez. SNP also extended Wilkie's approach to a wide variety of new areas: voting patterns, the role of the Roman Catholic Church, urbanization, and foreign trade patterns. Moreover, SNP developed the rationale for revising the format of the annual *Statistical Abstract of Latin America* (SALA). In 1976 Wilkie became editor of SALA and its Supplement Series. SALA abstracts data from over 400 worldwide sources; the SALA supplements combine narrative and quantitative analysis on specific social, political, and economic themes.

Since 1976 SALA has contained a section titled "Development of Data," where several important studies have appeared. For example, in SALA 18 Kenneth F. Johnson revised and brought forward data originally gathered by Russell H. Fitzgibbon that redefine the U.S. scholarly image of democracy in Latin America since 1945. In SALA 19 Peter L. Reich examined U.S. government data that had attempted to measure the "Communist menace" in Latin America. In SALA 20 Richard W. Wilkie presented hitherto unpublished data on the rural population of Argentina, data basic to our understanding of that country's development. In SALA 21 Thomas M. Millington tested James Wilkie's theory about the recentralization process by examining Bolivian budgets in a case study.

SALA 21 and 22 contain Stephen Haber's significant studies on rural and urban Mexico. In SALA 21 Haber put Mexican community studies since 1930 into a historical and statistical framework. In SALA 22 he developed measurements to understand the rapid social change of Mexican cities, communities, and villages since 1930. Haber continued his work in a dissertation that quantified the structure of Mexican industrial capital in the late nineteenth century (1985).

Concerning Wilkie's own development of data in SALA, he has treated individual countries such as Mexico (for example, his research on class structure in SALA 23) and Bolivia (his research on U.S.-Bolivian financial relations in SALA 22 as well as a periodization of the Bolivian National Revolution from 1952 to 1985 in SALA 25). Furthermore, he has undertaken new approaches to understanding Latin America as a whole (his study of food production in the twenty countries of Latin America in SALA 23).

In the preface to SALA Wilkie has drawn together relevant themes from the data assembled for publication in the yearly volume. For example in SALA 22 he placed Mexico's "new" financial crisis of 1982 into historical perspective. In SALA 23 he defined the concepts of "Latin America" and the various numbers of countries which comprise it according to different viewpoints. In SALA 25 he showed how Latin America's debt has been redefined over time under the pressure of international agencies.

In the pages that follow, Wilkie and four of his students carry forward quantitative historical analysis of modern Mexico into new areas. In Chapter 1, "Six Ideological Phases of Mexico's 'Permanent Revolution' since 1910," Wilkie presents a significant reinterpretation of the Mexican Revolution. He carries forward two of the field's deepest traditions: (1) the tendency to consider the Mexican Revolution an ongoing process to date rather than a violent confrontation that ended in 1920; and (2) the identification of distinct phases within the process that is the Mexican Revolution, so that one can make sense of Mexico's development from 1910 to the present.

Wilkie defines the Mexican Revolution in terms of the ruling elite's changing ideological tendencies. He argues that ruling class ideology in Mexico since the Revolution is not fixed but rather has substantially changed in response to challenges to or crises in the Mexican political system. Although Wilkie criticizes some of their reactions and overreactions to crises, he also provides ample recognition of the ruling elite's capacity to hold power and direct the country.

Making use of abundant historical quantitative data, Wilkie also shows how nonpolitical tendencies have interacted with elite decisions to shape Mexican history in the twentieth century. Most importantly, he argues that economic growth has been the fundamental constraint upon the country's ruling groups, and that their continued rule depends on their capacity to construct an adequate growth model. He also contends that statism, which became the dominant ideology in the 1970s, must be jettisoned if the Partido de la Revolución Institucional (PRI) is to continue to preside over a growing economy and consensual polity.

Wilkie's chapter is, among other things, a response to the development of the field since the books by Reynolds and Solís. While a few studies, like those by Smith and Camp, have looked at noneconomic variables, most have concentrated on narrow economic areas. Wilkie argues that politics and economics must be viewed together, and that time series are necessary for understanding their interplay.

In Chapter 2, "The Development of Engineering for Social and Economic Modernization in Mexico since 1929," David Lorey uses a combination of published and unpublished statistical data on Mexican education to develop new quantitative indicators of Mexico's development process in the twentieth century. Lorey contends that previous studies use data that are too aggregate to understand the complexities of Mexican education. He generates fresh data on the evolution of engineering education to argue that Mexico's revolutionary governments have supported social and educational development less than economic growth. This has generated a new bottleneck in the country's modernization process—a lack of professionals for social modernization. Lorey's conclusions go beyond previous studies to show how changing government development strategies have influenced career choices of university students.

Chapter 3, "Class Structure in Mexico, 1895–1980," by Stephanie Granato and Aída Mostkoff, extends the original Wilkie-Wilkins measurement of changing class structure in Mexico. In that earlier quantification, Wilkie and Wilkins used modified census data to measure changing class composition from 1895 to 1970. Since then the 1980 census has appeared, and Granato and Mostkoff use the new data to establish a longer series. The authors include a detailed methodological discussion, covering concepts and methods of measurement as well as sources.

Their methodology leads to the conclusion that the middle class made the greatest increases from 1970 to 1980. The lower class significantly declined in size during the decade. If true, on the one hand, this indicates that Mexico's revolution has indeed succeeded in creating an increasingly modern, middle-class society despite high inflation and foreign debt. On the other hand, it may turn out that upper, middle, and lower are categories too broad to capture the essence of Mexico's rapidly changing social structure of the 1970s.

In Chapter 4, "Complexities of Measuring the Food Situation in Mexico: Supply versus Self-Sufficiency of Basic Grains, 1925–86," Aída Mostkoff and Enrique C. Ochoa present historical time series in four areas: production, trade, and supply data of four basic grains; per capita supply data; import and export series; and real price series.

The authors use a variety of published sources to construct their series. The new time series are then used as the basis for a criticism of studies, like those by Sanderson and Barkin, which have argued that Mexico has lost food self-sufficiency. Mostkoff and Ochoa argue that their series demonstrate that Mexico's food production has kept pace with population growth. They strongly criticize the self-sufficiency school for concentrating on short-run tendencies, thus missing the point on Mexican agricultural development. In arguing that production must be distinguished from the politics of food consumption, Ochoa and Mostkoff follow in the vein established by Wilkie in his article on food production in Latin America (SALA 23).

Chapter 5, James Wilkie's "Borrowing as Revenue: The Case of Mexico, 1935–82," provides a new theoretical basis for showing patterns of revenue generation by central governments. It applies the theory to the case of Mexico, 1935 to 1982. Wilkie argues that the standard reasons for ignoring debt as revenue are misleading. They do not allow for a full understanding of the role of the executive, leading to a misunderstanding of government everywhere, particularly in the Third World.

Wilkie uses a variety of published and unpub-

lished sources to show that the official statistics claim that income tax has been the greatest source of revenue. Revising Mexico's official presentation of data, he factors Mexico's borrowing into the analysis, demonstrating that debt has provided the greatest source of income since López Mateos.

He then argues that Mexico had been overborrowing heavily since the 1960s, making inevitable the financial crisis of 1976 and the subsequent debt crisis of 1982. Wilkie states that if policymakers had employed his method rather than the standard method, perhaps they would have foreseen the dangers of becoming overreliant on debt as income, and thus might have avoided Mexico's current economic crisis.

Chapter 6, "The Dramatic Growth of Mexico's Economy and the Rise of Statist Government Budgetary Power, 1910–82," argues that the Mexican government's economic role increased from 1910 to 1982 in dramatic fashion, eventually generating the statist economic policies that dwarfed the private sector.

Staying with quantitative sources, Wilkie indicates that government income and spending accounted for increasing shares of gross domestic product from 1910 to 1982. Government expenditures accounted for more than a quarter of GDP under López Portillo, whereas they had been only 5 percent under Obregón. Finally, in 1982 López Portillo nationalized the banks. According to Wilkie, that placed more than half the Mexican economy under government control.

Despite characterizing the Mexican economy as having achieved statism by 1892, Wilkie cautions against a simplistic analysis. He carefully shows that the parastate sector and the central government may operate in different fashions, generating more pluralism than one might think. He also indicates that the 1982 economic crisis may have the beneficial effect of inducing economic realism into the system, so that recovery may not be as distant as most observers think.

Society and Economy in Mexico is timely and challenging. The field of Mexican studies has been moving toward greater sophistication of quantitative methods since the 1960s. These studies demonstrate the utility of quantification and the need for greater sophistication. They also challenge the conventional views of Mexico's social and economic development in the twentieth century.

Preface

The purpose of this volume is to present new ways to understand the extent and pace of Mexico's social and economic development in the twentieth century, especially as related to politics. The focus is on quantitatively measuring Mexico's historical change, which at times seems to confound observers with its complexity.

Analysts around the globe today justifiably see Mexico as one of Latin America's leading countries and an increasingly important nation in the world, and strong interest in the Mexican system has emerged. Living under the direction of an Official Party system which governs with the goal of carrying out ongoing, state-directed change, Mexico gained fame during the 1960s and 1970s for its economic success, when the gross domestic product expanded by an average of 6.8 percent yearly. Some of that growth was fueled by the discovery of new oil deposits in the mid-1970s, which by 1979 gave Mexico the seventh largest reserves in the world and by 1980 made it the fourth largest petroleum producer.[1]

But since the 1980s, Mexico has received less favorable attention. In 1988 Mexico is contending with Brazil for the highest foreign debt (over 100 billion dollars) in Latin America, and in 1985 Mexico had the world's fourth highest payments on the debt (329 percent) in relation to total exports of goods and services.[2] With the collapse of world oil prices in 1982, Mexico found its international reserves exhausted and the government nationalized the foreign-owned banking industry in order to protect the private sector from going bankrupt. The resulting economic crisis lasting since 1982 has led to speculation that the country may default on its foreign debt payments, throwing the world banking system into disruption.

If Mexico's economic crisis of the 1980s were not enough, its capital, Mexico City, is experiencing a crisis of size. Given the rapid population growth, it is projected that by the year 2025 Mexico City will be the world's largest (over 30 million inhabitants) and most polluted city. In the meantime, Mexico City's size (18 million persons) apparently was a factor in intensifying the effects of two major earthquakes that struck in September 1985, measuring 8.1 and 7.8 on the Richter scale. The height and weight of the city's hundreds of buildings interacted with the soil instability to create a harmonic resonance. Structures from six to sixteen floors had a natural tendency to vibrate at the same rate as the shock waves of the earthquakes, causing nearly 1,000 buildings to fall and damaging over 1,000 other buildings so badly that they have to be demolished.[3] Property damage amounted to 4.3 billion dollars, and the death toll reached at least 6,000.[4]

Although Mexico's affairs of the 1980s seem quite dramatic, they are only part of a much larger picture which needs to be studied in depth. The intent of this volume is to show how quantitative research into change in Mexico can lead to new findings as well as to refinements in methodology for investigating Mexico's past and present—both critical areas if we are to fathom the nature of Mexico's alternative futures.

The approach here is twofold. It involves the formulation of, first, a framework to understand the

EDITOR'S NOTE: For financial support to carry out my own research developed here, gratitude is expressed to the William and Flora Hewlett Foundation and to the Historical Research Foundation.

[1] Coincidentally with Mexico's becoming the fourth largest producer, Iran dropped out of contention for that position, owing largely to its war with Iraq (1980–88). Production data are from Nacional Financiera, *La Economía Mexicana en Cifras, 1981* (México, D.F.), p. 356; data on reserves are from ibid., 1986, p. 382.

[2] SALA, 25, pp. xv and 643.

[3] Robert A. Jones, "New Lessons from Quake in Mexico," *Los Angeles Times*, September 26, 1986.

[4] Economic Commission for Latin America, *Damage Caused by the Mexican Earthquake and Its Repercussions Upon the Country's Economy* (Santiago, 1985), pp. 3–19.

ideological periods of Mexico's "Permanent Revolution" under an Official Party and, second, the development of time series data needed for interpretation. It is my view that by charting yearly or periodic statistics across time we can discover patterns that are otherwise hidden.[5] The idea is not simply to use statistics as presented by official data-gathering agencies but also to test the data by juxtaposing alternative series and reorganizing official data into new categories for interpretation.

It is appropriate to mention at the outset that the six studies on change in Mexico presented here are only illustrative of the kinds of new research that needs to be undertaken into the complex realities of a country which will have grown from 15 million persons in 1910 to about 104 million by 2000. Nevertheless, I believe that the statistical series presented help us to better understand the magnitude of current problems facing Mexico where, by the early 1980s, the sheer size of the economy had increased in real terms almost 21 times compared with the size of the economy under the dictator Porfirio Díaz and over 12 times since the late 1930s.

Use of historical statistics to develop new insights into the past not only enables us here to better understand the present but also helps others make more realistic projections into the future. Projections of the future that do not take into account the baseline of the past and its relation to the present cannot reflect any plausible possible futures. For example, alternative projections of high, medium, or low levels of change have meaning only insofar as they are built upon carefully defined assumptions about and parameters for analysis of past trends.

That studies about the past and present as well as the future have limitations should be manifest to readers; however, unless those limits have been addressed precisely one does not know how assumptions fit together and the extent to which parameters influence interpretation. What becomes clear through quantitative studies is that interpretation is valid only

to the extent that the reader accepts the premises of the data within the given definitions, limits, and reorganization necessary to achieve consistency from one time to another.[6] If readers disagree with part of the quantitative analysis, they may adjust the data and develop their own conclusions.

Because the quantitative view requires explicit statement of and rationale for assumptions, the reader understands more fully the limitations of the data than is often the case with nonquantitative studies. Indeed, in qualitative studies, the limitations on meaning may only be implied, perhaps even leading specialists astray in their interpretation.

With regard to premises on which data analyses are developed in this book, in Chapter 1 I offer a new interpretation of Mexico's twentieth-century history by setting forth six ideological periods. This view is based upon long-term statistical series which integrate the economic and social approaches with the political approach.

In Chapter 2, "The Development of Engineering Expertise for Social and Economic Modernization in Mexico since 1929," David Lorey develops the premise that study of the engineering profession is needed to shed light upon the ability of Mexico to create and maintain a modern social and economic infrastructure ranging from potable water to telecommunications networks. Thus Lorey offers new statistical series that define and measure the size of the engineering pool as it has developed under different presidential approaches to national modernization.[7]

To test presidential policies for developing Mexico's engineering capacity, Lorey develops three different methods for tracking the growth of the engineering profession. The series complement each other and enable Lorey to analyze university problems in the production of specialists, problems that will increasingly jeopardize Mexico's drive to construct a social and economic base for permanent social mobility.

Chapter 3, "Class Structure in Mexico, 1895–1980," by Stephanie Granato and Aída Mostkoff, illustrates the role of definition of terms in statistical studies. Although all researchers make assumptions about and formulate the parameters of their study, generally those who adopt a quantitative approach

---

[5] In defining the field of quantitative history, I distinguish between classificatory (or descriptive) statistics and inductive (or predictive) statistics. The classificatory approach involves systematically organizing and reorganizing data into categories needed for analysis and emphasizes the measurement of proportion, central tendency, and adjustment for real meaning. The inductive approach utilizes inferential model building and emphasizes techniques such as correlation, regression, and factor analysis. Although inductive statistics tend to be unintelligible to persons without an extensive background in mathematics and probability theory, most readers with a background in social sciences are able to understand classificatory statistics, which are presented in the form of numerical summaries of comparable data. On the theory of quantitative history applied to twentieth-century state policy in Latin America, see James W. Wilkie, *Statistics and National Policy* (Los Angeles: UCLA Latin American Center Publications, 1974), pp. 6–9.

[6] In the annual SALA, readers are cautioned that "all data for any topic vary according to definition, parameters, methods of compilation and calculation, and completeness of coverage as well as date gathered, date prepared, and/or adjusted." Thus, in presenting data from many sources, SALA offers alternative views of the same phenomena measured differently according to differing criteria.

[7] For a related study by David E. Lorey, see "Professional Expertise and Mexican Modernization: Sources, Methods, and Preliminary Findings," in SALA, 26, chapter 34.

define more fully their methodology than those who do not use such an approach. For example, many authors have written about the "middle class" in Mexico, but quantitative researchers Mostkoff and Granato, building upon previous SALA research,[8] explain as precisely as possible how:

1. class structure (i.e., upper, middle, and lower) is defined according to occupation, income, or both;

2. groups or parts of them are distributed in the scheme of class structure according to different job titles, income levels, or both;

3. official statistical data are reorganized and/or abstracted to tell us what we need to know;

4. data are adjusted through time to achieve consistency in interpretation.

The latter factor involves not only taking into account such matters as changing job definitions in the decennial population and economic censuses but also deflating income levels across time to fairly compare life in one decade with life in another.

Chapter 4, "Complexities of Measuring the Food Situation in Mexico: Supply versus Self-Sufficiency of Basic Grains, 1925–86," by Aída Mostkoff and Enrique Ochoa, shows the complexity of assessing food statistics. By developing an independent analysis of government data on food production in relation to exports and imports of food, the authors show that the issue of Mexico's food self-sufficiency is a false issue. In examining the theoretical framework for that false issue, they also question the government's concept of food production per capita and recalculate the data to offer a view based upon academic research rather than implicit government propaganda.

Chapters 5 and 6 illustrate ways of redefining the roles of government activity. They also help to show how Mexico reached its politico-economic crisis by 1982 with subsequent need since then to reform the role of government in the economy. These two chapters, reprinted from two issues of *The Mexican Forum*, develop several arguments. In Chapter 5, "Borrowing as Revenue: The Case of Mexico, 1935–82," I posit the view that if we do not compare government borrowing to other sources of income, the result is a distorted view of the importance of such a major aspect of raising revenue as the role of income taxes. Although the current practices of excluding borrowing from revenue is important for calculating government deficit spending, from another point of

view we also need to know the share of borrowing in relation to total funds available to government.

In Chapter 6, "The Dramatic Growth of Mexico's Economy and the Rise of Statist Government Budgetary Power, 1910–82," I attempt to measure, among other factors, the rising importance up to 1982 of the public sector, which includes the central government (executive, legislative, and judicial branches of activity) and the parastate or decentralized government. The parastate sector is defined as including:

1. autonomous agencies, such as Petróleos Mexicanos and the Instituto Mexicano de Seguridad Social;

2. mixed private and public companies with majority state ownership, such as Teléfonos de México and Fertilizantes Mexicanos;

3. mixed companies with minority state ownership, such as Cobre de México and Cigarros La Tabacalera;

4. trust funds, such as for Caminos y Puentes Federales and for the Fondo Nacional de Fomento al Turismo.

Because of Mexico's bureaucratic confusion, it has not been possible to measure directly the importance of the public sector, so I have done so indirectly.[9]

In other studies published elsewhere, I have also measured change indirectly through proxy indicators. For example, in research into the extent of social change in Mexico from 1910 through 1970,[10] I settled upon measuring the extent of poverty as defined by seven items in the national population censuses: persons who are ill-fed (one item), ill-clothed (two items), ill-housed (one item), and living in educational or geographic isolation (three items). (See Fig. 3 in Chapter 1.) These items do not measure poverty per se but rather serve as proxies to understand social aspects of poverty. To examine economic aspects of poverty, one would consider income statistics, as Jeffrey Bortz has done in a recent study.[11]

Beyond qualifications about the meaning of time series statistics, readers are reminded that although the studies published here do cover many years, once they are completed time does not stand still. As suggested in Chapter 1, the pace of events in Mexico

---

[8] See James W. Wilkie and Paul D. Wilkins, "Quantifying the Class Structure of Mexico, 1895–1970," in SALA, 21, chapter 36.

[9] For a related study, see James W. Wilkie, "Changes in Mexico since 1895: Central Government Revenue, Public Sector Expenditure, and National Economic Growth," SALA, 24, chapter 34.

[10] See James W. Wilkie, *La Revolución Mexicana (1910–1976): Gasto Federal y Cambio Social* (México, D.F.: Fondo de Cultura Económica, 1978).

[11] See Jeffrey Bortz, *Industrial Wages in Mexico City, 1939–1975* (New York: Garland, 1987) and *El Salario en México* (México, D.F.: Ediciones El Caballito, 1986).

seems to quicken with each decade and to contest the stereotype of a "timeless" Mexico. The research presented here examines part of the rapid long-term change which Mexico has been undergoing for many years.

To suggest the major change that Mexico has undergone since 1982, when the Official Party stretched its political power to a maximum and the parastate sector reached its economic zenith, Chapter 1 examines in preliminary fashion challenges to both. Given the rapidity of change and the fact that these essays were written before the Mexican presidential election in July 1988, Chapter 1 contains a postscript, written in October 1988. Although interpretation ends in 1988, I have added data to tables up to 1989 where possible.

J.W.W.

Cerro de Chipinque, Nuevo León
June 1987

Mazatlán, Sinaloa
April 1988

Tables

Chapter 5, Borrowing as Revenue: The Case of Mexico, 1935–82

Chapter 6, The Dramatic Growth of Mexico's Economy and the Rise of Statist Government Budgetary Power, 1910–82

Figures

Abbreviations and Symbols

kg	kilogram
PC	percentage change
PI	per inhabitant
SALA	*Statistical Abstract of Latin America* (Los Angeles: UCLA Latin American Center Publications, University of California). References are given in abbreviated form. For example, SALA, 26–3400, refers to volume 26, table 3400.
WPI	Wholesale price index
~	Data not available in source
†	Estimate by or in source
@	Estimate made herein
*	Link (splice) in series or technical change
——	Source does not specify whether data are recorded separately, not applicable, zero, or negligible

1

The Six Ideological Phases of Mexico's "Permanent Revolution" since 1910

JAMES W. WILKIE

To provide a broad political context into which fit the economic, social, and political elements of Mexican twentieth-century history, I offer here a conceptual framework for periodizing Mexico's idea of "Permanent Revolution" since 1910. My interpretation divides the course of events and debates into six phases of ideology which have guided Mexico's ongoing experiment in state-directed socioeconomic change. The phases are as follows:[1]

    I. Political Revolution, 1910–30
       A. Violence, 1910–19
       B. Reconstruction, 1920–30
    II. Social Revolution, 1930–40
    III. Economic Revolution, 1940–60
    IV. Balanced Revolution, 1960–70
    V. Statist Revolution, 1970–82
       A. Political, 1970–76
       B. Economic, 1976–82
    VI. Restructured Revolution, 1983–
       A. Economic, 1982–88
       B. Political, 1988–

The Official Party of the Mexican Revolution, which has governed the country implicitly since the late 1910s and explicitly since 1929, justifies its continued rule on the basis of the need for a strong government to serve as the engine required to forge a modern society and economy as well as to overcome successive crises in national development. The Mexican Revolution began in 1910; seven years of violence followed before a constitution could be achieved that would elaborate the movement's long-term goals. Although the 1917 charter accorded to the private

sector an important role in national affairs, implementation of the constitution has seen the state assume an ever expanding role—at least through 1982.

Established as the Partido Nacional Revolucionario (PNR) in 1929, the Official Party organized regional strongmen to end the need for them to try to seize power. In return for assured positions of importance in the national government, the regional bosses agreed to resolve their differences behind the scenes thus allowing the Official Party to present a united image to the public.

The Official Party was transformed into a popular front in 1938 as the Partido de la Revolución Mexicana (PRM). The PRM shifted the base of Party strength to four sectors: organized peasants, organized labor, the military, and popular groups (including the middle and upper classes), each being represented in Congress. Although the moneyed sectors were left out of the PRM, their real influence in the government was provided for under legislation that required all businesses above a certain size to join into chambers of a national network of trade associations, which eventually organized into two national groups (CONCANACO and CONCAMIN, discussed below).

The Official Party's final transformation came in 1946 when it became the Partido de la Revolución Institucional (PRI). The PRI dropped the military sector from its formal organization, but by that time all of the formal groups had lost influence to the trade associations.

Under the Official Party the Congress and judiciary have been subordinate to the presidency in all major policy decisions. Although theoretically independent, in fact the Congress and courts have been very careful not to offend the executive branch of government because the president of Mexico has emerged with the influence of a king, albeit one who

---

[1] This periodization draws upon an earlier analysis developed in my study titled "La Rivoluzione Messicana e la Sua Eredità," in Nicola Tranfaglia and Massmo Firpo, eds., *La Storia—I Grandi Problemi dal Medioevo all'Età Contemporanea*, vol. 9, no. 4 (Torino: Unione Tipografico-Editrice Torinese, 1986), pp. 56–72.

cannot be reelected. In 1940 supreme court justices won a change in their term, which had been limited to the term of office of the Mexican president who appointed them. Now the justices have tenure but no real power in matters of interest to the nation's chief executive.

Whereas Mexican leaders sought political solutions from 1910 to 1930 and looked to electoral "answers" to complex problems, during the 1930s they rejected the purely political approach and turned to social solutions. Under the banner of Social Revolution, the left-wing of the Official Party rose to ascendancy. Pushing such programs as land reform for the peasants and the right to strike for laborers, the government undertook the nationalization of major industry and transporation. Less overtly, the government laid the basis for loaning funds to private industry.

Not until the period from 1940 to 1960 did the government emphasize openly a call for economic revolution. Under this ideology, the government was able to convert manufacturing subsidies into the scale required to launch the country's industrial expansion. Further, state policy emphasized the nationalization of industry and creation of state-run enterprises such as railways, airlines, and steel mills. State corporations were decentralized into the parastate sector so as to allow the enterprises to operate as businesses independent from the central government, with the idea that profits would help develop Mexico's public sector rather than the private sector. Unfortunately, such enterprises usually operate at a loss and Mexico's parastate corporations were no exception, requiring subsidies from the central government.

State policy also focused on building the economic infrastructure needed for industrialization, including hydroelectric projects. Thus the ideology of the period turned away from land reform to emphasize irrigation, for example.

In the 1950s the Official Party adopted a monetarist policy subsequently known as "stabilizing development." This policy, which lasted from 1954 to 1970, was based upon a stable peso and low inflation. Gross domestic product (GDP) grew steadily. Stability for economic growth was also provided by tacit pacts which the Official Party had begun to make with an increasing number of socioeconomic sectors beginning in the late 1930s.

By the 1960s many in Mexico sought a new path that would overcome disenchantment with successive state policy shifts from emphasizing political themes (1910–30), to social ideas (1930–40), and then economic themes (1940–60). Hence there arose the concept of Balanced Revolution, which from 1960 to 1970 sought to harmonize the desires of each of the three preceding periods. During this period the para-

state sector of government expanded into numerous industries, including nationalization of Mexico's electricity and telephone networks.

Following the failure of Balanced Revolution, punctuated by the government-student battle in 1968 at Mexico City's Plaza of the Three Cultures, the Official Party turned to the Statist phase of the Revolution, 1970–82. During this period the idea was advanced in the first subperiod from 1970 to 1976 that a legal revolution would make possible new state power for national development. This first Statist subperiod called for government-sponsored redistribution of wealth domestically and independence from the United States internationally. The subperiod from 1976 to 1982 emphasized rapid economic change to take advantage of Mexico's new oil-based wealth.

With the collapse of world oil prices in 1982, Mexico was forced in 1983 to adopt the present ideology of Restructured Revolution. Realizing that the bloated parastate sector of government could no longer be supported in its many money-losing businesses, since 1983 the Official Party has sought to reduce the parastate sector in favor of an increased role for the private sector. Too, all government activity is subject to revamping in order to deregulate and rationalize decisions in the Mexican economy. And the government is dismantling the private sector's protected Mexican market, forcing private industry into the world market place.

Through the historical course of these six periods, an implicit theory of state policy has emerged to justify continued one-party rule: the government has had to identify (or if necessary to create) a series of crises that require its continuation in power until the Constitution of 1917 can supposedly be fully implemented and the country's population can live in harmonious well-being by overcoming Mexico's troubled historical antecedents. The crises themselves are not seen by the Official Party as indicating the Revolution's failures but as representing new problems that will always be caused by the unforeseeable conjuncture of events.

Thus for the Official Party each new crisis offers the kind of stimulus needed to advance Mexico to ever higher stages of development from the past into the future in a country where since independence 167 years ago, the population has grown from 6 to 80 million. This view of crisis has been tested by the economic depression of Mexico since 1982. That a major group split from the Official Party for the national elections of 1988 suggests that the Official Party may have become involved in a crisis of more damaging proportions than it realized.

Antecedents to the Revolution[2]

Nineteenth-Century Mexico

Mexico's independence from Spain did not come in 1821 as a result of the country's having built a strong preindependence economic and political infrastructure, as had the United States. Rather, independence came as the result of a chaotic civil war after 1810 that had seen freedom won by those who originally opposed the break with Spain. In the end, events in Spain had dictated that the Spanish conservatives in the colonies could protect their privileges only by breaking with the liberal reforms in the homeland.

Ill-prepared for independence economically and politically, Mexico fell into civil war that continued for the next half century and caused the destruction of the country's silver, gold, and other mining bases for wealth. Loss of mining production hampered consolidation of the new nation, shattering confidence in the credit and investment system. In the confusion of civil war, Mexico could not defend against U.S. incursions into the north. As a result of war with the United States (1846–47), Mexico was forced in 1848 to yield half of its territory to the United States, including the gold of California which would help to fund U.S. industrialization. To complicate matters, Mexico engaged in ruinous struggles with the Roman Catholic Church between 1853 and 1867 for control of civil society (including registry of birth, marriage, and death), land and property, and credit.

Not until the era of the dictator Porfirio Díaz (1876–1911) was the country returned to order in the name of achieving progress. Utilizing the slogan "bread or the stick," Díaz ended the chaos that had engulfed Mexico since independence. Too, his programs halted Mexico's long slide into economic depression that had coincided with the destruction of the mines. By providing the country's first credit, investment, and commercial codes, Díaz laid the basis for economic recovery. Capitalizing on the fact that Mexico was far behind the United States, with whom so many of Mexico's leaders compared their country's unfavorable position of material wealth, Díaz helped to overcome Mexico's disadvantageous geography by building railways to export raw materials. Lacking the coast-to-coast transportation systems that the United States enjoyed, Mexico had been especially vulnerable to competition once the world needed U.S. agricultural and industrial goods more than Mexico's mining output, which had also lost out to U.S. production.

During the Díaz administration, Mexican mineral and agricultural exports allowed economic recovery and attracted foreign capital to establish modern industry. As part of his program to stimulate the economy, Díaz settled the postindependence struggle over land ownership by opting against the liberal idea of backing the medium-sized rural farm owner; he reinforced the growth of the great hacienda that had survived since Spanish colonial days. The peasants suffered grievously under the Díaz solution, the large entrepreneurs in town and countryside profiting at the expense of the masses. Under Díaz, the basis was laid for the emergence of the middle class in Mexico, which constituted an estimated 8 percent of the population by 1895.

Crisis of the Díaz Dictatorship, 1899–1910

Consequences of Díaz's long-term economic pattern were several. Mexico found itself short of cash needed by the banking system to finance and refinance mortgages held by growing numbers of economically powerful landowners, who faced serious problems in repaying loans during a time of increasing world economic instability. At the same time, the rural middle class and Indian peasants were feeling the cumulative effects of the decline in the possibility of their owning land—during Díaz's more than thirty years in power, one-quarter of Mexico's land surface was transferred into large landholdings to develop export-oriented agriculture and ranching products. Hence, the vast majority of rural people faced decline in food supply owing to export production, loss of their own lands, and indebtedness of Indians to the large landowners. Beyond the rural sector, some middle class employees and professionals were affected by a general decline in real wages.

---

[2] Colin M. MacLachlan and Jaime E. Rodríguez O., in *The Forging of the Cosmic Race: A Reinterpretation of Colonial Mexico* (Berkeley: University of California Press, 1980), have reinterpreted findings to argue that on its own terms the colonial period involved a balanced, integrated economy and that its legacy did not cause the organizational failures of newly independent Mexico; rather, those failures should be attributed to the collapse of silver mining and the inability of the government to pay the costs required for national development. Although their argument is persuasive about the colonial period, its silver-analysis theory about the post-1821 era must be supplemented because the era lacked an institutional and legal legacy for development. See John H. Coatsworth, "Obstacles to Economic Growth in Nineteenth-Century Mexico," *American Historical Review* 83:1 (1980), pp. 80–100. Also important is Jaime E. Rodríguez O., ed., *The Independence of Mexico and the Creation of the New Nation* (Los Angeles: UCLA Latin American Center Publications, 1989). For positive reinterpretation of the Díaz era, see Raymond Vernon, *The Dilemma of Mexico's Development: The Roles of the Public and Private Sectors* (Cambridge, Mass.: Harvard University Press, 1963), and Fernando Rosenzweig, "El Desarrollo Económico de México de 1877 a 1911," *El Trimestre Económico* 32 (1965), pp. 405–454. The emergence of Mexico's industrial base during the era of President Porfirio Díaz (1876–1911) is postulated by Stephen H. Haber, *Industry and Underdevelopment: The Industrialization of Mexico, 1890–1940* (Stanford: Stanford University Press, 1989).

Matters were complicated for the Díaz dictatorship by the erratic performance of the Mexican economy after 1899. GDP had a high growth rate in 1901, 1903, 1905, and 1907, but those gains were offset by negative growth rates in 1899, 1902, 1906, and 1908. This whipsawing of the economy was further complicated by the very low growth rates of GDP in 1900, 1904, and 1910 (Table 1).

When in Mexico's presidential election of 1910 the new upwardly mobile middle class and economi-

cally powerful entreprenuers found themselves definitively closed out of political influence, Francisco I. Madero and other critics of Díaz moved to resolve the problem of dictatorship by calling for the establishing of political democracy, which seemed to be the basis for the economic success of such countries as the United States and England. Even Díaz had entered office with the slogan "effective suffrage and no reelection," which he had soon chosen to forget.

Table 1

YEARLY CHANGE IN MEXICO'S REAL GROSS DOMESTIC PRODUCT,[1] 1896–1988

Year	PC	Year	PC	Year	PC
1896	3.1	1935	7.4	1965	6.5
1897	6.7	1936	8.0	1966	6.9
1898	5.8	1937	3.3	1967	6.3
1899	− 4.8	1938	1.6	1968	8.1
		1939	5.4	1969	6.3
1900	.8				
1901	8.6	1940	1.4	1970	6.9[a]
1902	− 7.1	1941	9.7	1971	4.2
1903	11.2	1942	5.6	1972	8.5
1904	1.8	1943	3.7	1973	8.4
		1944	8.2	1974	6.1
1905	10.4				
1906	− 1.1	1945	3.1	1975	5.6
1907	5.9	1946	6.6	1976	4.2
1908	− .2	1947	3.4	1977	3.4
1909	2.9	1948	4.1	1978	8.2
		1949	5.5	1979	9.2
1910	.9				
1921	7.7	1950	9.9	1980	8.3
1922	2.3	1951	7.7	1981	8.8
1923	3.4	1952	4.0	1982	− .6
1924	− 1.6	1953	.3	1983	− 4.2
		1954	10.0	1984	3.5
1925	6.2				
1926	6.0	1955	8.5	1985	2.5
1927	− 4.4	1956	6.8	1986	− 3.8
1928	.6	1957	7.6	1987	1.5
1929	− 3.9	1958	5.4	1988	1.1
		1959	3.0		
1930	− 6.3				
1931	3.3	1960	8.1		
1932	− 14.9	1961	4.9		
1933	11.3	1962	4.7		
1934	6.8	1963	8.0		
		1964	11.7		

1. GDP data in Chapter 5, below, may vary slightly owing to revisions given here.
a. Improved data, 1970–.

SOURCE: Calculated from latest revisions of Banco de México constant-peso data in market prices:

To 1925   Instituto Nacional de Estadística e Informática, *Estadísticas Históricas de México*, 2 vols. (México, D.F.), I, p. 311.

1925–58   Nacional Financiera, *La Economía Mexicana en Cifras, 1986*, p. 80.

1958–77   International Monetary Fund, *International Financial Statistics—Yearbook, 1986* and *1987*.

1978–81   Banco de México, *Indicadores Económicos*, May 1987.

1982–88   Nacional Financiera, *El Mercado de Valores*, June 1, 1989

Phase I. Ideology of Political Revolution, 1910–30

The Violent Stage,[3] *1910–20*

Given the mixed social and economic situation, both the urban and rural sectors had reason to support the call of Francisco Madero for peaceful political change in the presidential election of 1910. Jailed to prevent his participation in the election, Madero then called for revolution against the old dictator. In 1911, after Madero captured Ciudad Juárez, Díaz realized that his army had aged with him and was unable to fight, so he agreed to leave office.

Elected to the presidency, Madero seemed oblivious to the fact that the political solution of electing new leaders could not resolve popular demands for dismantling the Díaz-backed hacienda system. Madero could not restrain leaders such as Emiliano Zapata, who led the movement to seize haciendas (many of which had been consolidated by foreigners) and divide them among their former owners. In the turbulence of threat to foreign investment Madero was overthrown in 1913 by General Victoriano Huerta, his chief of staff who had the support of U.S. Ambassador Henry Lane Wilson. However, Ambassador Wilson could not convince the new U.S. president, Woodrow Wilson (no relation), that the fall of Madero was justified. Horrified by the murder of Madero, who had been "shot while attempting to escape," Woodrow Wilson not only refused to recognize Huerta but recalled Henry Lane Wilson and then set about trying to teach Mexicans that the threat to democracy could not be rewarded.

Within Mexico, the death of Madero provoked four years of upheaval. Venustiano Carranza (of the northeast), Francisco Villa (of the north center), Alvaro Obregón (of the northwest), and Zapata (of the center south) maneuvered their armies in shifting coalitions to see who would win the continuing civil war. Carranza won with the backing of Obregón. Subsequently Obregón imposed a constitution radical for its time upon Carranza, who did not implement much of it. The Constitution of 1917 went beyond prohibiting reelection of presidents. Among other things, it provided for land reform, workers' rights (including profit sharing), and secular education. Although the state was declared the owner of Mexico's subsoil mineral wealth and responsible for re-creating and protecting the *ejido* (communal farm, discussed below), the Constitution of 1917 also provided for private property rights. Given the foreign and domestic interests threatened by the legislation (which was never ratified by Mexico's thirty-two political entities), and given the possibility of U.S. intervention, regulatory laws to implement the constitution have taken many years to emerge.

The Stage of Reconstruction,[4] *1920–30*

To stop Obregón's rise in politics and certain presidential victory, Carranza tried to impose his successor on Mexico. The ploy failed and Carranza was assassinated in 1919, thus opening the way for Obregón's election in 1920.

President Obregón finally brought relative peace to the country by incorporating dissident generals into the regular army. Zapata, who had remained in rebellion to call for land reform ever since he declared himself against Madero in 1911, had been killed by Carranza's troops in 1919 and that left only a few powerful leaders, such as Juan Andreu Almazán, to be co-opted. Once incorporated into the regular army, Almazán went into the construction business. With public works contracts awarded by Obregón and subsequent presidents, Almazán began by building a model military base in Monterrey before turning to road construction. Such co-option not only brought peace to Mexico but also reconstruction of the country's damaged economic infrastructure.

Obregón began the process of land reform slowly because his government did not receive U.S. diplo-

[3] For bibliography, see James W. Wilkie and Albert L. Michaels, eds., *Revolution in Mexico: Years of Upheaval* (Tucson: University of Arizona Press, 1984). The detailed story is told in, for example, Arnaldo Córdoba, *La Ideología de la Revolución Mexicana* (México, D.F.: Ediciones Era, 1973); Ramón Ruiz, *The Great Rebellion: Mexico, 1905–1924* (New York: Norton, 1980); and John Mason Hart, *Revolutionary Mexico: The Coming and Process of the Mexican Revolution* (Berkeley: University of California Press, 1987). See also Alan Knight, *The Mexican Revolution*, 2 vols. (New York: Cambridge University Press, 1986), who examines the teens; and Linda B. Hall, *Alvaro Obregón: Power and Revolution in Mexico, 1911–1920* (College Station: Texas A&M University Press, 1981), who treats the rise of General Obregón. Essential reading is Friedrich Katz, *The Secret War in Mexico: Europe, the United States, and the Mexican Revolution* (Chicago: University of Chicago Press, 1981). Michael C. Meyer reappraises the role of Huerta, the General who overthrew President Madero to become president in 1913, in *Huerta* (Lincoln: University of Nebraska Press, 1972). An important statistical view of political careers from 1900 to 1976 is developed by Peter H. Smith, *Political Recruitment in Twentieth-Century Mexico* (Princeton, N.J.: Princeton University Press, 1979).

[4] The best descriptive work for 1920–30 is the detailed chronology provided in John W. F. Dulles, *Yesterday in Mexico: A Chronicle of the Revolution, 1919–1936* (Austin: University of Texas Press, 1961), but the period remains open to analysis. The classic account in Ernest Gruening, *Mexico and Its Heritage* (New York: Century, 1928). An interesting thread of inquiry involves the life of General Almazán which carries from the 1910s through his rise to military power in the 1920s, his role in building the railway link of "mainland" Mexico to the Yucatán peninsula, his influence on the presidential election of 1940, and his role in building tourism after 1940. See James W. Wilkie, "El Complejo Industrial-Militar en México durante la Década de 1930: Diálogo con el General Juan Andreu Almazán," *Revista Mexicana de Ciencia Política* 20:77 (1974), pp. 59–65.

matic recognition until 1924. Obregón's support for the formation of peasant leagues throughout the country to petition for land in an organized way helped him remain in the presidency because, when in 1923 some of his generals rebelled, he was able to mobilize the peasants against the dissident military. This first success of the peasant leagues signaled the beginning of a peasant role in politics that would expand in the 1930s.

With peace established again by 1924, Obregón and his successor in the presidency, Plutarco Elías Calles (1924–28), could proceed on a number of fronts not only to rebuild Mexico but also to frame new institutions. José Vasconcelos, Minister of Education (1921–24), firmly established a new role for educators and stimulated the pedagogical contributions of Mexico's famous muralists, such as Diego Rivera. Manuel Gómez Morín wrote the law for the country's first Agricultural Credit Bank (1925).

Calles established the government's administrative structure. The Banco de México was founded, as were the national commissions for roads, irrigation, and electricity. Calles, who increased the tempo of land reform, found that implementing the constitution was quite problematic, especially to foreigners (who feared losing their subsoil petroleum rights) and to foreign and domestic Catholics (who were angered by limitations on the historical power of the Church in Mexico).

Facing the Cristero War (1926–29) in which lay Catholics rebelled against the government after the Church hierarchy ceased administering the sacraments in Mexico, Calles also had to contend with rebellious generals in 1927 and 1929, the latter of whom were rumored to be trying to link up with the Cristeros. In this complex situation, Calles maintained his power by (*a*) calling on the peasant leagues to help do battle with rebellious soldiers, (*b*) toning down his rhetoric about the rights of labor over capital, and (*c*) accepting the friendship of U.S. Ambassador Dwight Morrow.

Morrow convinced Calles that additional land not be expropriated without previous payment; in turn, Morrow oversaw a softening in the U.S. position that Mexico was dangerous in its "drift toward Bolshevism." Indeed, Calles moderated land reform, labor programs, and support of the Sandino cause against the U.S. marines fighting in Nicaragua.

Morrow also tried to help end the Cristero War, but that work was undone with the assassination of President-elect Obregón in 1928 by a Catholic fanatic. Obregón had been convinced to seek peace with the Catholics, especially because he was scheduled to return to the presidency after changing the constitution to allow for his controversial presidential reelection following an intervening term.

To stifle any doubts that the assassination was religious and not political, Calles (who stood to gain most politically if he did not have to give power back to Obregón), called for the creation of an Official Party of the Revolution, which emerged in 1929 to represent all political wings among the so-called Revolutionary Family. Calles announced that he would never again seek the presidency.

Interim-President Emilio Portes Gil (1928–30) established the Official Party (Partido Nacional Revolucionario), which was based upon the power of regional political bosses. In power fourteen months (the time needed to nominate and elect Obregón's successor, Pascual Ortiz Rubio, for the period 1930–34), Portes Gil defied Calles's main policy goal of merely espousing radical rhetoric.

With regard to revolutionary policy, Portes ignored Calles's wishes and mobilized the country to develop a draft labor code, but it was aborted before it could finally implement the pro-labor provisions of the constitution. Even before Calles left for Europe in June 1929 to assess the world situation, for example, Portes overrode his view that there was no need for labor activism. Calles had argued that the rights of labor were protected by Luis Morones, who was not only the powerful boss of organized labor but also former Minister of Labor under Calles. In theory the workers were protected, but in practice Morones represented the quintessence of labor union corruption.

With Calles in Europe for seven months until December 1929,[5] President Portes Gil acted freely, especially pushing land reform. He and his Minister of Agriculture, Marte R. Gómez, refurbished the image of Zapata, still considered by many to have been a troublesome bandit during the course of his life. Portes and Gómez described Zapata as a heroic guerrilla who fought tenaciously for the right of the peasants to own land. The monthly rate of definitive land distribution to ejidos rose to an average 1.4 times the averages of Obregón and Calles combined, and the rate for persons benefited has never been surpassed (Table 2).

---

[5] Interview with Emilio Portes Gil in James W. Wilkie and Edna Monzón de Wilkie, *México Visto en el Siglo XX; Entrevistas de Historia Oral: Ramón Beteta, Marte R. Gómez, Manuel Gómez Morín, Vicente Lombardo Toledano, Miguel Palomar y Vizcarra, Emilio Portes Gil, Jesús Silva Herzog* (México, D.F.: Distribuido por el Instituto de Investigaciones Económicas, 1969), 512.

Table 2

LAND REFORM IN MEXICO,[1] 1916–88

PART I. Hectares[2]

Date Term Ends[3]	President	Approx. Months in Office	Resolutions Published[4]			Definitive Actions[5]		
			Number	Hectares[7]	Hectare /Month	Number	Hectares[7]	Hectare /Month
May 21, 1920	Venustiano Carranza	48.4⎫	326	224,393	4,636⎫	188	134,239	2,774
Nov. 30, 1920	Adolfo de la Huerta[6]	6.1⎭		157,533	25,825⎭		33,696	5,524
Nov. 30, 1924	Alvaro Obregón	48.0	748	1,730,686	36,056	628	1,133,813	23,621
Nov. 29, 1928	Plutarco Elías Calles	48.0	1,622	3,186,294	66,381	1,573	2,972,876	61,935
Feb. 4, 1930	Emilio Portes Gil	14.1	1,350	2,438,511	172,944	1,156	1,707,757	121,118
Sept. 3, 1932	Pascual Ortiz Rubio	30.8	540	1,225,752	39,797	852	944,538	30,669
Nov. 29, 1934	Abelardo L. Rodríguez	27.0	1,581	2,060,228	76,304	596	790,694	29,285
Nov. 29, 1940	Lázaro Cárdenas	72.0	11,334	20,145,910	279,804	10,744	17,906,430	248,700
Nov. 30, 1946	Manuel Avila Camacho	72.0	3,074	5,970,398	82,922	3,485	5,944,450	82,562
Nov. 30, 1952	Miguel Alemán Valdez	72.0	2,245	5,429,528	75,410	2,385	4,844,123	67,279
Nov. 30, 1958	Adolfo Ruiz Cortines	72.0	1,745	5,771,721	80,163	1,864	4,936,665	68,565
Nov. 30, 1964	Adolfo López Mateos	72.0	2,375	9,308,149	129,280	2,887	11,361,270	157,795
Nov. 30, 1970	Gustavo Díaz Ordaz	72.0	3,912	23,055,619	320,217	2,769	14,139,560	196,383
Nov. 30, 1976	Luis Echeverría Alvarez	72.0	2,208	12,243,317	170,046	2,202	13,328,852	185,123
Nov. 30, 1982	José López Portillo	72.0	3,415	6,347,425	88,159	1,975[a]	6,728,797[a]	93,456
Nov. 30, 1988	Miguel de la Madrid Hurtado	72.0	2,103	4,448,754	61,788	1,298	2,981,519	41,410
	Total	870.4	38,578	103,744,209[b]	119,191	34,602	89,889,279	103,274

1. Revises most data given in Mexico's presidential reports (which tend to be unreliable when compared to detailed data given by the land reform agency); Instituto Nacional de Estadística, Geografía e Informática, *Estadísticas Históricas de México*, I, p. 277; and data for presidents Díaz Ordaz and Echeverría given in James W. Wilkie, *La Revolución Mexicana (1910–1976); Gasto Federal y Cambio Social* (México, D.F.: Fondo de Cultura Económica, 1978), p. 323.
2. Land reform rights distributed as grants to, restitutions to, and enlargements of collective and individual ejidos; grants for new ejidal population centers; and confirmation of existing communal land rights (which recognizes de jure rights of ejidatarios historically holding de facto rights with unregistered legal papers).
3. Because presidential reports to congress customarily take place September 1 and presidents leave office December 1, data for the final three months in office for any president may be credited to the following president.
4. Presidential resolutions become preliminary actions when published in the Mexican government's *Diario Oficial*; resolutions are subject to appeal by persons affected and do not become effective until presidential definitive actions are signed. Resolutions here exclude those signed by one president but not published until one or more succeeding presidents have also taken into account political considerations, technical details, and bureaucratic delays.
5. Definitive actions finalize previously published presidential resolutions; they are also known as "resoluciones ejecutadas" or "resoluciones definitivamente entregadas." Definitive actions take into account appeals, technical adjustments, and changing circumstances to often modify the resolutions. Definitive actions may be based on resolutions signed by earlier presidents. Pending definitive actions are here excluded.
6. Data for De la Huerta are separated here from data for Carranza.
7. One hectare equals 2.47 acres.

a. These definitive data are from Secretaría de Reforma Agraria (SRA), *Avance en Materia Agraria*, cited in Source, below. These figures should be used with caution because the López Portillo government did not leave records fully documenting definitive actions, according to Alfonso Casillas Romahn, MMH's head of the SRA Dirección General de Documentación e Información Agraria, interviews August and October 1988. De la Madrid's *Quinto Informe Económico; Apéndice Estadístico*, 1987, p. 412, gives the following erroneous figures for the JLP period: 3,321 definitive actions distributing 13,904,924 hectares.
b. Excludes 65,023,310 hectares resolved for distribution by one president but published under another (1920–80), according to Casillas.
c. The only figure available is from De la Madrid's *Quinto Informe*, cited in note a, above. Although this figure seems logical in relation to the historical series, it should be used with caution because of the erroneous data given in the *Quinto Informe* for the number of hectares distributed to these persons.
d. Excludes 1,346,759 beneficiaries resolved under one president but published under another (1920–80), according to Casillas.
SOURCE: Secretaría de Reforma Agraria (SRA), *Avance en Materia Agraria, 1983–1987* ([México, D.F.]: Dirección General de Programación y Evaluación, n.d.); James W. Wilkie, *The Mexican Revolution: Federal Expenditure and Social Change Since 1910* (Berkeley: University of California Press, 1970), p. 188; and SRA chart "Resoluciones Presidenciales Publicadas, Ejecutadas y Pendientes de Ejecutar por Período Presidencial, 1915–1980," photocopied in José Luis Mares, "Diagnóstico del Sector Agropecuario y Forestal; Estructura Social: La Reforma Agraria en México, 1915–1980; Un Nuevo Enfoque Analítico," manuscript, n.d., except all De La Huerta data are from Departamento Agrario, *Memoria de Labores, 1945–1946* (statistical section), figures subtracted from total for Carranza in source above. JLP data for resolutions are from SRA, Dirección General de Documentación e Información Agraria, "Resoluciones Presidenciales Publicadas en el Período de José López Portillo," computer printout October 1988, supplied by Alfonso Casillas Romahn; for JLP definitive data, see note a, above. MMH data are from SRA, "Resoluciones y Ejecuciones en el Período de Miguel de la Madrid Hurtado," computer printout August 1988, supplied by Casillas Romahn.

(PART II on overleaf)

Table 2 (Continued)

PART II. Beneficiaries[1]

Date Term Ends[3]	President	Approx. Months in Office	Resolutions Published		Definitive Actions	
			Persons	Persons /Month	Persons	Persons /Month
May 21, 1920	Venustiano Carranza	48.4	59,848	1,237	40,068	828
Nov. 30, 1920	Adolfo de la Huerta	6.1	17,355	2,845	6,330	1,038
Nov. 30, 1924	Alvaro Obregón	48.0	164,128	3,419	134,798	2,808
Nov. 29, 1928	Plutarco Elías Calles	48.0	302,539	6,303	297,428	6,196
Feb. 4, 1930	Emilio Portes Gil	14.1	187,269	13,281	171,577	12,169
Sept. 3, 1932	Pascual Ortiz Rubio	30.8	57,994	1,883	64,556	2,096
Nov. 29, 1934	Abelardo L. Rodríguez	27.0	158,393	5,866	68,556	2,539
Nov. 29, 1940	Lázaro Cárdenas	72.0	764,888	10,623	811,157	11,266
Nov. 30, 1946	Manuel Avila Camacho	72.0	122,941	1,708	157,836	2,192
Nov. 30, 1952	Miguel Alemán Valdez	72.0	108,625	1,509	97,391	1,353
Nov. 30, 1958	Adolfo Ruiz Cortines	72.0	226,292	3,143	231,888	3,221
Nov. 30, 1964	Adolfo López Mateos	72.0	289,356	4,019	304,498	4,229
Nov. 30, 1970	Gustavo Díaz Ordaz	72.0	374,520	5,202	240,695	3,343
Nov. 30, 1976	Luis Echeverría Alvarez	72.0	223,250	3,101	206,452	2,867
Nov. 30, 1982	José López Portillo	72.0	245,488	3,410	264,532[c]	3,674
Nov. 30, 1988	Miguel de la Madrid Hurtado	72.0	184,213	2,559	105,920	1,471
	Total	870.4	3,487,099[d]	4,006	3,203,682	3,681

1. For notes, see Part I, above.
SOURCE: Resolutions, SRA chart, "Resoluciones Presidenciales Publicadas, Ejecutadas y Pendientes de Ejecutar por Período Presidencial, 1915–1980," given in Mares, slightly revising data in Nacional Financiera, *La Economía Mexicana en Cifras, 1977*, p. 45; except data for De la Huerta from Departamento Agraria, *Memoria de Labores, 1945–1946* (statistical section), subtracted here from data for Carranza. JLP data are from SRA, Dirección General de Documentación e Información Agraria, "Resoluciones Presidenciales Publicadas en el Período de José López Portillo," computer printout October 1988, supplied by Alfonso Casillas Romahn (see note a, above).

MMH data are from SRA, "Resoluciones y Ejecuciones en el Período de Miguel de la Madrid Hurtado," computer printout August 1988, supplied by Casillas Romahn.
Definitive Actions, SRA chart for 1915–80 (as for resolutions, above), slightly revising Wilkie, *The Mexican Revolution: Federal Expenditure and Social Change Since 1910*, p. 194; except JLP data for definitive actions are from MMH, *Quinto Informe de Gobierno; Apéndice Estadístico, 1987*, p. 412. MMH data are from SRA, "Resoluciones y Ejecuciones en el Período de Miguel de la Madrid Hurtado," computer printout August 1988, supplied by Casillas Romahn.

PART III. Certificates of Inaffectability Granted to Protect Agricultural and Ranching Lands from Land Reform,[1] 1934–88[a] (Number)

Period	President	Agricultural		Ranching	
		Issued	Pending	Issued	Pending
1934–40	Lázaro Cárdenas	865	0	69	0
1940–46	Manuel Avila Camacho	13,350	0	126	0
1946–52	Miguel Alemán	73,694	0	575	0
1952–58	Adolfo Ruiz Cortines	82,366	0	445	0
1958–64	Adolfo López Mateos	8,627	0	54	0
1964–70	Gustavo Díaz Ordaz	2,055	0	749	0
1970–76	Luis Echeverría Alvarez	1,496	0	361	0
1976–82	José López Portillo	7,715	0	481	0
	Subtotal	190,235	0	2,862	0
1982–88	Miguel de la Madrid Hurtado	222,816	1,257	31,572	451
	Total	413,051	1,257	34,434	451

1. For farm lands, certificates are permanent; for ranching, some certificates are permanent and some are for 25 years. Data include certificates issued as renewal of protection granted earlier.
a. Between 1901 and 1933, 67 certificates were issued for agricultural lands, 2 for ranching lands.

SOURCE: SRA, Dirección General de Documentación e Información Agraria, "Inafectabilidad: Concentrado de Certificados por Período Presidencial," computer printout August 1988, supplied by director general Alfonso Casillas Romahn.

Table 2 (Continued)

**PART IV. Agricultural Lands Protected
by Certificates of Inaffectability, 1936–88[a]
(Hectares)**

Period	President	Type of Land[1]		Total[1]
		Irrigated	Rainfed	
1934–40	Lázaro Cárdenas	12,040	41,555	53,595
1940–46	Manuel Avila Camacho	115,474	292,712	408,186
1946–52	Miguel Alemán	387,397	455,416	842,813
1952–58	Adolfo Ruiz Cortines	94,197	1,229,526	1,323,723
1958–64	Adolfo López Mateos	150,340	34,704	185,044
1964–70	Gustavo Díaz Ordaz	60,796	52,413	113,209
1970–76	Luis Echeverría Alvarez	14,892	15,089	29,981
1976–82	José López Portillo	48,392	37,654	86,046
1982–88	Miguel de la Madrid Hurtado	343,906	1,476,657	1,820,563
Total		1,227,447	3,635,736	4,863,183

1. May include some renewal of certificates granted early in the program.
a. Between 1901 and 1933, 23 hectares were protected, 13 irrigated and
   10 rainfed land.
SOURCE: SRA, Dirección General de Documentación e Información
   Agraria, "Inafectabilidad: Superficie Amparada por Certificados Agrícolas Emitidos," computer printout August 1988, supplied by director
   general Alfonso Casillas Romahn.

**PART V. Ranching Lands Protected
by Certificates of Inaffectability, 1934–88[a]
(Hectares)**

Period	President	Total
1934–40	Lázaro Cárdenas	114,369
1940–46	Manuel Avila Camacho	736,148
1946–52	Miguel Alemán	2,316,743
1952–58	Adolfo Ruiz Cortines	945,577
1958–64	Adolfo López Mateos	71,944
1964–70	Gustavo Díaz Ordaz	2,262,575
1970–76	Luis Echeverría Alvarez	262,024
1976–82	José López Portillo	70,387
1982–88	Miguel de la Madrid Hurtado	9,311,582
Total		16,091,890

1. Includes renewal of certificates.
a. Between 1901 and 1933, 54 hectares were protected, 472 of low quality and 69 of medium quality.
SOURCE: SRA, Dirección General de Documentación e Información
   Agraria, "Inafectabilidad: Superficie Amparada por Certificados
   Ganaderos Emitidos," computer printout August 1988, supplied by
   director general Alfonso Casillas Romahn.

Phase II. Ideology of Social Revolution,[6] 1930–40

The limits to the political solution to Mexico's problems had become all too clear by the end of the 1920s. Not only was there a continuing difficulty in achieving peaceful transition between Mexican presidents but also the U.S. politico-economic model (which had provided a resistant force to new socialistic and communistic models) seemed to have fallen along with the collapse of Wall Street in 1929. Calles ignored the climate of opinion that had so many politically aware Mexicans turning away from the U.S. model to the Soviet model of development, which would also tend to support the development of the ejido.

Although the Mexican economy entered a depression between 1929 and 1932 (Fig. 1), Calles rejected calls to adopt aspects of communalist models coming into vogue. His outlook on political economy was strengthened by his 1929 travel to Europe, which proved influential for Mexico. The trip, which effectively allowed Portes Gil to speed up land reform, spurred Calles to act against Portes Gil's important agrarian program. Upon his return from Europe in December 1929, Calles argued that land reform creates tiny parcels which cannot take advantage of mechanization and modern techniques. He called for a halt to further land reform in Mexico.[7]

With regard to Calles's past record in land reform, as president he had undertaken to encourage small farms while restoring land to the ejido or community-owned agricultural and ranching units which had lost their holdings under Díaz. But Calles preferred only one of the ejidos' two manifestations. By law, the ejido can be worked individually or collectively, and Calles favored the individual ejido wherein each head of family (ejidatario) is allotted a specific parcel (with common land set aside for common use such as meetings, sports, grazing, etc.) rather than the group ejido wherein farm and pasture land is worked by all the people. For Calles, individuals working their own ejido plots were destined to graduate to the status of peasant proprietors with their own titles.

Calles was especially critical of the ejido system for two reasons. First, in both of its forms the ejido is community owned and cannot be sold or mortgaged, thus being ineligible for private bank credit. Private banks require collateral in order to make loans, and Calles was more concerned than ever about the lack of public funds available to supply credit.

Second, on his trip to Europe Calles was impressed by French small private farmers. He saw them as the bulwark of France's stable development —the type of bulwark needed by Mexico.

Having returned to Mexico for the early 1930 inauguration of President Ortiz Rubio, Calles was determined to reassert his authority. As the Strong Man of Mexico, he imposed his will upon a compliant President Ortiz Rubio. Calles ordered land reform to be terminated within a short time, and Ortiz Rubio called for state agrarian commissions to finish their work and dissolve themselves within months.

But with economic conditions reaching a trough in Mexico by 1932, when GDP declined by nearly 15 percent (Table 3), Calles soon realized that if the Official Party were to remain in power he would have to cede to its left wing. Forcing Ortiz Rubio from office in 1932 after only 2.5 years, Calles named a temporizer as interim-president, Abelardo Rodríguez. Although Rodríguez halted strikes on the grounds that they disrupted the Revolution, he eliminated the time constraint on completing land reform. Most importantly, he facilitated the naming of Calles's choice for president from 1934 to 1940—General Lázaro Cárdenas.

The Calles decision about whom to name president was somewhat constrained. Needing to appeal to the left wing of the Official Party and to choose a general with whom he could work to establish a stable political system, Calles selected Cárdenas, his protégé. Cárdenas not only had the advantage of Calles's support but the additional advantage of being a hero of the left, which was impressed with his reforms as governor of Michoacán from 1928 to 1932. There

---

[6] For a work which shows implicitly the complexity of events of the 1930s, see ibid. On politics, see Lyle C. Brown, "General Lázaro Cárdenas and Mexican Presidential Politics, 1933–1940" (Ph.D. dissertation, University of Texas at Austin, 1964). Also useful is the view on the Cárdenas presidency in Nora Hamilton, *The Limits of State Autonomy: Post-Revolutionary Mexico* (Princeton, N.J.: Princeton University Press, 1982). For the most important single reference work on politics, see Roderic A. Camp, *Mexican Political Biographies, 1935–1981*, 2d ed. (Tucson: University of Arizona Press, 1982). See also Camp, *Intellectuals and the State in Twentieth-Century Mexico* (Austin: University of Texas Press, 1985). Camp's most recent work is his insightful *Entrepreneurs and Politics in Twentieth-Century Mexico* (New York: Oxford University Press, 1989). Other views of industrialists are provided by Dale Story, *Industry, the State, and Public Policy in Mexico* (Austin: University of Texas Press, 1986), and Betsy L. Link, "Spirit of Entrepreneurship: Octaviano Longoria and the Rise of Industry in Mexico" (Ph.D. dissertation, University of California, Los Angeles, 1989); on the economy in the 1930s, see *La Industrialización Mexicana durante la Gran Depresión* (México, D.F.: El Colegio de México, 1987).

[7] See Eyler Newton Simpson, *The Ejido, Mexico's Way Out* (Chapel Hill: University of North Carolina Press, 1937), pp. 89–90 and 113 ff. On the history of land problems, see also Clifton B. Kroeber, *Man, Land, and Water: Mexico's Farmlands Irrigation Policies, 1885–1911* (Berkeley: University of California Press, 1983); Paul L. Lamartine Yates, *Mexico's Agricultural Dilemma* (Tucson: University of Arizona Press, 1981); and Jeffery Brannon and Eric Baklanoff, *Agrarian Reform and Public Enterprise in Mexico: The Political Economy of Yucatán's Henequen Industry* (Tuscaloosa: University of Alabama Press, 1987).

Figure 1
YEARLY CHANGE IN MEXICO'S GDP, 1896–1986

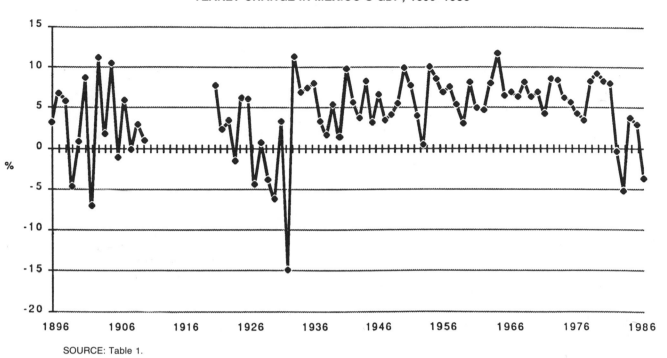

SOURCE: Table 1.

Cárdenas had organized workers and peasants to improve their conditions, and did not follow Calles's order to halt land reform.

Although Calles thought Cárdenas would be a deferential president, Cárdenas immediately accelerated land reform, and he allowed labor to use the strike as a political weapon to take over factories. When those policies brought Calles's wrath, in 1936 Cárdenas expelled Calles and Morones from Mexico.

To solidify support, Cárdenas created a giant new labor central organization under Vicente Lombardo Toledano; at the same time Cárdenas won the peasants to his cause by stepping up monthly definitive actions distributing land to ejidos at a rate more than double that under Portes Gil (Table 2). Using the labor and peasant sectors to counterbalance the power of the military, he reorganized the Official Party in 1938 as a Mexican Popular Front.

Drawing from European models, Cárdenas's Partido de la Revolución Mexicana (PRM) shifted from the base of regional political bosses to a corporate system with four sectors: labor, peasants, militarymen, and popular sector representatives. A major sector omitted was the private capital group which wielded the real economic muscle of the country. Cárdenas required that this group organize into chambers representing its components (such as commerce, manufacturing, etc.) in order to consult with the government. With many interest groups to mobilize, Cárdenas effectively neutralized the military as the key decision maker in Mexican politics.

Yet Cárdenas did not organize monolithic political sectors. Thus, he prevented Lombardo Toledano from merging his labor sector with the peasant sector, and he sought to prevent any one faction in each from becoming too strong. That the private capital group would not emerge in monolithic form is illustrated by the role of the manufacturers component. Within the Confederación de Cámaras Industriales (CONCAMIN), a subcomponent of small manufacturers organized to form the Cámara Nacional de la Industria de Transformación (CNIT). While CONCAMIN traditionally was dominated by interests who could generate credits on their own and thus sought to restrain broad activity by government intervention in the economy, CNIT's interests tended to be those of newer firms which, concerned about competition from foreign capital, also lacked the ability to generate adequate credit, and therefore favored broad government economic intervention.[8] These opposing views within the private capital sector gave the government much leeway to expand the role of state policy.

[8] See Vernon, *The Dilemma of Mexico's Development*, pp. 18–19.

Table 3

DOLLAR VALUE OF THE PESO[1] AND MEXICO'S INFLATION RATE[2]

PART I. Average Peso Market/Free Rate
Compared to Average Inflation Rate,[3] 1950–88

Year	Peso[4] A. Average Pesos per Dollar	B. % Devaluation[6]	Inflation[5] C. Average Yearly Consumer Price Index % Increase[7]
1950–1953	8.65[a]	0	7.8[c]
1954	12.50	30.8	5.2
1955–1975	12.50[b]	o	6.4[d]
1976	15.43	19.0	15.8
1977	22.57	31.6	29.0
1978	22.77	.9	17.5
1979	22.81	.2	18.2
1980	22.95	.6	26.4
1981	24.51	6.4	27.9
1982[e]	56.40	56.5	58.9
1983	150.30	62.5	101.8
1984	185.19	18.8	65.5
1985	310.17	40.3	57.7
1986	637.38	51.4	86.2
1987	1,405.80	54.7	131.8
1988	2,290.00	38.1	114.2

1. For the peso, Part I gives the average market/free rate, also used for foreign trade conversion to dollars through 1981; Part II gives the controlled conversion rate for foreign trade, which was established in 1982; Part III gives the end of year free-market rate; Part IV gives rates for major devaluations on the free market.
2. For inflation since 1968, the International Monetary Fund (IMF) uses the Bank of Mexico national consumer price index; prior to 1968, the IMF uses the food price index for Mexico City; cf. Jeffrey Bortz, *Industrial Wages in Mexico City* (New York: Garland, 1987), pp. 331–332.
3. Inflation and devaluation do not involve one-to-one relationships because in the former case the percentage change is unlimited and in the latter case it is limited to 100 percent. For example, inflation of 233 percent would require a 70 percent devaluation in order to maintain parity.
4. Mexico's "market" or "free" rate has been subject to support by Mexico's Banco Central and/or to the Banco Central's manipulation by "dirty floats" wherein the rate is in reality a regulated rate. Since 1982 the free rate is used for non-foreign trade transactions. The free rate has not always meant free convertibility of pesos to dollars, e.g., for a time beginning in 1982 residents of Mexico's interior could buy no more than 1,500 dollars per person yearly and residents in the border area could purchase no more than 1,500 dollars monthly; see *IMF Survey*, November 15, 1982.
5. Inflation calculated from yearly average indexes in contrast to indexes for December to December given in Part III.
6. Devaluation is calculated by figuring percentage change from later year to prior year; for example, the average devaluation for 1983 (average peso value = 150.30) compared with 1982 (average peso value = 56.40) is calculated as follows: (56.4/150.3) − 1 × 100. Alternatively, it can be calculated as follows: (150.30 − 56.40) = 93.9/150.30 × 100, which yields the same result.
7. National percentage increase or change is figured from earlier year to following year; for example, from 1982 (average index number 203.3, not given in Part I) to 1983 (index 410.2) as follows: (410.2/203.3) − 1 × 100).

a. Stable exchange rate for 4 years, 1950–53.
b. Stable exchange rate for 21 years, 1955–75.
c. Accumulated average percentage change of 31.2 percent divided by 4 years = 7.8 percent per year; the Bortz worker cost of living index (see note 2, above) shows 31.3 percent for the four years or 7.8 percent per year.
d. Accumulated average percentage change of 134.0 percent in index divided by 21 years yields an average 6.4 percent per year; the Bortz worker cost of living index (see note 2, above) differs slightly, showing 114.8 for the 21 years or an average of 5.5 percent per year.
e. "Free" or floating rate begins in 1982 (as does the "controlled" rate given in Part II, below), but free rate is pegged within narrow limits by the Banco de México. The Banco de México set gradual devaluation of the peso at 7 centavos daily from December 20, 1982, through September 21, 1983, then at 13 centavos into December 1984, at 13 centavos into April 1985, and at 21 centavos into August 1985. In August 1985 the rate was "freed" to allow market forces to influence higher devaluation, but still regulated by the Banco de México. (See Juan Raymundo Rocha, "Evolución del Tipo de Cambio, 1976–1987," *Comercio Exterior*, September 1987, pp. 724–729.) On December 16, 1987, the free-market peso was frozen at 2,225 until January 8 when minor slippage permitted it to slowly reach 2,295 by May 1988 (*Indicadores Económicos* 104, March 1988, pp. 30–31), the Banco de México committing its dollar reserves to provide peso stability at least until fall 1988.

SOURCE: A, International Monetary Fund, *International Financial Statistics—Yearbook, 1980* and February 1988 (line "wf" for 1980–1982, line "xf" since 1983); and Banco Nacional de México, *Review of the Economic Situation of Mexico*, July 1989; see also Banco de México, *Indicadores Económicos*, October 1987, p. IV–9, which clarifies the data.
B, Calculated.
C, 1950–58: International Monetary Fund, *International Statistics—Yearbook, 1980*, pp. 60–61.
1959–88: ibid., *1987*, pp. 114–115; and *El Mercado de Valores*, January 15, 1988, June 15, 1988, and August 15, 1989.

Table 3 (Continued)

PART II. Average Controlled (Foreign Trade)[1] Peso Rate, 1982–88

Year	Average Pesos per Dollar
1982	57.44[a]
1983	120.09
1984	167.83
1985	256.87
1986	611.77
1987	1,378.00[b]
1988	2,273.00

1. The controlled rate, established in 1982, is used for most import-export transactions, and it cannot be used for private investments, debt payments, or tourist exchange transactions. For the rate of slippage against the dollar (which was the same as that of the free rate from 1982–85), see note e in Part I, above. Beginning in February 1988, the gradual slippage was increased to 3-peso "minidevaluations" each business day.

a. Nacional Financiera, *La Economía Mexicana en Cifras, 1977* (México, D.F., 1984), p. 221.
b. The controlled peso stood at 1,705 on November 18, 1987, when the free-market peso was dramatically devalued (*Los Angeles Times*, November 19, 1987). The controlled peso had slipped to 1,801 by December 14, 1987, when it was devalued sharply to 2,200 to bring it to about the same level as the free-market peso (*Los Angeles Times*, December 18, 1987).

SOURCE: International Monetary Fund, *International Financial Statistics*, February 1988 (line "wf" since 1983); *El Mercado de Valores*, February 15, 1988; Banco de México, *Indicadores Económicos*, January 1989, pp. 146 and 147; and Banco Nacional de México, *Review of the Economic Situation of Mexico*, August 1988; see also Banco de México, *Indicadores Económicos*, February 1988, which clarifies the data.

PART III. Year-End Peso Market/Free Rate,[1] and Year-End Inflation, 1970–88

Year	Peso — A. Year-End Pesos per Dollar	Peso — B. % Devaluation December to December	Inflation — C. National CPI December to December
1970	12.50	0	4.8
1971	12.50	0	5.2
1972	12.50	0	5.5
1973	12.50	0	21.3
1974	12.50	0	20.7
1975	12.50	0	11.2
1976	19.95	37.3	27.2
1977	22.74	12.3	20.7
1978	22.73	0	16.2
1979	22.80	.3	20.0
1980	23.26	2.0	29.8
1981	26.23	11.3	28.7
1982[a]	149.25	82.4	98.8
1983	161.35	7.5	80.8
1984	209.97	23.2	59.2
1985	450.75	53.4	63.7
1986	914.50	50.7	105.7
1987	2,227.50	58.9	159.2
1988	2,295.00	2.9	51.7

1. On the limits to the concept of the "market/free" rate in Mexico, see note 3 in Part I, above.

a. The "free" rate begins in 1982 (as does the "controlled" rate in Part II, above); the free rate is in reality pegged within narrow limits by the Banco de México.

SOURCE: A, 1975–85: International Monetary Fund, *International Financial Statistics—Yearbook, 1987* (line "ae" for 1975–1981).
   1982–88: idem, *International Financial Statistics*, November 1987 and February 1989 (line "xe" since 1982). See also Banco de México, *Indicadores Económicos*, May 1987; and *El Mercado de Valores*, February 15, 1988.
B, Calculated.
C, National Consumer Price Index (CPI) given in Nacional Financiera, *La Economía Mexicana en Cifras, 1986*, p. 301, and (since 1980) *El Mercado de Valores*, October 26, 1987, January 15, 1988, and February 15, 1989.

(PART IV on overleaf)

Table 3 (Continued)

PART IV. Major Devaluations of the Peso on the Free Market,[1] 1948–87

Year	Date	Pesos per Dollar	% Devaluation
1948	June 21	4.86	
	22	6.45	24.7
1949	June 17	8.22	
	18	8.65	5.0
1954	Apr 18	8.65	
	19	12.50	30.8
1976	Aug 31	12.50	
	Sep 1	20.00	37.5
	Oct 26	20.00	
	27	26.00	23.1
1982[a]	Feb 17	27.00	
	18	38.00	28.9
1987	Nov 17	1,712.00[b]	
	18	2,200.00[c]	22.2

1. On the limits to the concept of the "free" rate in Mexico, see note 3 in Part I, above.

a. By December, the Banco Central begins open intervention in the free market to devalue the peso at a regular and gradual rate against the dollar; see note e in Part I, above.

b. The rate stood at 1,625 on October 19, 1987—Wall Street's "Black Monday."

c. In a highly volatile day of trading for some transactions, on November 18 the buying rate of the peso reached as high as 2,700 to the dollar and the selling rate as high as 3,000—according to the *New York Times*, November 24, 1987.

SOURCE: 1948–54, Nacional Financiera, *La Economía Mexicana en Cifras* (México, D.F., 1977), pp. 216–217, except 1948–49 from Ricardo Torres Gaytán, *Un Siglo de Devaluaciones del Peso Mexicano* (México, D.F.: Siglo XXI), p. 308.

1976, *Los Angeles Times*, September 9 and October 28, 1976.

1982, ibid.; James W. Wilkie, "Problems and Processes of Developing Research on a 'New' Area," in Stanley R. Ross, ed., *Ecology and Development of the Border Region* (México, D.F.: Asociación Nacional de Universidades e Institutos de Enseñanza Superior, 1983), p. 301.

1987, *Barron's*, November 23, 1987, p. 72.

Meanwhile, Cárdenas resolved the problem of the Catholic Church's continuing challenge to the Mexican state. The Church was attempting to defeat two programs of the Ministry of Education. The first involved so-called sex education dating from the early 1930s; the second involved so-called socialist education begun by Cárdenas. The very titles of the programs sparked Church enmity, but Cárdenas strongly favored both as part of his plan to teach the masses about their situation in life, his goal being to enable them to make more effective demands so that Mexico could eventually become a socialist country.

By the middle of his presidency, Cárdenas sacrificed these educational programs for several reasons. Because the population was still two-thirds illiterate in the 1930s, the program depended upon highly sophisticated teachers, few of which existed. Also his ability to retain power was being severely tested by multiple economic problems, including disruptions in the countryside as land reform proceeded, confusion in the cities as strikes cut off even electricity, and impending trouble with the foreign-owned oil companies.

Therefore, Cárdenas was willing to develop a new Church-state relationship that would allow each to tacitly support the other. This arrangement was made possible when the bishop of Michoacán, Church moderate Luis Martínez, became archbishop of Mexico in 1937. Cárdenas and Martínez had coexisted peacefully when Cárdenas had been governor of Michoacán, and both laid the basis for an implicit Church-state reconciliation that has lasted to the present. Although the anticlerical provisions of the Constitution of 1917 remain, they are purely symbolic and are not enforced. Leaders of both sides have moderated their language as trust has replaced distrust in Church-state relations.[9]

Cárdenas resolved problems with the Church at an opportune moment because in 1938 he had to turn his attention fully to problems with the foreign-owned oil companies. In a confrontation over the amount of wages paid to workers, Cárdenas nationalized the oil companies. The Church hierarchy backed that action just as it would the nationalization of the privately owned banking system in 1982.

Cárdenas now faced new political problems, however, because the right wing within the Official Party did not like the socialistic direction Mexico was taking. General Almazán broke with the PRM to run for the presidency in 1940 and could count on support from such widely different groups as the Sinarquistas (far right lay Catholics who claimed Mexico

---

[9] Peter L. Reich, "Mexico's Hidden Revolution: The Catholic Church in Politics Since 1930," University of California, Los Angeles, n.d., manuscript.

was falling into anarchy) and former supporters of General Saturnino Cedillo (who in 1938 unsuccessfully led Mexico's last military rebellion reputedly instigated by the former owners of the oil companies).

By the late 1930s Cárdenas realized that immediate social benefits for the masses would not solve Mexico's long-term problems. Even as he began government loan and subsidy programs to help private industry expand under government supervision, he chose a moderate to follow him in the presidency. In the bloody contest of 1940, Cárdenas's candidate, moderate Manuel Avila Camacho, was elected for the term from 1940 to 1946.

Phase III. Ideology of Economic Revolution,[10] 1940–60

With Avila Camacho in the presidency, General Almazán, who had lost the election of 1940, did not rebel as he had promised; rather, he retired to Acapulco where he pursued his construction business by building the port city's first luxury hotel and establishing the basis for the emergence of Mexico's tourist industry. Tourism would be aided by the onset of World War II; no longer able to travel to Europe, the U.S. elite discovered Mexico by air and the middle class followed by auto in the 1950s until they too were affluent enough to travel by air beginning in the 1960s.

Mexico's industry also benefited from World War II. Mining production and industrial output were guaranteed export to the United States. Prices were pegged low as part of Mexico's contribution to the war effort, but in turn the United States bought most everything Mexico could produce. The resulting boom in the economy brought about an industrial revolution that absorbed governmental energies.

Cárdenas himself, who served as Minister of War under Avila Camacho, believed that the land reform had been completed by the time he left office. Indeed over 40 percent of the agriculturally employed population had received land from the government so the country was free to turn from agriculture to industry.

The political framework for this shift was dictated by President Miguel Alemán, who in 1946 modified the concept of Revolution by reshaping the Official Party as the Partido Revolucionario Institucional (PRI). Institutionalization deemphasized party militancy by downplaying the role of labor and elim-

inating the military sector. Henceforth civilians, mainly lawyers, would focus on development of the economic infrastructure, conferring on private investment the task of industrializing the country. The "revolutionariness" of the Official Party now incorporated Economic Revolution.

Under presidents Alemán (1946–52) and Adolfo Ruiz Cortines (1952–58), nation building emphasized construction of dams and hydroelectric and massive irrigation projects, instead of land reform. The expanding road and rail network provided further infrastructure for the development of a heavily protected industry, which set the pace for steady growth in GDP (see Table 1).

This era of ideology stressing economic development looked for its ideas, capital, and technology in close relations with the United States. During this "Era of Good Feeling" between the two countries,[11] both nations were disposed to resolve problems rather than create them. With Mexico's liberal investment laws, U.S. companies rushed to Mexico where they could become co-owners with Mexican capital of factories producing for a captive market. As the *Handbook for the Foreign Investor*, published about 1960, put it:[12]

Today . . . Mexico is one of the three most stable nations, politically and economically, in the Western Hemisphere. The years of violent revolution, from 1911 to 1921, ended almost forty years ago. The subsequent period of economic unrest was over before the Second World War. . . .

Individuals or countries afflicted with an "inferiority complex" are likely to behave in illogical and unpredictable ways. National confidence is an asset to the foreign investor. A feeling of insecurity makes nations very touchy about foreign influence and makes it very easy to enlist popular sentiment against foreign firms. In a nation that has gained confidence in its own destiny, this danger to foreign capital is no longer present.

In Mexico, concern about possible discrimination against foreign capital tends to be minimized by the growing number of joint foreign and Mexican enterprises. Where foreign and Mexican investors are associated in joint ventures, there is little incentive to this sort of discrimination.

Coming to Mexico, the foreigner discovers that investments which appear to meet every criterion of the conservative investor nevertheless yield high returns. They are suspicious and incredulous. . . . Actually there is no mystery and no inconsistency between low risk and high return. . . . Where capital is in short supply compared with demand in the form of promising investment opportunities, there is nothing illogical about a situation which offers high returns with safety.

---

[10]On the 1940s and 1950s, see Frank R. Brandenburg, *The Making of Modern Mexico* (Englewood Cliffs, N.J.: Prentice-Hall, 1964), who puts these decades into a historical perspective. See also Howard F. Cline's classic work, *The United States and Mexico* (Cambridge, Mass.: Harvard University Press, 1953).

[11]See Howard F. Cline, *Mexico: Revolution to Evolution, 1940–1960* (New York: Oxford University Press, 1963), pp. 304–398 and passim.

[12]John Morris Ryan, ed., *Handbook for the Foreign Investor in Mexico*, 2d ed. (México, D.F.: John Morris Ryan, n.d.), pp. 11–13 and 16–19.

The *Handbook* went on to show (p. 16) that the share of government investment in total investment (private plus government) was 39 percent in 1953 compared with 34 percent in 1958. In indicating that "the principal function of government ownership in Mexico today is not to compete with private enterprise," the *Handbook* reminded readers that there was "no shortage of opportunities for private initiative," investment being closed to Mexicans and foreigners only for petroleum; limited to Mexicans for inland transport, fishing, bottling, radio and cinema, and advertising and publishing; and excluding more than a 49 percent foreign investment in a few cases.[13]

The ideology of Economic Revolution involved the policy of stabilizing development, that is, economic growth that was neither too fast nor too slow. Monetary policy offered the means to this end, with the peso stable and inflation low. From 1954 to 1976 the peso was pegged at 12.50 to the dollar, with inflation averaging an amount low for Latin America—about 6 percent yearly (Table 3, Part I).

Under the policy of stabilizing development, Mexico encouraged private and foreign capital to substitute goods manufactured in Mexico for imported goods, the government imposing high tariffs to protect Mexican private industry to which it extended subsidies. When foreign capital was not willing to cooperate with Mexico's private sector in joint ventures, the government either did so or encouraged domestic and foreign industrialists to join in developing the country's manufacturing base.

At the same time, political stability was encouraged as the Official Party entered into implicit alliances with various socioeconomic sectors in Mexico. Tacit pacts had been developed with sectors since the Cárdenas era in order to create the basis for the Official Party, and, as the economy grew, the number of pacts expanded (more fully discussed below). For example, manufacturers enjoyed the privilege of exemption from import taxes on needed equipment. The government's selection of whom to grant (or not to grant) such permits gave it leverage to gather private support of the Official Party, as did the selection of who would receive credits and subsidies to build plants and distribution networks.

Increasingly rapid population growth spurred the economic expansion of Mexico after 1940. World War II hastened the development and marketing of miracle drugs such as penicillin, which soon meant the control of many diseases and a declining death rate. The advent of modern refrigeration permitted

[13] Ibid., pp. 16, 18–19, and 114. Revised data on public investment (see table 14, below) show 37 percent for 1953 and 32 percent for 1958.

Figure 2

SOCIAL POVERTY INDEX FOR MEXICO, 1910–70

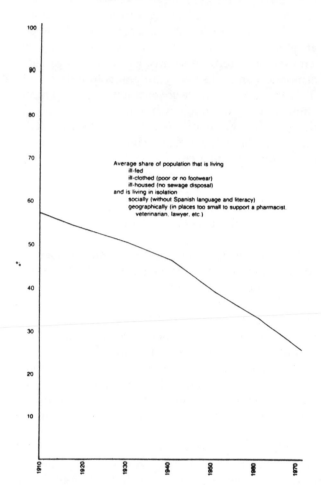

Average share of population that is living
ill-fed
ill-clothed (poor or no footwear)
ill-housed (no sewage disposal)
and is living in isolation
socially (without Spanish language and literacy)
geographically (in places too small to support a pharmacist, veterinarian, lawyer, etc.)

SOURCE: James W. Wilkie, *La Revolución Mexicana (1910–1976): Gasto Público y Cambio Social* (México, D.F.: Fondo de Cultura Económica, 1978), p. 384.

the development of the tropics, which had remained unfit for habitation until the introduction of sulpha drugs in the 1930s.

Where population had fallen during the 1910s from 15 to 14 million after a decade of civil war that either killed people or forced them to leave Mexico, by 1930 the population had regained its upward trajectory, reaching 17 million. In 1940 the total was 20 million, increasing to 26 million in 1950. By 1960 the population reached 36 million—double the 18 million figure which Cárdenas believed in 1935 was too low to achieve dynamic national growth. Indeed, by 1970 when the total reached 51 million, the population was growing faster than the country's ability to supply services and create jobs. Although new population policy established plans to slow the growth rate (discussed below), Mexico's population reached 69 million in 1980 and may, perhaps, reach 84 million in 1990.

Although the benefits of Economic Revolution were supposed to slowly trickle down to the masses, the results were mixed. On the one hand, the Social Poverty Index for Mexico showed much improvement. It had stood at 56.9 percent in 1910, but improved to 46.0 percent in 1940 and to 33.1 percent in 1960 (Fig. 2). The decrease in social poverty meant that Mexico's masses were prepared to mobilize in a sustained way for the first time. On the other hand, income distribution seemed to become increasingly unfair.

By the end of the 1950s, the gap in income distribution led to a strong demand for change in government policy. The impetus for change came from the masses as well as the new generation of university graduates. The tremendous expansion in the number of university students begun under Alemán meant the rise of the first large base for articulate social criticism in Mexican history. Thus, in a 1960 book titled *La Distribución del Ingreso y el Desarrollo Económico de México* published by the National School of Economics, Ifigenia M. de Navarrete argued that the incomes of the poor and middle class had fallen from 48 percent to 43 percent of total income between 1950 and 1957.

Demand for change in government policy coincided with events in Cuba after 1959 where Fidel Castro undertook to put the social aspect into the process of development, which for so long had been dominated by economic theory. Former president Cárdenas demanded deemphasis of Economic Revolution.

Phase IV. Ideology of Balanced Revolution,[14] 1960–70

In the early 1960s Cárdenas seemingly threatened to break with the Official Party as he sought to rally Mexico behind Cuba in its struggle with the United States. In reality Cárdenas was merely organizing the left in Mexico to pressure the Official Party to shift away from the ideology of Economic Revolution. Reiterating his loyalty to the Revolutionary Family, Cárdenas praised its "discipline" in deciding matters inside the Official Party—discipline which had long since made General Saturnino

[14] On the 1960s, see James W. Wilkie, Michael C. Meyer, and Edna Monzón de Wilkie, eds., *Contemporary Mexico: Papers of the IV International Congress of Mexican History* (Berkeley: University of California Press, 1976), which provides important insights on all of Mexican history as well. On the passing in Mexico of Octavio Paz's important interpretation of the country's so-called inferiority complex, see James W. Wilkie, "The Historical View of Octavio Paz: A Critique of the Washington Address," *New Scholar* 9 (1984), pp. 1–11.

Cedillo's 1938 attempt to overthrow Cárdenas the last such move. Like most Mexicans, Cárdenas knew that the Cuban Revolution was not a suitable model for Mexico, which had developed a socially responsible constitution even before the Russian Revolution of 1917.

To make the transition from overt Economic Revolution, the PRI had broken with its tradition of selecting presidents from the Ministry of War (through 1940) or from the Ministry of Interior (through 1952) and had chosen as its standard bearer for the term from 1958 to 1964 the Minister of Labor, Adolfo López Mateos (ALM). The choice was made with the realization that the PRI would be hard pressed to continue to contain strike activity, which it had done so successfully after 1940.

Labor strife broke out with pent-up explosiveness in 1958. Major strikes that year and for the next several years led by railroad, telephone, and telegraph workers as well as by teachers, for example, seemed to mark the end of "Permanent Revolution." ALM's response was two-pronged. He offered new benefits to workers, including the implementation of profit-sharing programs which were promised in the constitution of 1917. Workers who continued to strike rather than accept benefits were jailed.

To win over critics of the PRI, ALM called for a shift from the economic phase of Permanent Revolution to the phase of "Balanced Revolution." He promised to balance economic factors with social and political ones. Industrial subsidies were continued by ALM, who also emphasized land reform, which he pushed to the highest monthly activity since Cárdenas (Table 2, above). While stressing expansion of tourism to meet his goal of one million persons (see Table 4), ALM moved to reform the political system. He made provisions for opposition political parties to win elections without costing the PRI victories. The political answer has been simple: an opposition party is entitled to one at-large seat in the country's Chamber of Deputies for each percentage point it wins in the national vote for deputies, providing that a minimum share is reached, as discussed below. Nationalization of the foreign-owned electricity industry in 1960 helped to establish ALM in the pantheon of Revolutionary Family heroes before he turned over power to his successor.

The new president, Gustavo Díaz Ordaz (GDO), served from 1964 to 1970. His programs emphasized continued state support of private business and an expanded parastate sector. Simultaneously, GDO continued to distribute land to ejidos at a fast pace, surpassing Cárdenas's resolutions per month and approaching his definitive actions. He has the fourth best presidential record for persons benefited. However, his programs were overtaken by events in 1968

Table 4

TOURISTS VISTING MEXICO'S INTERIOR,[1] 1929–88

Year	Number	Year	Number
1929	14	1960	761
		1961	803
1930	24	1962	941
1931	42	1963[a]	1,058
1932	37	1964	1,210
1933	40		
1934	64	1965	1,350
		1966	1,499
1935	75	1967	1,629
1936	92	1968	1,879
1937	130	1969	2,065
1938	103		
1939	128	1970	2,250
		1971	2,509
1940	126	1972	2,915
1941	166	1973	3,226
1942	90	1974	3,362
1943	127		
1944	120	1975	3,218
		1976	3,107
1945	157	1977	3,247
1946	255	1978	3,754
1947	240	1979	4,134
1948	254		
1949	306	1980	4,144
		1981	4,038
1950	384	1982	3,767
1951	425	1983	4,749
1952	443	1984	4,655
1953	420		
1954	505	1985	4,207
		1986	4,618
1955	537	1987	5,400
1956	588	1988	5,696
1957	614		
1958	640		
1959	682		

1. Excludes tourists crossing from the United States into Mexico's border region—such tourists do not need documentation for short stays within about 70 miles of the border.

a. Raymond Vernon suggested in 1963 that by the early 1960s the prospects for tourism to Mexico did not seem to offer any new continued impetus for economic growth; see Vernon, *The Dilemma of Mexico's Economic Development* (Cambridge, Mass.: Harvard University Press), pp. 116–117.

SOURCE: 1929–1980, Instituto Nacional de Estadística, Geografía e Informática, *Estadísticas Históricas de México*, II, pp. 702–703.

1981–1986, idem, *Cuadro de Información Oportuna*, February 1988, p. 103; and *El Mercado de Valores*, September 26, 1987.

1987–1988, Banco Nacional de México, *Review of the Economic Situation of Mexico*, March 1988 and July 1989.

when students in Berkeley, New York, Paris, and Tokyo made non-negotiable demands for a voice in national political decision making and condemned the United States for its "criminal" war in Vietnam.

Mexican students were not to be outdone. University and preparatory students added to the international list of nonnegotiable issues their own demands that:

1. the universities be opened to the popular sector regardless of formal entrance requirements;

2. abusive police be fired;

3. the government cease "wasting" funds on building a subway in Mexico City and divert that money instead to help solve the problems of the rural poor;

4. the government resist "U.S. imperialism";

5. the government agree to these demands or face student disruption of the Olympic Games scheduled for October 1968 in Mexico City.

Failing to realize that the essence of politics is negotiation, the students amassed several hundred thousand persons in successive protest parades through downtown Mexico City.

To stop this heretical protest against the Official Party, which claimed that the students were too immature to understand the costly gains of the violent period of the Permanent Revolution, on October 2 the government cracked down at the Plaza of the Three Cultures where thousands of students gathered in defiance of a government ban on their assemblies. Who opened fire first, skittish soldiers or student snipers seeking to create martyrs to the cause, is unclear, but the soldiers killed between 50 and 600 students and confiscated a huge student arms cache. Even as the Official Party maintained its power at the high political cost of undermining in 1968 much of the democratic political credibility that it could ostensibly claim, the economic underpinning of Balanced Revolution was in trouble. Beneath the surface of economic growth and rising urban prosperity, the Official Party's monetary policy had put the country's exports at a price disadvantage, deemphasizing exports and promoting imports by consistently overvaluing the peso. (The historical value of the peso is shown in Table 3.) The stage was set for the shift away from "stabilizing development."

Phase V. Ideology of Statist Revolution,[15] 1970–82

Political Stage,[16] 1970–76

The secretary of interior who had crushed the student revolts in 1968, Luis Echeverría Alvarez (LEA), became president of Mexico for the period from 1970 to 1976. Upset at having been named as CIA contact "Litempo-14" by former CIA officer Philip Agee in his 1975 exposé of CIA activities in Latin America, LEA was also determined to live down his role as chief of internal security at the time of the massacre at the Plaza of the Three Cultures. Too, he seems to have seen himself as a sympathizer of the leftist labor leader Vicente Lombardo Toledano, who had helped make the Cárdenas programs successful in the 1930s. Therefore, LEA opened the government to young, recently graduated intellectuals, some of whom, like Porfirio Muñoz Ledo, had studied in Europe and favored increased state power, to be used to combat imperialism and dependency relations among nations.

LEA's youthful appointees proceeded to undertake a legal revolution that attempted to "regulate" the foreign role in the economy and foreign transfer of technology. The LEA group considered private investments in Mexico, be they national or foreign, as making too great a profit (the high profit defended by

the *Handbook for the Foreign Investor in Mexico*, above), and LEA saw those high profits as contributing to income inequalities. He believed that with a booming economy, Mexico had enough power and experience to bring the private sector under government control, expand the role of the state (which would manage investments for the good of the nation rather than for a few stockholders), and redistribute the national income more equally. In short, LEA and his group believed that it was time for Mexico to shift from "stabilizing development" to "shared development" in which the benefits of an expanding GDP would be distributed to the masses under the aegis of the state. Too, LEA felt that his government had to create jobs at a faster rate than was possible under the policies of stabilizing development.

Beyond establishing himself as a distinctive president of Mexico's Permanent Revolution, LEA assumed the ideological stance that he had lacked in order to establish himself as Mexico's first international leader. True, Cárdenas had played a brief role on the world stage when he became the only leader in the Western Hemisphere to support the Spanish Republic against Franco, but LEA's group could argue that Cárdenas's actions were more humanitarian than political.

In 1973 LEA took his "political and moral" concerns about development of the Third World to the Club of Rome, a private group of 85 influential intellectuals and international businessmen holding its fifth meeting to assess the limits of economic growth. LEA argued that if the Club's call for limited growth were implemented without taking into account the Third World's disadvantageous position in the global economic scheme, the Third World would be frozen into an unfair distribution of international income.

LEA won support from the Club of Rome for his Charter of the Economic Rights and Duties of States, which established a framework for protecting nationalistic economic policies in the Third World and for preventing exploitation by multinational companies while assuring fair and stable prices of raw materials. Although the Charter was approved by the United Nations in 1974 with a vote of 120 in favor and 10 abstentions, it was opposed by 5 key industrial countries led by the United States.

With regard to Western Hemispheric development policy, in 1975 LEA founded (with President Carlos Andrés Pérez of Venezuela) the Sistema Económico Latinoamericano (SELA). The goal of SELA is to integrate Latin America economically and to counter the influence of the U.S.-dominated Organization of American States.

By turning away from the United States and by backing a series of laws drafted to control U.S. influence in Mexico, LEA argued that Mexico could

---

[15] Statism is the trend toward government control of economic life, especially through nationalization of industries considered to be strategic for national development. Statism involves an expanding government structure and bureaucracy to carry out state planning and the execution of plans. In my view, statist systems are achieved when the public sector (central government plus parastate sector of nationalized enterprises) controls nearly half or more of a country's GDP (see Chapter 6, below). On the role of the state in twentieth-century Mexico before and after 1982, see James W. Wilkie and Jesús Reyes Heroles González Garza, "Industria y Trabajo en México: Antecedentes y Perspectivas," UCLA Program on Mexico, manuscript, 1989. For a general view on statism, see Harold S. Sloan and Arnold J. Zurcher, *Dictionary of Economics* (New York: Barnes and Noble, 1970), p. 416; and for a specific view of the state in Mexico and in the Third World, see Judith A. Teichman, *Policymaking in Mexico* (Boston: Allen and Unwin, 1988).

[16] On the early 1970s, see Samuel Schmidt, *El Deterioro del Presidencialismo Mexicano: Los Años de Luis Echeverría* (México, D.F.: EDAMEX, 1986). For the period from the early 1970s into the early 1980s, see Alan Riding, *Distant Neighbors: A Portrait of the Mexicans* (New York: Random House, 1984), which also offers insights into the development of Mexico's oil industry and corruption in government. On Mexico's oil trade, see SALA, 26–3518; on Mexico's oil industry, see George W. Grayson, *The Politics of Mexican Oil* (Pittsburgh: University of Pittsburgh Press, 1980). On the problems of "stabilizing development" and "shared development," see Clark W. Reynolds, "Why Mexico's 'Stabilizing Development' Was Actually Destabilizing," *World Development* 6 (1978), pp. 1005–1018. On the Sistema Económico Latinamericano (SELA), see *¿Qué es el SELA?* (N.p.: SELA, 1984). On population change, see Banco Nacional de México, *México Social, 1984: Indicadores Seleccionados*.

overcome dependence upon U.S. foreign investment, U.S. tourism (2 to 3 million visitors yearly), and U.S. trade (two-thirds of which had been with its northern neighbor). Laws were passed, for example, to control the importation of technology and patents, register foreign investment, require Mexican majority share-holding in foreign-owned companies, and strictly control foreign residence in Mexico. To show internationally Mexico's revolutionariness, LEA opened Mexico's doors to defeated guerrillas from other Latin American countries and to the former leaders in the Salvador Allende government overthrown in 1973 by General Augusto Pinochet.

Arguing that Mexico's own economy had been too long distorted by conservative monetary policy, LEA moved to increase Mexico's external debt and the amount of money in circulation to stimulate domestic policy in favor of the masses. The resulting inflation ended the peso's stability vis-à-vis the dollar (Table 2).

Claiming that Mexico was finally strong enough economically to divert resources into income redistribution, LEA said that he would halt economic growth if that was what was necessary to finally help Mexico's financially poverty-stricken population. In any case, while LEA stopped governmental investment to develop a national plan for economic growth, the economy declined. Panicking at the result and realizing that the national plan that emerged was so general as to be useless, LEA accelerated public investment and overheated the economy. This indecisive policy of turning government investment off and on continued in alternate years and created a chaotic situation for Mexico, especially as LEA expanded the public sector by doubling the number of decentralized agencies even as he tried to bring all of them under central government control in order to double the power of the presidency.

Given the increasing economic confusion, the private sector and LEA soon confronted each other. Fearful of the results of contradictory investment and governmental organizational schemes, and to successfully block LEA's plan for tax reform, the private sector began to shift funds out of Mexico to protect itself against the inevitable devaluation of the peso. Infuriated, LEA claimed that the private sector was engaging in un-Mexican activities in order to destabilize his government. LEA's declarations further alienated the right wing of the Official Party and the chambers of commerce and industry which advise it.

LEA's conflict with and attempts to regulate domestic and foreign capitalists, however, did not win him the support of Mexico's left inside or outside of the PRI. In spite of LEA's support of Castro and the Allende group and appeals to Mexico's left through his woeful understanding of economic theory, the left thought that LEA had not gone far enough in creating a statist system.

Further, LEA could not live down the massacre of 1968 as he now moved to defeat the students who had been forced underground and into guerrilla activity. To LEA's embarrassment, ultrarightists in the government employed paramilitary groups to seize the initiative against the "left." When students protested, justifiably, the fact that many students remained jailed or had disappeared after their arrest in 1968, the paramilitary group visciously attacked them on June 10, 1971, beating or killing without mercy. LEA's own strategy was to focus on combating guerrillas who had set up armed refuges in the countryside. To sway the peasants, LEA pumped funds into labor-intensive rural road building, but his leftist critics remarked that those roads destined to integrate the rural sector had another function—at their termination point the military was building helicopter pads to deploy troops rapidly against the guerrillas. LEA's political programs lacked support from either the far left or the far right even as they alienated the middle and upper classes which considered his policies to be erratic and leading the country toward economic disaster.

LEA's economic problems were compounded when OPEC's shocking increase of petroleum prices in 1973 cost Mexico dearly because production by the state oil company (PEMEX) had not satisfied demand since it was created in 1938. By 1947 Mexico was importing almost as much oil as it was exporting. Starved for funds because the government had kept the cost of oil and gas low for consumers in order to control inflation and assure low-cost food and transportation for the masses, PEMEX did not have the resources to explore and modernize production. Stung by the need to import oil at high cost (and by the need to import more than it exported between 1971 and 1974), LEA pushed expansion of PEMEX. With the increased value of oil, LEA decreed in 1974 an increase in domestic prices charged by PEMEX (the first in fifteen years), and development could begin in earnest.

In developing the oil industry LEA was reluctant to use Mexico's black gold as a weapon for direct export expansion that could help U.S. industry. He felt that the oil should fuel Mexico's own industrialization and indirect export expansion through manufacturers, as California gold had done for the United States. Although increased oil production did bring rich rewards from world sales, it required increasing Mexico's foreign debt to provide the investment funds needed by PEMEX. In spite of oil investment credits flowing into Mexico and Mexico's own printing of money, LEA insisted on holding the peso at 12.5 to the dollar, causing inflation.

Further economic problems arose in 1975 when Mexico voted in the United Nations with the Arab bloc to declare Zionism as racism. The U.S. Jewish community undertook a very effective boycott against tourism to Mexico which did not end until Mexico apologized.

With economic problems mounting in 1976, LEA desperately sought a propaganda coup to secure his place in history. To cast himself in the Cárdenas mold, LEA increased the definitive rate of monthly ejidal land distribution to an amount exceeded only by Cárdenas and Díaz Ordaz. (See Table 2.)

Further, LEA made a dramatic expropriation of land in northwest Mexico, which ironically backfired because large numbers of day laborers claimed that the implementation of the inefficient ejido system would cost them their jobs on the large export-oriented farms being expropriated. Many had long before abandoned their ejidos which soon became too small for the extended families which generation by generation grew larger than the fixed land size could support. Others had left ejidos because they could no longer tolerate the corruption of "elected" ejidal leaders, who used their power to entrench themselves, favor their cronies, and exploit the mass of ejidatarios who in effect became day laborers working for subsistence wages and who lived without hope for advancement. In a logical new alliance, day laborers joined with large landowners against the discredited ejidatarios who, if they won the land, would not only throw thousands of day laborers out of work but also would fail to produce the food needed for export or to feed Mexico's rapidly growing urban population (cities over 35,000), which had gone from 11.0 percent in 1910 to 40.1 percent in 1970.

If LEA hoped to keep the rural labor force in Mexico instead of seeing much of it move to the United States, his land policy in northwest Mexico was counterproductive. Although he had hoped to achieve a new temporary-labor pact with the United States to control the flow of Mexicans across the northern border (the pact of 1942 had expired in 1964), LEA did not choose to go ahead with the pact after the oil discoveries because (among several reasons) he feared that in return for fair treatment of Mexican workers he would have to bargain away Mexico's oil at low prices. In any case, in the complexities of Mexico's situation, out-migration of workers has meant that the United States has served as Mexico's escape valve for the unemployed and underemployed, a reality that would have to continue until (and perhaps beyond) the U.S. attempted to control its borders through the Immigration Reform and Control Act of 1986.

With regard to demographic issues, LEA's Law of Population Control gave the government authority to encourage smaller families and to slow Mexico's population growth rate, which had reached 3.8 percent yearly during the 1960s. The government supported family planning programs which helped to reduce the population growth rate to 2.8 percent during the 1970s. Population control came too late, however, and by the 1980s between 800,000 and one million persons were entering the job market each year.

Given such a tremendous expansion in the labor force and his own fitfull investment policies, LEA did not create a Shared Revolution but Statist Revolution, which did less to benefit the nation and the nongovernmental sectors than it did to benefit the government sphere. While the latter benefited with ever higher salaries, the masses were not so lucky. Although in the short term, minimum wage levels had outpaced the inflationary policy favored by LEA and his successor, by the 1980s the reverse would come true with a vengeance.

In running the state, LEA was handicapped compared with his predecessors because he could not pretend that projected expenditures were the actual expenditures, as had been possible prior to my book *The Mexican Revolution: Federal Expenditure and Social Change* (1967 and 1970).[17] Whereas actual expenditures of presidents after 1940 had risen from an average of 35 to 83 percent more than projected amounts (Fig. 3), LEA reduced the difference to 22 percent. (The difference fell to 19 percent under LEA's successor.) Both LEA and his successor used the budget to continue support of private and parastate industry.

LEA's break with the policy of stabilizing development is clearest in his monetary policy, which established the trend into at least 1988. The long-term change in the M_1 money supply shown in Table 5 is revealing. (M_1 = currency held outside banks + demand deposits held by the private sector.) During the 21-year period of stabilizing development (1955–76), yearly growth of the money supply exceeded 14 percent only twice—1955 and 1964, when it reached 19.8 percent. After 1972 LEA stepped up monetary emissions to a growth rate of almost 22 percent during his last four years in office. His successor was even less restrained, accelerating the growth in M_1 by 27 percent in 1977 and to the thirtieth percentile until 1982, when the rate of increase went up to nearly 44 percent.

[17](Berkeley: University of California Press). This book could not be published in Mexico and updated through 1976 until the government reformed its budgetary system for 1972 to reduce the discrepancy between projected and actual expenditures. See *La Revolución Mexicana (1910–1976): Gasto Federal y Cambio Social* (México, D.F.: Fondo de Cultura Económica, 1978), pp. 343–349.

Figure 3

**ACTUAL GROSS EXPENDITURE COMPARED TO
PROJECTED GROSS EXPENDITURE IN MEXICO,
BY PRESIDENT, 1900–82
(PC)**

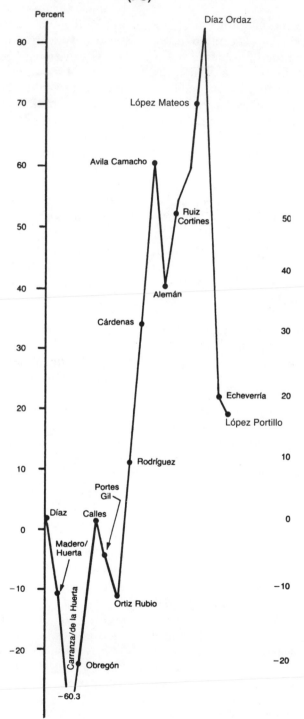

SOURCE: SALA, 24–3403.

Table 5

CHANGE IN MEXICO M₁ MONEY SUPPLY,[1] 1926–88

Year	PC	Year	PC
1926	16.2	1960	12.1
1927	− 8.9	1961	6.0
1928	28.4	1962	8.3
1929	4.5	1963	14.0
		1964	19.8
1930	4.3		
1931	− 60.2	1965	9.0
1932	31.3	1966	8.4
1933	15.4	1967	10.1
1934	13.8	1968	12.3
		1969	12.6
1935	7.9		
1936	23.9	1970	11.3
1937	5.9	1971	8.1
1938	10.8	1972	13.5
1939	19.8	1973	22.8
		1974	19.2
1940	20.2		
1941	19.8	1975	21.5
1942	37.8	1976	22.3
1943	52.7	1977	26.6
1944	23.8	1978	37.2
		1979	31.4
1945	6.9		
1946	− 2.2	1980	31.1
1947	− .6	1981	36.8
1948	13.8	1982	43.5
1949	11.2	1983	44.1
		1984	53.2
1950	38.4[a]		
1951	11.7	1985	53.7
1952	4.2	1986	51.3
1953	10.9	1987	106.5[b]
1954	11.9	1988	106.0
1955	19.6		
1956	11.2		
1957	6.7		
1958	6.6		
1959	13.1		

1. M₁ = currency, coin, and checking accounts held by the public. For absolute data on M₁ and expansion of definition to M₂, see SALA, 22–2.

a. Shift from Banco de México calculations to International Monetary Fund calculations (Banco de México datum for 1950 is 37.6 percent). The International Monetary Fund converts end of period stock series to averages from which it then calculates indexes and percentage changes.
b. With regard to single-month rates, International Monetary Fund calculations show that November 1987 reached at least 141.0 percent—the highest such rate in decades.

SOURCE: SALA, 26–3500; and International Monetary Fund, *International Financial Statistics*, June 1988 and July 1989.

During the last four years of LEA's term, accumulated statist activity had resulted in consumer-price inflation averaging 20 percent for December. This meant that in 1976 LEA had to devalue the peso from 12.50 to 20 per dollar (Table 3, Part III). LEA's legacy of increased money supply, inflation, and devaluation was to be expanded upon in the following presidential term. He and his successor denied that this legacy would harm the economy.

The Economic Stage of Statism,[18] 1976–82

José López Portillo (JLP), who served as president from December 1, 1976, through November 30, 1982, took Mexico to its apogee in statism. As part of that trajectory, he increased M₁ by an average of 34.4 percent (Table 5), setting off a six-year average inflation rate for December of nearly 36 percent. Ironically, JLP was at first welcomed by Mexico's private sector to enter into an Alliance for Production with the government.

As a corollary to the Alliance, in 1981 JLP signed a new land reform law that legalized cooperation between private and communal farmers—the first law aimed at helping ejidos obtain the private capital needed to help them become productive. Given the credit needs of Mexico, the government has never been able to supply the credit needed by the ejidal sector, which is prohibited from mortgaging its lands and hence ineligible to receive private loans. Cooperative farming using private capital and ejidal workers provides a way to circumvent the bottleneck in ejidal credit.

To stimulate the economy, JLP adopted some of LEA's policies. On the one hand, he rejected LEA's concern about exporting oil to the United States and expanded sales rapidly in order to stimulate the economy and create jobs. On the other hand, he followed LEA's lead in using the prospect of Mexico's seemingly inexhaustible supply of petroleum to attract foreign loans needed to expand oil production and public and private industry.

JLP also followed LEA's policies of developing tourist growth poles, continuing to invest in Cancún, Cabo San Lucas, and Puerto Vallarta. Interested in modernizing facilities in Acapulco, Mazatlán, and Zihuatenejo, JLP opened Ixtapa as a twin resort to enhance development of the Zihuatenejo area.

JLP's contribution to the development of economic growth poles for Mexico originated in his plan

[18] See Roberto Newell García and Luis Rubio F., *Mexico's Dilemma: The Political Origins of Economic Crisis* (Boulder, Colo.: Westview Press, 1984); Riding, *Distant Neighbors*; Teichman, *Policymaking in Mexico*; and Chapter 6, below.

to gain the confidence of the private sector. JLP invested in seventeen regional growth poles based in twenty new industrial cities: three in Baja California; two in Guanajuato; and one each in Aguascalientes, Coahuila, Durango, Guerrero, Jalisco, Hidalgo, Michoacán, Nayarit, Nuevo León, Querétaro, Tabasco, Tamaulipas, Tlaxcala, Yucatán, and Veracruz. Growth did not come easily, however, and the plan to make such places into industrial growth was hampered by the lack of such basic infrastructure as a commercial aiport; many important cities in Mexico lack a commercial airport (such as Puebla) or acquired one only recently (such as Zacatecas, 1983).

The real external debt of Mexico (public sector plus private sector debt) has not been easy to analyze because every few months the government seems to revise the series upward, as can be seen by comparing data in parts I and II of Table 6. The latest revision (upon which I base my calculations in part II) shows that the total in 1971 stood at 16.8 billion in standard dollars of 1980, and reached 37.1 billion under LEA by the end of 1976, an unprecedented 121 percent increase, which the Official Party had difficulty justifying. By 1982, under JLP, Mexico's external debt increased to 79.3 billion or 114 percent (Table 6).

While the real foreign debt was expanding 4.7 times under LEA and JLP, their publicists continued to deceive most Mexicans and foreigners alike (as had presidents since the 1960s) into believing that the country's biggest source of revenue was income taxes. The truth was, however, that Mexico had come to look upon foreign loans as a form of normal revenue; loans became far more important in the Mexican budgetary scheme than income taxes.[19]

If oil prices had continued to increase from 35 dollars to 50 dollars a barrel as expected, given the Iran-Iraq War (1980–88), Mexico would have been able to service its foreign debt. But OPEC's 1979 increase in oil prices (which compounded the problematic increase of 1973) meant that the world had to absorb that arbitrary rise in energy costs, causing the subsequent weakening of oil prices that continues to plague Mexico into the present.

With the recession in world economic output beginning in 1980 and the impact in 1982 of a long-term shift by industrialized countries from import of raw materials to development of synthetic materials, Mexico suffered a concomitant decline in prices for most of its export commodities. Mexico's export price index, which had reached at least a twenty-year high in 1981, experienced dramatic decline (Table 7). The export price index fell almost 26 percent in 1982 and another 37 percent by 1988.

In the meantime, the government's policy of shared development (with which JLP had associated himself as Secretary of Treasury under LEA) would follow two equally disastrous economic tracks. First, public sector employment exploded by 82 percent in the eight years from 1975 to 1983 (Table 8). From the time of LEA through JLP and into the first year of Miguel de la Madrid Hurtado, positions for central government and parastate workers increased from 2.2 million jobs in 1975 to 4.0 million in 1983. Whereas 14 percent of the positions were located in the public sector in 1975, that total was 20 percent by 1983. While the public sector's total contribution to GDP rose from 15 percent in 1975 to 26 percent in 1983, its share in Mexico's total salaries rose from 30 percent to 40 percent.

Second, the government ignored the need to drastically devalue the peso in order to discourage Mexican shopping trips to the United States and to encourage Mexican exports. Rather, the government only gradually devalued the peso, thus giving cause for Mexico's middle class (about 31 percent of the work force by 1980) and upper class (about 6 percent in 1980) to live on the dollar standard. Even the lower class (some 64 percent by 1980) knew that it was safer to save dollars than pesos amid the heady inflation and exploding economy under JLP. Mexicans paid less for electronic goods and manufactures with dollars in the United States than with pesos in Mexico, where import tariffs further complicated purchase prices. The growing Mexican middle class was able to take several foreign vacations a year for buying sprees. Domestically, Mexicans took advantage of nominal interest rates which lagged behind inflation, allowing them to purchase real estate at a negative or low real interest rate.

As a consequence of such distorted monetary policies, Mexican industrial output had a declining consumer base even as the GDP shown in Table 1 averaged 8.4 percent in real growth between 1978 and 1981. This was one of the highest growth rates in the world, Japan averaging 4.4 percent and the United States and West Germany only 2.5 percent during those four years. By 1982, Mexico could no longer service its debt and declared an internal emergency which involved freezing dollar bank accounts and converting them into peso accounts as well as devaluing the peso to 150 to the dollar. Trying to avoid leaving office in total disgrace, finally JLP nationalized Mexico's commercial banking system and restricted payments on Mexico's private and public debt. Although the private sector was furious about the nationalization of the banks and the loss of easy peso convertibility into dollars, JLP's program saved it from bankruptcy—the private sector could not have paid its debts.

[19] See Chapter 5, below.

Table 6

MEXICO PUBLIC AND PRIVATE FOREIGN DEBT, 1970–88
(Year-End, Billions of Dollars)

PART I. Unrevised Data, 1971–86

Year	A. Total	B. Public	C. Private	D. B/A	E. U.S. Export Price Index (1980 = 100)	F. Real Total Debt[1] A/E
1971	6.6	4.6	2.1	69.7	39.4	16.8
1972	7.7	5.1	2.6	66.2	40.7	18.9
1973	10.3	7.1	3.2	68.9	47.4	21.7
1974	14.5	10.0	4.5	69.0	60.5	24.0
1975	20.1	14.4	5.6	71.6	67.6	29.7
1976	25.9	19.6	6.3	75.7	69.9	37.1
1977	29.3	22.9	6.4	78.2	72.4	40.5
1978	33.4	26.3	7.2	78.7	77.4	43.2
1979	40.3	29.8	10.5	73.9	88.1	45.7
1980	50.7	33.8	16.9	66.7	100.0	50.7
1981	74.9	53.0	21.9	70.8	109.2	68.6
1982	87.6	58.9	28.7	67.2	110.4	79.3
1983	93.8	65.6	28.2	69.9	111.6	84.1
1984	96.7	69.4	27.3	71.8	113.1	85.5
1985	98.7	72.1	26.6	73.0	113.3	89.1
1986	100.5	75.4	25.1	75.0	113.3	89.7

1. Billions of dollars of 1980; may exclude short-term loans under 90 days.
SOURCE: A–D, 1971–79: Roberto Gutiérrez R., "El Endeudamiento Externo del Sector Privado de México," *Comercio Exterior*, April 1986, p. 338.
           1980–87: *El Mercado de Valores*, October 26, 1987, p. 1131.
    E,   SALA, 26–3231; and International Monetary Fund, *International Financial Statistics*, June 1988.
    F,   Calculated.

(PARTS II and III on overleaf)

Table 6 (Continued)

PART II. Revised Data, 1971–88

Year	A. Total	B. Public	C. Private	D. B/A	E. U.S. Export Price Index (1980 = 100)	F. Real Total Debt[1] A/E	G. Total Debt as Share of GDP (A/GDP)
1971	6.4	4.6	1.8	71.9	39.4	16.8	16.3
1972	6.2	5.1	1.1	82.3	40.7	18.9	13.5
1973	9.1	7.0	2.1	76.9	47.4	21.7	16.5
1974	12.2	10.0	2.2	82.0	60.5	24.0	16.9
1975	19.9	15.4	4.5	77.4	67.6	29.7	21.5
1976	26.1	19.6	6.5	75.1	69.9	37.1	29.4
1977[a]	30.9	24.1	6.8	80.0	72.4	40.5	37.7
1978	34.7	27.5	7.2	79.3	77.4	43.2	33.8
1979	40.3	29.8	10.5	73.9	88.1	45.7	29.9
1980	50.7	33.8	16.9	66.7	100.0	50.7	26.0
1981	74.9	53.0	21.9	70.8	109.2	68.6	29.9
1982	92.4[b]	68.5	23.9	74.1	110.4	79.3	54.2
1983	93.8	74.7	19.1	79.6	111.6	84.1	63.8
1984	96.7	78.2	18.5	80.9	113.1	85.5	55.0
1985	96.6	79.9	16.7	82.7	112.2	86.1	52.4
1986	101.0	84.9	16.1	84.1	113.3	89.1	77.8
1987	107.5	92.4	15.1	86.0	115.3	93.2	75.4
1988	100.4	93.3	7.2	92.9	123.3	81.4	56.8

1. Billions of dollars of 1980; may exclude short-term loans under 90 days.
   For a view of real public sector debt, see SALA, 26–3504.

a. Beginning in 1977 explicitly includes International Monetary Fund loans.
b. Since 1982 includes nationalized banking system, data on which are
   often not included in government presentations.
SOURCE: A–D, G 1982–88: *El Mercado de Valores*, May 1, 1989.
        E,   SALA, 26–3231; and International Monetary Fund, *International Financial Statistics*, June 1988 and July 1989.
        F,   Calculated.

PART III. Sectors Owing the Foreign Debt, 1988
(Estimated Year-End)

Sector	Millions of Dollars		Percent	
	Subtotal	Total	Subtotal	Total
Total		100,384		100.0
Public Sector				
Government	81,003		80.7	
Banking System	7,481		7.4	
Central Bank	4,786		4.8	
Subtotal	93,270		92.9	
Private Sector	7,114		7.1	

SOURCE: *El Mercado de Valores*, May 1, 1989.

Table 7

BANCO DE MEXICO EXPORT PRICE INDEX, 1960–88
(1970 = 100)

Year	Unadjusted	Adjusted[1]
1960	87.8	87.2
1961	89.6	88.3
1962	83.9	82.0
1963	89.1	87.3
1964	85.7	84.8
1965	84.1	83.5
1966	85.2	85.1
1967	83.9	84.1
1968	89.0	90.4
1969	88.0	91.2
1970	96.7	100.0
1971	100.0	100.0
1972	103.3	100.7
1973	115.2	121.2
1974	110.1	118.9
1975	97.8	95.8
1976	113.0	119.3
1977	113.0	121.9
1978	104.1	115.7
1979	113.1	111.7
1980	127.6	125.6
1981	124.3	127.5
1982	108.2	94.7
1983	99.0	77.9
1984	97.1	66.0
1985	91.9	70.5
1986	66.2	54.4
1987	73.1	66.4
1988	66.1	59.7

1. Adjusted to take into account international interest rates.

SOURCE: *El Mercado de Valores*, May 15, 1989. Cf. SALA, 26, Chapter 34.

Table 8

PUBLIC SECTOR EMPLOYEES AS SHARE OF
MEXICO'S EMPLOYED POPULATION, 1975–83
(Average Number of Salaried Positions, in Millions)[1]

Year	Subtotal Public Sector	Central Government	Local Government	Social Security[2]	Parastate Agencies[3]	% of Total Mexican Employees
1975	2.2	1.2	.3	.1	.5	14.0
1976	2.3	1.3	.4	.2	.6	15.1
1977	2.5	1.3	.4	.2	.6	15.3
1978	2.7	1.4	.4	.2	.6	15.8
1979	2.9	1.6	.5	.2	.7	16.4
1980	3.2	1.7	.6	.2	.7	17.0
1981	3.5	1.9	.6	.2	.8	17.5
1982	3.7	2.0	.6	.3	.9	18.7
1983	4.0	2.1	.7	.3	1.0	20.4

1. An employee may hold more than one position; may exclude consultants; detail may not
   add to subtotal because of rounding.
2. Separated out of parastate agencies.
3. Here excludes social security employees.

SOURCE: Instituto Nacional de Estadística, Geografía e Informática, *Participación del Sector Público en el Producto Interno Bruto de México, 1975–1983* (México, D.F.: Secretaría
de Programación y Presupuesto, 1984), p. 5

Phase VI. Restructured Revolution,[20] 1982–

Economic Stage, 1982–88

Taking office for the period 1982–88 as the newest savior of Mexico was Miguel de la Madrid Hurtado (MMH), JLP's Secretary of Planning and Budget. When MMH was sworn into office December 1, 1982, he was more aware than most of where the Permanent Revolution stood in positive as well as negative terms.

Positively, during the 1970s real GDP had doubled, just as it had in the 1960s. Per capital GDP had quadrupled between the presidencies of Díaz and JLP. With the world's seventh largest world oil reserves, Mexico may rise above fourth place in world petroleum production—especially if the Middle East dissolves into all-out war, which seems inevitable to some observers.

Negatively, however, when oil and other commodity prices declined in the early 1980s, MMH increased the supply of money at a tremendous rate even compared with JLP. Under MMH, growth of M_1 went from 43.5 when JLP left office in 1982 to 50 percent through 1986 and then shot up to more than

108 percent in 1987.[21] In 1982 consumer-price inflation reached a 12-month average of 59 percent, causing the devaluation of the peso by 56 percent (Table 3, Part I). Between December 1981 and December 1982, consumer prices rose nearly 99 percent, with the peso devalued by 149 percent (Table 3, Part III). At the same time, during 1982 Mexico suffered a private capital flight of perhaps 8.4 billion dollars.[22] The resulting crash of Mexico's economy in 1982 provoked an economic crisis which has yet to be fully measured or resolved. MMH knew that he would face a loss of jobs in the Mexican economy, which would hurt all of Mexico's socioeconomic classes, at least in absolute terms.

With regard to the post-1982 effect of the crisis, the labor force has suffered a severe jolt. The masses saw the real general minimum salary (direct plus indirect social services) decline by 42.1 percent between 1981 and 1986, with a 9 percent decline in 1982.[23]

---

[20] For a sophisticated start in measuring the status of the Mexican economy before and after Mexico's economic crisis in 1982 as well as in 1976, see Newell García and Rubio, *Mexico's Dilemma*, especially Part III.

[21] On M_1 and export prices, see tables 5 and 7, respectively below.

[22] As measured by the errors and omissions category in Mexico's balance of payments. Although this 8.4 billion loss was partially offset by the entry of new long-term capital to Mexico, the reserves of the Bank of Mexico declined in 1982 by 4.7 billion dollars. Also, during 1981 Mexico also lost 8.4 billion dollars in the flight of private capital compared to a 4 billion loss in 1981, according to data in Nacional Financiera, *La Economía Mexicana en Cifras, 1986*, p. 315.

[23] For an innovative index developed to show Mexico's real general minimum salary directly paid as well as the benefits indirectly paid to workers through social expenditures (education, hous-

Also, the middle and upper classes have found it more feasible to travel within Mexico using pesos than outside using dollars; with the devaluation of November 1987 the peso's value fell from 26 to the dollar at the end of 1981 to 2,200 (a 98.8 percent decline).

The depth of Mexico's current economic crisis can be appreciated by examining the yearly percentage change of real GDP (Table 1). Whereas from 1970 to 1981 real GDP increased by a yearly average of 6.8 percent, from 1982 to 1988 the average changed by zero percent, with the years 1983 and 1986 posting changes of about − 4.0 percent.

Although in popular lore Mexico's current economic crisis is often considered to be the worst since the Mexican Revolution of 1910–20, in reality the impact of the present crisis has not yet exceeded that of the Great Depression. Between 1927 and 1932 Mexican GDP averaged − 4.3 percent yearly, with serious declines of − 4.4, − 3.9, − 6.3, and − 14.9 percent in 1927, 1929, 1930, and 1932, respectively (Table 1).

Between the Great Depression and the Crisis of the 1980s, Mexico's real GDP made gains every year. From 1933 through 1981 no negative rate was reported, the lowest gains being 1.6 percent in 1938, 1.4 percent in 1940, and .3 percent in 1953 (Fig. 1). Indeed GDP gains of 8 percent or more were frequent: 1936, 1941, 1944, 1950, 1954–55, 1960, 1963–64, 1968, 1972–73, 1978–81. During this long period from the early 1930s to the early 1980s, GDP gained on the average 6.3 percent yearly, which made Mexico's achievement the envy of most of the developing world.

Forty-nine years of growth from 1933 through 1981 had provided funds to benefit certain sectors of society, benefits typified in government generosity toward higher education. The government built in the early 1950s a modern new campus for the Universidad Nacional Autónoma de México (UNAM) and in the 1960s and 1970s began to pay its professoriate the highest salaries in Mexican history. The country was proud to establish university positions on a full-time basis, so that professors for the first time could dedicate themselves to teaching and research.

The university case exemplifies how, since the post-1982 economic crisis, Mexico's social affairs have been forced into a restructuring process, albeit often implicit rather than explicit. Through real budgetary reductions for the university system in the face of rapid inflation, the ability of Mexico's professoriate to educate future generations of experts needed for the country's development has been severely compromised.[24] In 1982 devaluation reduced the top monthly professor's salary from 2,450 dollars of 1982 to 1,243 dollars for a loss of 43.9 percent. (Pesos are converted into dollars figuratively if not literally by Mexican citizens who seek to measure and protect the value of their income.) Top salaries declined to the 500-dollar level in 1983, 1984, and 1985. Then they fell drastically into the 300-dollar range in 1986 and 1987, when they hit a low of 321 dollars. By 1989, the top monthly salary regained somewhat, reaching 597 dollars. Although this amount has stabilized, the relative decline in the top salary was 76 percent between early 1982 and early 1989 (Table 9).

The incredible decline in the top salary level at UNAM has meant that many professors have had to leave the university or take on several "full-time jobs," in addition to their university post. To overcome this problem and preserve the integrity of Mexican university education, UNAM now needs to pay professors enough to conduct research and teach on a "full-time, exclusive" basis.

With regard to cuts in UNAM's budgets, in 1986 the university received from the government half the subsidy it was allocated in 1978, after taking into account inflation. UNAM, which conducts 30 percent of the country's scientific research, saw its real budget for 1988 fall by 60 percent compared with 1987 when scientific salaries were 80 percent less than in 1981. UNAM estimates that scientists in the United States average 15 times more in salaries than in Mexico, attracting Mexican faculty to positions out of the country.[25]

In the meantime, students at UNAM have rejected a 1986 reform proposal to explicitly restructure the university by raising academic standards.[26]

---

ing, health, and public service outlays divided by the economically active population), see Albert Dogart and Rafael Sánchez, "De Tal Tijera, Tal Salario," El Cotidiano 14 (1986), pp. 54–57. (El Cotidiano is published by the Universidad Autónoma Metropolitana, Azcapotzalco.) For direct data which show a 9.7 percent decline of Mexico City's real minimum wage in 1982, see Nacional Financiera, La Economía Mexicana en Cifras, 1986, p. 53. On cost of living indexes for Mexico, see my "From Economic Growth to Economic Stagnation in Mexico: Statistical Series for Understanding Pre- and Post-1982 Change," SALA, 26, pp. 922–926.

[24] Data in nominal terms on the top scale of UNAM salaries between 1982 and 1988 for "Titular C, Tiempo Completo, Profesores/Investigadores" were supplied by Dr. Samuel Schmidt, Jefe de la División de Estudios Profesionales e Investigación, Facultad de Ciencias Políticas y Sociales.

[25] According to a letter from Ronald B. Nigh of UNAM's Coordinación de Investigación Científica, January 26, 1988. On the departure of UNAM scholars, see also Debra Beachy, "Serious 'Brain Drain' Said to Afflict Top Mexican University," Chronicle of Higher Education, December 5, 1984.

[26] On the UNAM reform proposals, see Debra Beachy, "Sweeping Reforms at Mexico's Autonomous U. Approved by Its Governing Board for 1986–87," Chronicle of Higher Education, October 1, 1986; and Pablo González Casanova, "Towards a University of the Future," Voices of Mexico (Mexico City) 4 (1987), pp. 12–26.

Table 9

EFFECT OF MEXICO'S ECONOMIC CRISIS ON TOP SALARY SCHEDULE AT
THE UNIVERSIDAD NACIONAL AUTONOMA DE MEXICO, 1982–89
(Pesos Converted to Real Dollars)

Salary Date	A. Monthly Peso Salary[1]	B. Average Pesos per Dollar	C. Nominal Dollar Salary	D. U.S. Consumer Price Index (1982 = 100)	E. Real Dollar Salary
Pre-devaluation					
Feb. 1, 1982	63,712	26.0	2,450	100.0	2,450
Post-devaluation					
Feb. 18, 1982	70,084	56.4	1,243	100.0	1,243
Feb. 1, 1983	87,604	150.3	583	103.2	565
Feb. 1, 1984[a]	113,008	185.2	610	107.7	566
Feb. 1, 1985	176,800	310.2	570	111.4	512
Feb. 1, 1986	275,824	637.4	433	113.7	381
Feb. 1, 1987	532,028	1,405.8	378	117.8	321
Oct. 1, 1987	1,101,840	1,677.0[b]	657	119.5[d]	550
Feb. 1, 1989	1,781,352	2,336[c]	753	126.1[e]	597

1. Top Scale = Titular C, Tiempo Completo, Profesores/Investigadores.

a. Beginning in 1984, salaries were adjusted several times yearly rather than once yearly.
b. Average for October 1987, according to Banco Nacional de México, *Review of the Economic Situation of Mexico*, April 1988.
c. Average for February 1989, according to ibid., July 1989.
d. Fourth quarter.
e. First quarter.

SOURCE: A, UNAM, Direcciones Generales de Personal y del Presupuesto por Programas, "Tablador Comparativo de Sueldos del Personal Académico, 1982–1987," y "1986–1989."
B, Table 3, above, Parts I and IV.
C, A/B.
D, International Monetary Fund, *International Financial Statistics*, January 1988 (base converted).
E, C/D.

For many students, the university is not a place of learning so much as the door to the middle or upper classes—a door that those students want kept open regardless of questions about the value of degrees received under questionable standards. That in 1987 the students could prevent implementation of a major reform proposed in 1986 had much to do, no doubt, with the fact that Mexico's Official Party desires a period of calm among the student body during 1987–88, as the government prepares for the transition to a new president for the 1988–94 term.

Although the Mexican government has faced mild disturbance on the part of university students during the current economic crisis, to date it has managed to avoid serious worker unrest. The government seems to have won worker acceptance of its claim that, because the crisis is due in the main more to the world collapse of prices for raw materials than to mismanagement by Mexican political leaders, wages must be sacrificed to help right the economy.[27]

[27] On reasons for lack of worker protest against the decline of its real wages since 1982, see Jeffrey Bortz, "The Dilemma of Mexican Labor," *Current History*, March 1987, pp. 105 ff.

MMH did not sit idly by watching implicit restructuring in Mexico, but rather he and his Secretary of Planning and Budget, Carlos Salinas de Gortari (CSG), utilized the concept to shift Mexico away from the Statist period of the LEA and JLP presidencies. The problem MMH and CSG have faced is how to reject the policies of statism without destabilizing the power of the Official Party, which has depended greatly on the patronage of an ever increasing pool of government employees.

Calling for Mexico's restructuring not only to escape from the present crisis but also to compete in the modern world, MMH has sought to rationalize the roles of the state and the private sectors. To deflect criticism away from the government's past management muddles, he has focused on the "failures" of Mexico's private sector.

Insisting since 1983 that many of Mexico's economic problems can be traced to the private sector's inability to compete in the world export market for manufactured goods, in 1986 MMH made Mexico a member of the General Agreement on Trade and Tariffs (GATT). Under GATT, Mexico has reduced its tariff subsidies which had protected the country's private industry. Indeed, industrial plants-had come since the 1940s to depend heavily on capital goods imports yet had little capacity or incentive to export, contributing (along with overvaluation of the peso and the fall in oil prices, for example) to the shortfall in the balance of payments that left the country with no foreign exchange reserves by 1982.[28]

Putting an end to national debate about how to establish Mexico's ability to compete in world markets, Mexico agreed under GATT to reduce its pre-GATT maximum tariff from 100 percent to a 1988 low of 30 percent. (Mexico's state-owned industries such as PEMEX are exempt from GATT rules.)[29] Prior to joining GATT, the government had protected the economy—in 1977 it controlled 77 percent of import categories and charged duties on 90 percent of all imports. Although by 1981 those totals had fallen to 26 percent and 85 percent, respectively, that antiprotectionist trend was reversed by the economic crisis of 1982, when those totals reached 100 percent as Mexico tried to prevent its dollars from being used to purchase goods abroad. Not until 1987, after Mexico joined GATT, did the share of protected import categories fall to 8 percent, with duties being collected on 31 percent of imports.[30]

Although the Mexican government itself has had to take some of the blame for the economic crisis of the 1980s, MMH attempted to distinguish between the central government (which is under his direct control) and the parastate sector (which is only under his indirect control). In admitting implicitly that the central government had lost control over parastate expenditures, he blamed the problem on the lack of an effective legal framework to exercise control over the sector.

The parastate entities (decentralized agencies, mixed public and private companies, and trust funds) had been established ostensibly to remove from the sphere of central government politics national activities that required long-term, private business–like decisions and investments going beyond any one presidential term. But since the 1950s the parastate entities had begun to increase in number throughout Latin America and to become powers unto themselves.[31] In 1930 Mexico had 16 parastate entities and

in 1976 the number was 760, after which the number skyrocketed.[32]

When MMH took office, the Mexican central government did not know how many parastate entities existed. The *Diario Oficial* for November 15, 1982, listed 849 entities,[33] but MMH's IV State of the Union Address in 1986 retrospectively listed the total for 1982 as 1,155 (Table 10), with more being created.

That the president did not know in 1982 the size of the parastate sector is understandable given the fact that without an appropriate legal framework the central government could not effectively register, supervise, audit, and evaluate the parastate entities. Although a number of laws had been enacted by the Congress since 1947 (when the first legislation was passed to offer legal rationale for and controls on the expanding number of parastate entities), those laws of 1966, 1970, 1975, and 1981 tried to improve matters to little avail.[34]

With the frequent changes in the laws governing the parastate sector, the legislation mainly managed to confuse the regulators as well as the regulated entities. The first attempt to register the entities came in 1970, and in 1976 they were assigned to subsectors, each subsector being placed under the "control" of an appropriate ministry or administrative department of the central government. But because each entity collected and expended its own revenues and did so without a common accounting system, the central government soon realized that it had only nominal control over the parastate sector.

Therefore, some new legal approaches to the parastate sector have emerged. In 1982 legislation was enacted which represented the first attempt to bring the parastate sector into the central government's process of planning, in the Secretariat of Planning and Budget (SPB), and into the process of audit, in the newly established Secretariat of the Controller General (SCG). Indeed, overall supervision and evaluation of the parastate sector have always been legally problematic. In 1947 the Secretariat of the Treasury (ST) was assigned those responsibilities; in 1970 the Secretariat of National Patrimony took over but was abolished in 1976. In 1986 the law gave the coordinating task jointly to the ST, SPB, and SCG; but in the same year the SCG was given control along with the first regulatory legislation to enable compliance.

[28] See Wilkie, "On Mexico's 'New' Financial Crisis."

[29] "Mexico: Out of the Sun," *The Economist*, September 5–11, 1987, pp. 3–22, especially p. 8.

[30] See Antonio Salinas Chávez, "Aspectos de la Apertura Comercial," *Comercio Exterior*, October 1987, pp. 808–809.

[31] See my study "Recentralization: The Budgetary Dilemma in the Economic Development of Mexico, Bolivia, and Costa Rica," in James W. Wilkie, *Statistics and National Policy* (Los Angeles: UCLA Latin American Center, University of California), pp. 101–131; and my "Bolivia: Ironies in the National Revolutionary Process, 1952–1986," in SALA, 25, pp. 912–928.

[32] Rosario Martínez, "El Origen de la Ley de Entidades Paraestatales," *El Cotidiano* 14 (1986), pp. 12 ff.

[33] For an incomplete 1980s listing in a more accessible source, see "Registro de la Administración Pública Federal Paraestatal, [December, 1980]," *El Mercado de Valores*, April 13, 1981, which included only 780 agencies.

[34] The nature of these laws is outlined in Martínez, "El Origen," pp. 17–19.

Table 10

ESTIMATE OF MEXICO'S PARASTATE ENTITIES, 1982

Category	Total	Decentralized Agencies	Companies with Majority State Ownership	Companies with Minority State Ownership	Trust Funds
Existing	1,155	107	750	65	233
In Process[1]	75	3	46	8	18

1. Some were in the process of being formed, others dissolved, and at least 27 cases represented entities the projects for which had been cancelled or never began operation.

SOURCE: Miguel Angel Romero and Francisco Robles Berlanga, "La Resestructuración de las Paraestatales," *El Cotidiano* 14 (1986), p. 29.

Table 11

DE LA MADRID PLAN FOR LIQUIDATION, SALE, OR FUSION OF 458 PARASTATE ENTITIES[1]
(December 1982–October 1986)

Category	Liquidation	Sale[2]	Transfer to States	Fusion	Total
Decentralized Agencies	2				
Companies, State Share:					
Majority-Owned	60	46			
Minority-Owned	3	19			
Trust Funds	34				
Unknown	170	36	30	58	
Total	269	101	30	58	458

1. For which plans are either completed or in process.
2. Includes companies eligible for debt-equity swaps.

SOURCE: Miguel Angel Romero and Francisco Robles Berlanga, "La Reestructuración de las Paraestatales," *El Cotidiano* 14 (1986), p. 26.

MMH's recognition of problems in the parastate sector gave him at least three advantages. He could justify the need for new legislation to bring the sector under central government control, thus recentralizing power. He could justify terminating central government subsidy of inefficient parastate enterprises, thus necessitating the liquidation, sale, transfer to state governments, or fusion of many entities. He could repay part of the foreign debt through debt-equity swap arrangements where foreign capital is used to purchase Mexican dollar loans at a discount and exchange them for pesos at the Banco de México, provided the pesos so exchanged are invested in a Mexican subsidiary (such as the U.S. Chrysler Corporation,[35]) or eligible enterprises among parastate entities being sold (Table 11).

Although some 40 percent of the parastate sector entities have been or are being liquidated, sold, transferred, or fused (458 out of 1,155), critics have

[35] Thus in 1986 Chrysler bought 100 million dollars of Mexico's dollar debt to foreigners for about 65 million dollars, including fees. Then Chrysler exchanged that debt at the Banco de México for pesos worth the full 100 million dollars. Finally Chrysler invested the pesos in Mexico as required. By investing in its Mexican plants, Chrysler received capital improvements at a 35 percent discount compared with what it would have cost to make the investment in U.S. currency. Mexico benefited by repaying its foreign debt in pesos, not dollars. See Edwin A. Finn, Jr., "There Goes the Neighborhood," *Forbes Magazine*, June 29, 1967, p. 37.

questioned the meaning of this contraction in relation to the value of sales. Of the 500 largest enterprises in Mexico in 1986, 49.4 percent of the sales were by 44 parastate agencies, among which only sixteen have been put up for sale. These sixteen entities constituted only 6.5 percent of the total sales of those 500 largest companies. Workers in the sixteen enterprises losing their affiliation with the public sector numbered only 83,799, or 14 percent of the 500 largest concerns.[36]

Yet the contraction of the public sector will take time, and it may be more comprehensive than the above figures suggest. During the last several years, MMH has sold or is selling to the private sector the impressive list of companies shown in Table 12. In addition, the government has announced that it plans to end its participation in 44 of the 49 mining properties in which it is now involved. According to this plan, the mining of minerals considered strategic (coal, iron, sulphur, potassium, and phosphorite) will remain under state control, but all other mining and refining will be opened to private enterprise or to ownership by individual state governments. Further, once the DINA automotive complex is sold, it is estimated that with regard to Mexico's total non-petroleum industrial activities, the state will have transferred to the private sector 35 percent of the work force and 30 percent of the value of production.[37]

In addition to reducing the size of the parastate sector, MMH has moved to constrict the role of Mexico City in national affairs by transferring some 70,000 central government workers to the regions of Mexico which their agencies serve.[38] In 1986 nearly 12,000 workers in the Ministry of Agriculture and Hydraulic Resources were transferred out of Mexico City, as were 15,000 employees of the ministries of Education and Health and 5,000 workers in other agencies. MMH's plan calls for another 38,000 to be relocated by the end of 1988. We await the results of that plan, which is scheduled to move nearly one-third of all basic education and teacher training and health personnel to the provinces.

Admirable as the goal may be to relocate some of the central government out of Mexico City, MMH has hampered economic and social planning and evaluation by moving to Aguascalientes a key agency

in Mexican development and the one agency upon which all others are dependent for basic data—the Mexican statistical agency. With the agency exiled from the locus of power (although safer from destructive earthquakes), perhaps recentralization will not be possible, information being the key to power.

Given the attempt since MMH to deconcentrate the central government and to reduce the role of the parastate sector, we do not yet know the extent to which the following irony will ensue: deconcentration will be offset by the new importance of the central government owing to the contraction of the parastate sector. Indeed, recentralization of power in the central government is not contradicted by deconcentration of the central government bureaucracy to the provinces.

With the restructuring of the state's role, by mid-1987 observers were adopting a more positive view about Mexico, especially because foreign reserves had increased fivefold compared with 1986. Reserves reached some 15 billion dollars owing to:[39]

1. increased earnings from higher oil prices, up from $10 to $20 per barrel;

2. a boom in tourism, owing to the undervalued peso;

3. the release of 7.7 billion dollars in new foreign-bank loans promised in 1986 after Mexico's successful renegotiation of nearly 43 billion dollars of its foreign debt, which in 1987 stood at only 17.5 percent more than in 1982 (Table 6);

4. the return of some dollars held abroad by Mexicans.

In this context of relative economic euphoria, the Official Party named Carlos Salinas de Gortari (CSG) as its presidential candidate in early October 1987 for the July 1988 election. The naming of CSG, Secretary of Planning and Budget and main architect of MMH's economic policies, implied that Mexico would continue the restructuring under way; and Salinas's nomination was welcomed by international bankers who were worried that Mexico might default on its foreign debt.

The circumstances of "euphoria" about the economy were conjunctural, however, and were being offset by an inflation rate of 132 percent during 1987, a public sector deficit expected to reach the pre-1982 levels, and an inordinately high increase in Mexico's money supply. MMH had taken the yearly

---

[36] Miguel Angel Romero and Francisco Robles Berlanga, "La Reestructuración de las Paraestatales," El Cotidiano 14 (1986), p. 27 and table 8.

[37] On MMH's plans for investment strategy for the mining industry, see Lloyds Mexican Economic Report, July 1988. On the share of work force and production left to the government, see María Amparo Casar, "La Reestructuración de la Participación del Estado en la Industria Nacional," El Cotidiano 23 (1988), pp. 28–38, especially pp. 37–38.

[38] El Mercado de Valores, May 25, 1987.

[39] For example, see Dan Williams, "$15 Billion Windfall Presents Mexico with New Fiscal Headaches," Los Angeles Times, August 17, 1987; and Lloyd's Mexican Economic Report, October 1987.

increases in money supply to about 53 percent from 1984 through 1986, and then seemed to lose restraint as the rates for 1987 and 1988 reached 106 percent (Table 5), the annualized figure for November 1987 increasing to 141 percent!

Not to be left out of the continuing real economic crisis, the commercial banking system has, since its nationalization in September 1982, presented serious problems to the government because real deposits declined drastically by 1986 to 65 percent of the pre-nationalization deposits (Table 13).

Thus pressure mounted on MMH to denationalize the banks as part of his process of opening the Mexican economy.

Although MMH has redefined drastically the strategic areas reserved for state ownership, the important factor concerns the state share, an issue in banking. MMH generally limited exclusive state control to petroleum, basic petrochemicals, electricity, nuclear energy, and certain (especially radioactive) minerals. In spite of the failure of the nationalized banks to attract deposits, however, MMH refused to

Table 12

**SAMPLE OF PARASTATE COMPANIES SOLD,
FOR SALE, OR RUMORED TO BE SOLD[1] BY
DE LA MADRID ADMINISTRATION TO PRIVATE SECTOR
(As of June 1988)**

Category/Branch	Company
Sold	
Hotels	Nacional Hotelera (including El Presidente hotels)
Chemicals	Cloro de Tehuantepec
Papermaking	Grupo Atenquique
General	48 companies owned by Nacional Financiera
	42 companies owned by Fomento Industrial Somex
Bicycles	Bicicletas Cóndor
Automotive	Renault de México
For Sale	
Automotive	Vehículos Automotores de México
	8 companies of Diesel Nacional (DINA)
Cotton	Algodonera Comercial Mexicana
Fishing	12 companies on west coast and Gulf
Petrochemicals	Petroquímica de México
Shipbuilding	Astilleros Unidos de Ensenada
Shipping	Compañía Naviera Minera del Golfo
Mining	Compañía Minera Cananea
	Barita de Sonora
	Gráfita de México
	Hierro y Acero del Norte
Steel	Siderúgica Nacional (Michoacán)
	Aceros Rossini
Sugar Mills	11 companies
Tractors	Fábrica de Tractores Agrícolas
Tobacco	Cigarrera La Tabacalera Mexicana
Rumored to be for Sale	
Fertilizer	Fertimex
Mining	Real del Monte
Steel	Altos Hornos de México
Sugar	Government sugar mills
Communications	Teléfonos de México
Airlines[2]	Mexicana de Aviación
Telephones	Teléfonos de México
Food	Industrias Conasupo

1. The government may retain a minority interest in some companies.
2. The government had offered to sell Aeroméxico, but there were no buyers and MMH precipitated its bankruptcy in April 1988. By year's end it was operating as a private company.

SOURCE: *Lloyd's Mexican Economic Report*, June and July, 1988; *El Cotidiano*, 14 (1986) and 23 (1988); and interviews.

Table 13

INDEX OF MEXICO'S REAL COMMERCIAL BANKING DEPOSITS, 1982–89
(January and August of 1982 = 100)[1]

Dec. Year	All Commercial Index[2]	Traditional Commercial Subindex[2]
1982[a]	100	100
1983	79	79
1984	85	83
1985	75	75
1986	73	65
1987	70	63
1988	61	29
1989[b]	50	20

1. Calculated from pesos of 1978.
2. Data are graphed in Figure 4, above. Nominal data for this subindex are given in Banco Nacional de México, *Review of the Economic Situation in Mexico*, line 50; real percentage change data are given in line 52. For full discussion of the subtotal of traditional commercial deposits, see SALA, 27, Ch. 37, "The Mexican Financial Imbroglio since 1982: Debt, Public Expenditure, and Nationalized Banking."

a. January and August.
b. April.

SOURCE: for 1982, data from Banco Nacional de México given in SALA, 26–3502; since 1983, Banco Nacional de México, unpublished computer series of banking data.

jettison the banks, as urgently demanded by the private sector so critical of the decline in loans, efficiency, and availability of credit.

To try to reestablish some public confidence in the commercial banking system, therefore, in early 1987 MMH permitted the private sector to repurchase 34 percent of the banks' stock. This sale of bank stock did not change the fact that the banks do not operate autonomously but under rigid control of the Ministry of Treasury and the Banco de México; and even CSG in his campaign supported the bank officials' complaints that any attempts to resolve problems in operation are caught up in overregulation by nonbank bureaucrats.[40] Theoretically, tight government controls assure all sectors access to credit; in reality, excessive controls defeat the all-important timing of loans, as well as the making of loans, especially in the venture capital markets. In any case, assertions are widespread that the banks have tended to favor public sector, rather than giving the private sector access to credit.

That the prerequisite for return to Mexico of the bulk of the capital which fled beginning in 1970 may be related to denationalization of the banking system is perhaps best illustrated in the following story which I heard in Tijuana, Baja California, while observing the CSG campaign in April 1988. It was rumored that CSG had met with the former owner of BANCOMER, Manuel Espinosa Yglesias, to ask him what it would take to encourage the return of the billions of dollars that had fled the country under LEA, JLP, and MMH—dollars needed to make domestic credit available to the private sector as well as to pay the foreign debt. Supposedly Espinosa Yglesias responded by saying:

Give us back our banks, and we will repatriate the billions of dollars that fled and that otherwise will never return. Give us back our banks and your economic problems are over.

In this story, Espinosa Yglesias is said to have reminded CSG that the real impediment to Mexico's economic recovery is not the foreign debt payment schedule, but the flight of capital that occurred especially with the nationalization of the banks.

Whether or not this story about Espinosa Yglesias is true, it is certain that would-be bank depositors lack confidence in Mexico's government-dominated banks, which have lived through difficult times of great increase in M_1 and inflation related to the flight of dollars. The traditional commercial banking system has continued to wither in spite of the sale of bank stock, real deposits having fallen in 1988 to 29 percent of the pre-nationalization balance (Fig. 4).

Although some funds have returned to Mexico for deposit in treasury bonds (CETES) or for investment in the Mexican stock market—both of which lack much liquidity—resolution of the bank issues is but one important part of a more complex policy question. How can liquidity be restored to the entire economic system?

With confidence in the peso dwindling, and declining deposits in the nationalized banks (where in any case deposits earned several percentage points less in interest than the rate of inflation), many of the limited dollars returning to Mexico were doing so only to take advantage of the dramatic rise in stock values on the Mexican stock exchange.[41] Mexico's

---

[40] On bank overregulation, see "Salinas Se Suma a la Crítica de Banqueros Oficiales al Banco de México," *Proceso*, February 22, 1988. On the sale of bank stock, see Banco Nacional de México, *Review of the Economic Situation of Mexico*, March 1987, p. 43.

[41] On the dramatic decline in bank deposits, see my "From Economic Growth to Economic Stagnation in Mexico," pp. 916–920; and Gustavo Lomelín and Enrique Quintana, "Reestructuración de la Banca, Es Necesario por la Baja Captación y Fuerte Descenso de Utilidades," *El Financiero*, April 18, 1988. On the Mexican stock market, see Dan Williams, "Mexico Moves to Prop Up Falling Market," *Los Angeles Times*, November 11, 1987, part IV, p. 1.

Figure 4

**INDEX OF MEXICO TRADITIONAL
COMMERCIAL BANKING DEPOSITS,
1982–88**

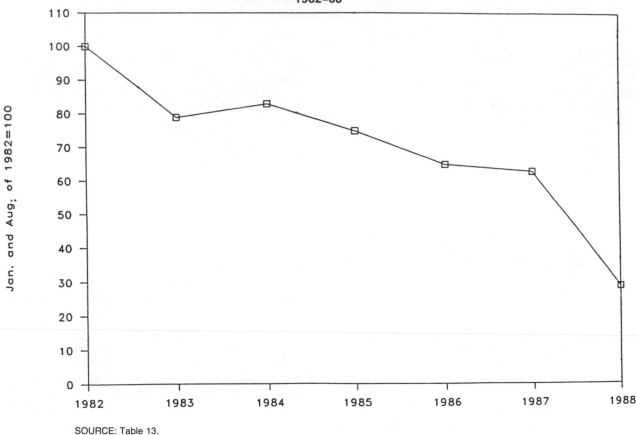

SOURCE: Table 13.

stock exchange was especially attractive to investors speculating in quick profits, and it became the fastest rising bull market in the world during the first nine months of 1987. As the value of stocks on Mexico's exchange ridiculously outpaced inflation, to reach 6 billion dollars in value by early October, the exchange found itself even more overvalued than Wall Street.

As long as Mexico's stock market held up, the government could continue to slowly devalue the peso. Following Wall Street's crash (and the crash of markets internationally) on October 19, 1987, however, Mexico's stock exchange went into a dramatic 70 percent decline. By November 18 the Mexican stock market's value fell to 2 billion dollars. The crash caused a rush to change pesos into dollars, and the rush soon became a panic.

To protect its reserves, the Mexican government withdrew its support of the peso by stopping the sale of dollars. With free convertibility effectively ended, the peso fell from 1,712 on November 17 to 2,200 on November 18—a devaluation of 22.2 percent (Table 3, Part IV).

In this context of obviously renewed economic crisis, CSG faced serious problems in his campaign for the presidency. At the beginning of the campaign, he had capitalized on the pre-crash financial optimism of summer and early fall 1987, and thus he generally ignored economic problems in order to stress pressing political issues. In calling for vague political restructuring, CSG seemed to be addressing opposition demands that the Official Party stop rigging elections. In briefly stating publicly that the era was over when the PRI could continue to win elections with a *carro completo* (or "full car" loaded with victories and leaving nothing for the opposition), CSG gave belated recognition to the split that his candidacy had caused within the Official Party. In calling himself a "progressive centrist," CSG positioned himself between the PRI right wing (led by labor chief Fidel Velázquez, who is angry about the contraction of the public sector) and the PRI left wing (much of which calls for cancellation of the foreign debt and cessation of oil shipments to the U.S. strategic reserve).

During the PRI's internal maneuvering to select its presidential candidate in late 1986 and 1987, the left wing, led by Cuauhtémoc Cárdenas (son of the former president of Mexico) and Porfirio Muñoz Ledo (former president of the PRI), had organized a "Democratic Current" intended to end the Official Party's tradition of allowing the president of Mexico to name his successor. Ostracized within the PRI for their heresy, these two dynamic leaders immediately established the Frente Democrático Nacional (FDN), or Democratic Front, to compete in the 1988 elections; Cárdenas would run for the presidency and Muñoz Ledo for the senate.

Upon resigning from the PRI on December 15, 1987, and flying to Los Angeles to tape-record his Oral History Memoirs with me, Porfirio Muñoz Ledo (PML) wrote an open letter to the Mexican people stating:

I consider the PRI to have abdicated its historical task and given up the vanguard role required to solve the crisis. Hidden behind its acronym is a plan to concede the national patrimony to foreign investors against the wishes of the people. . . . The PRI, subdued by the counterrevolutionary group [of monetarists] in power and imprisoned by the failure of leadership, has lost the genuine loyalty of its followers as well as the confidence of the citizenry, and as a consequence the PRI has lost the rationale for its existence.[42]

In his Oral History Memoirs, PML argues that even in the epoch of antimonetarist LEA, the monetarists, traditionally centered in the Banco de México and the Ministry of Treasury, had begun to reaccumulate the influence they had enjoyed within the PRI under a policy of stabilizing development, hence challenging him in his capacity within the PRI and combating him in his role as LEA's ideologist. PML attempted to sidestep this group by developing national plans from his Ministry of Labor and seeking to influence policy by keeping monetarists in the minority. According to PML, the antistatist monetarists gained more momentum when he was named ambassador of Mexico to the United Nations, ending his influence in Mexico as the leader of the antimonetarists. Under JLP, MMH created the Ministry of Planning and Budget, wherein the monetarists strengthened their position.

In PML's view, the monetarists could not have assumed complete power within the PRI, which remained a pluralist organization representing the interests of diverse groups ranging from the statists to the antistatists, but JLP named MMH to the presidency. That action gave exclusive power to the monetarists, led by CSG who in 1982 became Minister of Planning and Budget. With CSG in charge of antistate policy, the broad gamut of thinking within the PRI was frozen out of planning. This had never happened in Official Party history, even when Antonio Ortiz Mena dominated Mexican economic policy as Minister of Treasury (1958–70).

Given this situation of the closed PRI, PML says that he and Cuauhtémoc Cárdenas had no choice but to abandon the Official Party and to create a new national consensus about the need for a strong state. According to PML, the Democratic Front will enjoy strong support from the broad base of PRI groups now excluded from policy decisions. Although PML has high expectations of winning many seats in the Chamber of Deputies and several seats in the Senate (including one for himself), he does not foresee the Democratic Front winning the presidency until 1994. He expects the six years of misguided CSG policies to provide the coup de grace to the PRI's power.

In the meantime, CSG's campaign goes on, with little mention of the economic crisis. By adopting the slogan "Let the People Speak!" CSG effectively became a listener rather than a speaker. Ironically, the last president to listen was Lázaro Cárdenas. By implication, then, CSG hoped to dilute the importance of having as his main opponent Lázaro's son Cuauhtémoc, the name alone constituting a historical conscience for many voters.

Although serious thought by CSG presumably has taken place behind the scenes, it has not been evident in most of his presidential campaign rhetoric, which at least at the outset closely resembled that of MMH's campaign six years earlier. Examples of the MMH/CSG rhetoric are given in Figure 5.

Not until over half way through his campaign did CSG focus on the problem of inflation. In March 1988 in Yucatán he called for a general mobilization against inflation. Because this anti-inflation stance was the first campaign issue to strike a cord with the electorate, CSG stated that "Now we have a banner, and we won't let go."[43] CSG proceeded to fully extol the virtues of MMH's Pact of Economic Solidarity, which had been announced December 15, 1987.

The Pact of Economic Solidarity, linking the government, labor, and farm and business organizations, called for limiting wage demands and price increases beginning in March 1988 in return for government moderation and even freezing of prices for essentials such as gasoline and tortillas. Beginning in March, the government would raise wages ahead of inflation rather than behind it. In the meantime, the government immediately raised minimum and con-

---

[42] Letter is reprinted in *Unomasuno* (Mexico City), December 16, 1987.

[43] Quoted by Carlos Acosta and Fernando Ortega Pizarro, in "Del Pacto Sacó Salinas Por Fin, Una Bandera: Combatir la Carestía," *Proceso*, March 7, 1988, p. 7.

Figure 5

POLITICAL CAMPAIGN QUOTES OF DE LA MADRID AND SALINAS DE GORTARI

Miguel de la Madrid Hurtado 1981–1982 Campaign	Carlos Salinas de Gortari 1987–1988 Campaign
It is told in some episode in mythology that when the Greek gods wanted to gain strength, they would come to Earth. I have come to touch the Earth in [my home State of] Colima.	[I will begin my campaign in the State of Nuevo León because], like the classic myths point out, one has to tread the earth of one's origins in order to renew vigor and strength.
We need women to modernize the country, to make a more just nation, to have a more full life from the human point of view.	The participation of women is required to modernize the country, to make the nation more just, to enrich democracy, and to obtain a more full life from the human point of view.

SOURCE: Dan Williams, "Voter Apathy Troubles Mexico's Ruling Party," *Los Angeles Times*, November 22, 1987.

tractual wages by 38 percent, but also authorized official price increases, the largest increases being about 85 percent (for gasoline, telephone service, and sugar) and 79 percent (for fertilizer).

Under the Pact, the government then announced that the "free-market" peso would be held at about 2,250 to the dollar, a rate that was to be maintained through the end of MMH's term. The Banco de México guaranteed that it would use the country's 15 billion in reserves to maintain the peso, thus providing the stability that could woo some dollars back to Mexico.

By early 1988 it was clear that the government's attempt to anticipate inflation by raising prices and wages beforehand would itself cause inflation; therefore the government abandoned that aspect of the Pact and relied mainly upon preserving the value of the peso. Although the peso soon became overvalued, hurting Mexico's tourism and export industries, the government hoped to avoid devaluation, which would infuriate the middle and lower classes.

Having served MMH as his close advisor since the 1970s,[44] CSG has not been in a position to criti-

cize the policies for which he and MMH have directly shared responsibility since 1982, when CSG became head of planning for the government. Although CSG has hinted in his campaign that the Official Party cannot continue to insist on winning most fixed-seats in the 1988 elections, he has done so only obliquely. Given the severe economic realities of post-crash Mexico in late 1987 (including a post-1910s high in the increase of money supply and a consequent rise in inflation projected for the last years of the 1980s), it appears that Mexico's economic problems cannot be ignored and will finally have political ramifications.

Although the Official Party's current ideology of Restructured Revolution calls for continued reduction of the public sector's influence in the economy, such reduction is not easily accomplished amid severe financial crisis. Private funds deposited in the nationalized banks have tended to be used to pay the nationalized foreign debt and not recycled to the private sector.

With the decline of funds available to the private sector since 1982, the public sector's share in national investment has risen rather than declined (Table 14). From 1951 through 1960 the public sector's share of investment held in the 30 percents (except for 1956 when it declined into the 20s); from 1961 through 1964 it rose into the 40 percents; from 1965 through 1974 it fell back to the 30 percents (except 1965 when it was 29 percent); since 1975 it has risen into the 40 percents (except for 1976 and 1984). Whereas in 1976 it was 39 percent, in 1984 it reached 51 percent, the high since 1950.

The most promising opportunity for Mexico to obtain productive private funding involves foreign investment in tourism and the in-bond (*maquila*) industry. Under MMH, tourists to Mexico exceeded 5 million in 1987 (Table 4).

[44] CSG was serving during the LEA administration as advisor to the Undersecretary of Public Finances in the Ministry of Treasury when in 1972 MMH became Treasury's Director General of Credit. As MMH made the transition to the JLP administration as Undersecretary of Treasury and Credit (1975–79), CSG held increasingly important posts in the Secretariat, including Chief of the Department of Economic Studies in the General Direction of Treasury Studies and International Affairs (1974–76), Deputy Director of Economic Studies in the same General Direction (1976–78), and Director General of Treasury Planning (1978–79). When MMH became Secretary of Planning and Budget under JLP, CSG became his Director General of Economic and Social Policy (1979–81), and when MMH became President of Mexico, CSG became his Secretary of Planning and Budget (1982–87). See *Quien Es Quién en la Administración Pública de México* (México, D.F.: Secretaría de la Presidencia, 1982), pp. 15 and 131. It is also important to note that CSG is part of the Ortiz Mena group, which explains his stance on the debt while serving as Minister of Planning and Budget.

Under the maquila system, non-Mexicans import and export equipment and materials duty free into and out of Mexico merely by posting a bond to assure that the imports are only temporary—hence the name "in-bond" industry. The maquila industry is also called the twin-plant or production-sharing industry, owing to the fact that U.S. firms (and now Japanese) move goods between their U.S. and Mexican plants. Dating from Mexican legislation of 1966, Mexico has sought to capitalize on the Far East's experience of attracting U.S.-owned plants to assemble goods for the U.S. market. The operation of U.S. assembly plants abroad had become possible through U.S. tariff schedules 806.30 and 807 of 1930 (as amended in 1956), which require payment of U.S. taxes only on the foreign value added (labor, overhead, and profits) to U.S.-made components assembled outside the United States.

Although the original idea had been to require foreign companies to operate within a border zone twelve miles wide, this restriction was eliminated by 1967 as the in-bond industry demonstrated immediate prospects for providing new jobs. Employment opportunities in the in-bond industry grew from 20,000 positions in 1970 to 173,000 in 1983 (Table 15). Although this new industry pays minimal Mexican taxes, it stimulates the entire economy. In 1983 Mexico allowed in-bond companies to sell between 10 and 40 percent of their goods in Mexico, provided that the goods have at least 15 percent Mexican content. By 1987 Mexico had 308,000 workers employed in 1,005 in-bond factories, a development that seems to promise a new boom for the country.[45]

Transition to the Political Stage of the Restructured Revolution, 1988–

Looking back at the six ideological phases during which the Mexican government has sought to guide social and economic change, we see that in the Official Party view the violent revolution after 1910 was only the beginning of a long process of implementing goals set forth in the Constitution of 1917. Although the constitution provided for private property rights, the role of government grew steadily until 1982, when Mexico found itself financially bankrupt.

As we have seen, however, the 1982 crisis was not the first one but rather one of many. The management style of the Official Party has been to capitalize on crises in order to justify its continued leadership.

[45] On the in-bond industry, see Ellwyn R. Stoddard, *Maquila: Assembly Plants in Northern Mexico* (El Paso: Texas Western University Press, 1987); and on the history of the term and how the industry developed on the U.S.-Mexican border, see my "From Economic Growth to Economic Stagnation in Mexico," pp. 930–931.

Table 14

PUBLIC SECTOR INVESTMENT AS SHARE OF TOTAL INVESTMENT,[1] 1950–88[a]

Year	%	Year	%	Year	%
1950	51	1965	29	1975	42
1951	36	1966	31	1976	39
1952	36	1967	36	1977	40
1953	37	1968	36	1978	45
1954	39	1969	36	1979	44
1955	34	1970	33	1980	45
1956	28	1971	26	1981	46
1957	30	1972	32	1982	46
1958	32	1973	39	1983	44
1959	32	1974	38	1984	51
1960	35			1985	47
1961	43			1986	45
1962	43			1987	31
1963	45			1988	29
1964	45				

1. Investment is defined as funding for production machinery and equipment as well as for the buildings, construction, infrastructure, and transport equipment needed to produce new goods.

a. The series is constructed from three sources, the methodology for which may vary.

SOURCE: 1950–64, Nacional Financiera, *La Economía Mexicana en Cifras, 1977*, p. 90.
1965–83, ibid., *1986*, pp. 68–70.
1984–86, *El Mercado de Valores*, October 23, 1987.
1987–88, Calculated from data in Banco Nacional de México, *Review of the Economic Situation of Mexico*, July 1989, p. 269.

Table 15

MEXICO IN-BOND INDUSTRY, 1970–88

Year	Number of Factories	Thousands of Employees
1970	120[a]	20[a]
1974	455	76
1975	454	67
1976	448	74
1977	443	78
1978	457	91
1979	540	111
1980	620	124
1981	605	130
1982	585	123
1983	600	173
1984	672	202
1985	760	218
1986	900	255
1987	1,259	323
1988	1,480	398

a. Excludes factories and employees not in the border states; for discussion of the maquila industry, see source.

SOURCE: SALA, 26, pp. 930–931 and table 3519; and *El Mercado de Valores*, May 15, 1989.

Since 1982 the PRI has defended its continuation in political power by citing the need to dismantle money-losing state operations. As in the past, the blame for the present crisis has been shifted away from the Official Party. Moreover, the Official Party has been able to remain in power by adapting to take advantage of new circumstances, such as developing tourism as a renewable resource since World War II or meeting the world need for oil during the 1970s.

In its effort to restructure the "Permanent Revolution," since 1982 the Official Party has sought to create a dynamic new role for the private sector by forcing it to redirect production from domestic sales to the international market. The booming in-bond industry seems to offer the latest opportunity for Mexico to develop a comparative economic advantage that will earn it the dollars needed for continued development.

The context of change faced by Mexico in its internal and external affairs is seemingly multifaceted. Although the stereotype of a socially timeless Mexico has been countered somewhat by accounts in the world press about the internal migration to Mexico City and the capital's emergence as one of the largest cities in the world, the idea persists that Mexico has undergone little change.

Much social change has indeed taken place, as my Poverty Index for Mexico shows. This index measures the share of Mexico's population living in social poverty from 1910 through 1970 (Fig. 3). The level improved from 56.9 percent in 1910, to 46.0 in 1940, and to 24.8 in 1970.

A complementary index developed by Stephen Haber—the Social Modernization Index (SMI)—expands upon the Poverty Index. The SMI goes below the state level to examine the extent of change in 103 sample *municipios* (counties), selected from among 2,367 rural, semiurban, and urban municipios between 1930 and 1970. The SMI data show a shift from a nonmodern condition of society everywhere to a modern condition, with only a minor exception in 1960 for the urban category (see Fig. 6).

The extent to which pre-1982 social gains have been compromised by events in the 1980s has yet to be measured. Owing to JLP's stupendous failure to reorganize the Mexican statistical agency and create a giant data bank as he had hoped, the government lost control of its statistical base.[46] In suppressing Mexico's longest statistical series on inflation (and the one that showed the most change in the cost of living), for example, JLP no longer had the information base to assess what was happening to prices in the

[46] See my "The Management and Mismanagement of National and International Statistics," in SALA, 22, Chapter 41.

Figure 6

MEXICO SOCIAL MODERNIZATION[1] INDEX,[2] 1930–70

Category[3]	1930[e]	1940	1950	1960	1970
Selected Rural[a]	69.1	67.7	61.1	54.6	46.2
Selected Semiurban[b]	34.0	30.8	25.6	20.7	16.5
Selected Urban[c]	10.5	7.2	5.9	6.1	5.2
National Average[d]	52.6	48.6	40.7	33.5	24.1

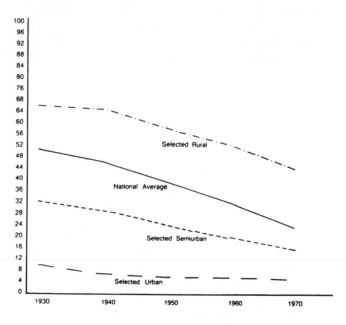

1. Zero indicates complete modernization. The Social Modernization Index (SMI) divides the total of seven components by five values instead of seven because non-Spanish speakers and bilingual persons are both part of a larger category of Indian speakers, and barefoot persons and sandal-wearers are subcategories of the larger category of shoeless persons.
2. Nonmodern persons live in social isolation (that is, are [1] illiterate, [2] speak Indian and Spanish, or [3] do not speak Spanish) and geographic isolation (defined as [4] living in localities of less than 2,500 persons), eat a nonmodern diet (measured by [5] share of persons who habitually consume tortillas instead of wheat bread), and have traditional dress patterns (those who [6] go barefoot or who [7] wear sandals instead of shoes). These seven items in the SMI are averaged with equal weight because there is no theoretical reason to assume that any one component is more important than the others as a measure of modernization.
3. Represents 103 sample municipios from the 2,367 Mexican municipios including the municipio in each state which had the highest percentage of illiterates in 1940, the capital of each of the 32 Mexican states, and 40 municipios represented in the community-study literature.

a. Municipios which in 1930 had more than 50 percent of the population living in localities of less than 2,500 persons.
b. Municipios not included in "Rural" or "Urban."
c. Mexico City, Guadalajara, and Monterrey.
d. Includes all of Mexico's population in 2,367 municipios.
e. Variance between seven-item average (seven items, five values) and four-item average (four items, three values) in 1940 is used to link the 1930 index to make it comparable to the post-1940 index.

SOURCE: Stephen Haber, "Modernization and Change in Mexican Communities, 1930–1970," SALA, 22, Chapter 40.

Mexican economy. Too, by disrupting basic data series JLP made it impossible to carry the Poverty Index and the SMI forward to 1980.

Could JLP have meant to break deliberately so many links of measurement over time or were he and his lieutenants simply incompetent and unable to gather the basic data needed for making decisions? Or was the JLP government so sure of its ability to start afresh that it believed that plans can be formulated without knowledge of real trajectories? Certainly JLP disliked statistics that challenged his propagandistic image of Mexico. Ironically, after having hampered our ability to understand contemporary Mexico, JLP prides himself on his writings which he sees as offering insights into Mexico's bygone history.

Regardless of the view of Mexico constructed consciously and unconsciously by the government, Mexico's image abroad has developed from two geographic perspectives. Measured by U.S. political, economic, and social standards, Mexico does not seem to have compared favorably with the United States to which it has been likened because of geographic proximity. Such comparisons, however, are unfair. In spite of their common border, in contrast to the United States, Mexican development has been impeded by difficult geographic and topographic conditions. Further, Mexico's colonial period did not prepare it for independence, as did the U.S. experience. Unlike the United States, Mexico has made a long and sincere attempt to assimilate the Indian population.

Viewed from South and Central America, Mexico seems to have created order for progress under the model of one-party democracy, which several other countries to its south have tried to emulate. Whatever the disadvantages of long-term rule under one-party democracy, Mexico's growing importance in the world is indisputable.

Taking advantage of Mexico's favorable image in Central and South America, LEA and JLP attempted to move the country onto center stage in international affairs and into a leadership role among Third World nations. They reminded one and all that Mexico could boast a peso that was more stable than the dollar and one that had not changed in value for over two decades. LEA even attempted in 1976 to position himself to become Secretary General of the United Nations, a plan that was to fail for many reasons.

LEA's campaign for the U.N. post deteriorated in the face of internal and external problems. Not only did Mexican inflation hit a post-1950 high that eroded the value of the peso, but also LEA had to overcome the consequences of the 1975 Jewish tourism boycott against Mexico. Further, he had become embroiled in the internal affairs of Spain when he called for worldwide sanctions against Franco to

penalize him for having executed political prisoners. LEA's ploy backfired because Franco claimed to be executing terrorists who had killed police, winning the sympathy of dictators throughout the world—all of whom fear international sanctions against their brutality.

JLP continued LEA's attempt to establish Mexico's role as a leader of the Third World, hosting at Cancún in 1981 the North-South Conference. In Western Hemispheric affairs, Mexico undertook diplomatic initiatives to negotiate an end to the Central American crisis caused, on the one hand, by the intervention of Cuban and Nicaraguan forces in El Salvador, and, on the other hand, by U.S. intervention in Nicaragua, El Salvador, and Honduras. By the late 1980s, however, Mexico was frustrated in many of its international initiatives, the government of MMH having had limited impact on resolving the Central American imbroglio.

For the government of CSG, Mexico's main contribution to hemispheric politics may involve finding a way to reduce the Third World foreign debt burden. For example, it could take the lead in convincing the U.S., European, and Japanese debt-holders that the debtor nations should pay interest not on the book value of loans but rather on the value of the loans on the world's secondary markets, where the loans are sold at 50–60 percent discount. In any case, Mexico must establish a means for reducing the payments on its foreign debt, which by the end of 1987 reached 92.4 billion real dollars of 1980 (Table 6, part II).

With the Mexican government turning its attention to world affairs, MMH did not share the same interest in land reform as many of his predecessors had. Perhaps he felt that the question of land ownership was too entangled to resolve food production problems. Too, it could be argued that if Mexico wishes to expand its export market in manufactures it might best hold its reciprocal imports to low-cost foodstuffs, resulting in a balance of payments surplus for Mexico.

With regard to land reform, MMH could argue, as have several of his predecessors including Cárdenas, that land reform measures can never keep pace with population growth, and that major landholdings must be set aside for commercial agriculture and ranching to feed the country's growing urban population as well as to export high-profit food supplies for dollars. Thus MMH reduced the monthly rate of presidential resolutions and definitive actions distributing land to a rate that had not been seen since Rodríguez in the early 1930s (Table 2, Part I).

Consistent with his philosophy of downplaying land reform and following Cárdenas's lead in protecting certain lands from distribution to ejidos, MMH emphasized the granting of certificates of inaffecta-bility to protect large commercial agricultural produc-ers against being divided through land reform. Such certificates, emphasized after 1936 by Cárdenas, as-sured that productive commercial farming, needed to provide a stable food supply for the domestic and for-eign markets, would not be disrupted. Alemán added certificates to protect livestock ranching, some per-manently and some for only 25 years. Whereas 190,235 certificates had been granted from 1936 through 1982, by 1987 MMH had granted 222,816, more than the combined total of his eight predecessors (Table 2, Part III). In terms of land protected, MMH reached the highest recorded (Table 2, Parts IV and V).

Despite land reform, and often because land re-form has resulted in tiny fragmented ejidal holdings incapable of supporting the numerous heads of fami-lies, many peasants and their offspring have migrated to the United States to remain at least part time. Meanwhile, the U.S. attempt in 1986 to control im-migration threatens the safety valve that has existed since the 1940s for Mexican laborers, for whom em-ployment opportunities in rural Mexico have become scarce as population has grown.

The rural scene has become more complicated because the course of land reform law has become somewhat confused since 1970. LEA's legislation in 1971 outlawed the subdivision of lands among members of any extended family which sought to seemingly create legal small farms that in reality con-stituted one large agricultural enterprise. JLP aban-doned the attack on such extended family farms and in 1980 legalized the common practice of cooperation between private farmers and the ejidos, the former needing land and workers and the latter needing credit. Having the legal right to rent land and labor from ejidos, the ejidatarios were perceived by critics as day laborers on their own lands, not borrowers of capital investing in their own future.

While the uncertainty over the direction of land reform legislation continued to befuddle the farm sec-tor, many ejidatarios had for years rented their lands to or worked as day laborers for private farmers. The shortage of government credit for ejidatarios and the fixed size of ejidal plots "pulverized" by the growing population have meant that since the 1960s the ejido has been increasingly unable to produce either for market or subsistence.

Given such complexities in the cumulative re-sults of socioeconomic change since 1910 and the financial problems facing Mexico since 1982, readers may ask two important questions: How has the Offi-cial Party managed to remain in power for six de-cades? Can the Official Party continue to dominate politics as it has?

Implicit Pacts between the Official Party and Sectors of Society

The Official Party, administered by successive Mexican presidents, was able to become strong enough to endure after 1929 because it developed im-plicit pacts with at least nineteen sectors of Mexican society (shown in Fig. 7). In return for benefits (often overlapping among these groups) that were granted with relative consistency by the government, the sec-tors (none of which are monolithic) pledged their loyalty to the Official Party. Together, members of these groups (including their extended families and in many cases their dutiful employees) represented well over half of the Mexican population, including the most influential sectors. Such backing assured the Official Party a broad base of self-interested support. (These implicit pacts should not be confused with the Official Party's 1987 explicit formulation of the Pact of Economic Solidarity intended to stabilize prices and wages, discussed above.)

Given the restructuring of the economy and contraction of the public sector since 1982, however, all the pacts have been threatened as money and patronage have been progressively restricted by the MMH-CSG "monetarist policy," which restricts credit. In the rural economy, for example, ejidata-rios, who benefited from land reform and stable agri-cultural prices for their products, have seen their credit (which was never enough) decline along with the value of their products bought at guaranteed prices by the government. Farmers have lost much of their incentive to produce for the domestic market because of price controls that do not provide suffi-cient profit margin; and peasants have seen their hopes for land wither as JLP and MMH lost interest in land redistribution to ejidos. The intended re-juvenation of agriculture under the now legal alli-ance of ejidatarios and private producers remains to be assessed.

In the urban areas, the middle sectors have suf-fered an erosion in their purchasing power in dollars; organized laborers have lost their purchasing power in pesos; slum dwellers and contractors have seen the number of jobs decline as the public sector has re-duced its investments in the country's infrastructure; the financial groups have seen their dollar loans be-come increasingly expensive to repay with devalued Mexican currency; and private manufacturers have lost most government credits to and investments in their industries.

Loss of purchasing power by such sectors as the bureaucracy and educators (where even university salaries entered into a state of collapse) has meant decline in demand for domestically manufactured goods, which by the late 1980s must compete with a flood of foreign imports. Where formerly Mexican manufacturers could not sell much abroad owing to the government's overvaluing of the peso, now manufacturers face a problem in selling domestically.

Perhaps the most influential group threatened by the Official Party's decision to join GATT are the manufacturers who gave private sector support to the government in return for a favored position in the economy of Mexico wherein foreign investment in any firm is limited to 49 percent or less. These industrialists benefited from high tariff protection for 45 years. Moreover, they received exemptions from the tariff code in order to import equipment and materials needed to develop the country's industrial base. Because of this close industry-government relationship (which also involved government subsidies, loans, and investments), Mexico's industry was not encouraged to operate efficiently and competitively in world markets, stunting both the domestic and export markets for Mexican goods.

Having accepted GATT-required elimination of preferential tariffs and dramatic reduction of import controls, the Mexican government cannot now use trade controls as major bargaining chips to assure private support for the Official Party, as it did so successfully in the past. Although losing important support from traditional manufacturers, the Official Party gains support from the new export-oriented manufacturers.

The country's potentially influential university graduates may present the most important long-term problem for the Official Party. The economic crisis since 1982 has reduced the supply of jobs for university graduates, who previously could count on government employment if they were not qualified for or interested in the private sector. Without jobs to offer this growing group seeking to enter the consumption-oriented middle class, the government will be confronted by an expanding pool of discontented and politically astute persons. Further, disillusionment has spread increasingly as students from humble backgrounds realize that the university no longer provides wide access to social mobility.[47]

Some sectors have not fared so badly. Mexico's export-oriented industrialists and farmers have benefited from legislation and loans but find their earnings down in dollars. Groups such as the military and the Church have not seen their privileges limited directly but have suffered a loss in buying power. Of the nineteen sectors listed in Figure 7, only foreign inves-

tors have benefited significantly since 1982, being especially attracted into the in-bond industry and activities related to foreign tourism to Mexico.

All sectors, however, have felt the government's drastic reduction in gasoline and electricity subsidies, the basis for all of the pacts, thus causing many supporters to question the extent of their support for the Official Party. Without these subsidies for energy, the cost of all Mexican goods and services has increased, from food to transport, from manufacturers to housing.

To capitalize on the weakening of the tacit pacts between the government and its once loyal allies, the Cuauhtémoc Cárdenas–Porfirio Muñoz Ledo team seeks to establish a social democratic party under a united center-left, the goal being to restore statist policies abandoned by the monetarists.[48] Drawing upon the experience of Cuauhtémoc Cárdenas, who served as governor of Michoacán, 1980–86 (as had Lázaro Cárdenas, 1928–32), and Muñoz Ledo, who as president of the Official Party in 1976 oversaw the transition from LEA to JLP, the Democratic Front will move to constitute itself as the Partido de la Revolución Democrática (PRD). Cuauhtémoc had established himself as a popular leader and Porfirio had won fame in 1976 for trying to extend the vote to Mexicans living outside the country.

In the Cárdenas–Muñoz Ledo view, as the Official Party pursues its monetarist policies to the detriment of sectors that have supported it, the pacts will rupture completely, benefiting the planned PRD, which will attract groups alienated from the PRI even as the PRD strengthens its own network for the 1994 presidential campaign. In the meantime, the Democratic Front seeks to win important representation permitted by the 1986 electoral reforms in which the PRI has foreseen its loss of majority status in the national Chamber of Deputies.

Most analysts have missed the real significance of Mexico's 1988 election campaign. Although observers agree that the PRI will win, they confine analysis to the highly visible presidential and gubernatorial elections—considered the "key" indicators. In discussing the disaffection facing the PRI, commentators speculate about corruption in vote counting under an electoral process dominated by bureaucrats affiliated with the Official Party.

Realizing that the PRI will win its twelfth consecutive presidential election by sweeping all supposedly key positions (including most senator seats) is not as important as understanding that beginning in

---

[47] See David E. Lorey, "The University and Economic Development in Mexico since 1929" (Ph.D. dissertation, University of California, Los Angeles, 1990), chapter 8.

[48] Drawn from James W. Wilkie et al., "Oral History Interviews with Porfirio Muñoz Ledo," Los Angeles, December 17–23, 1987.

Figure 7

IMPLICIT PACTS BETWEEN THE OFFICIAL PARTY
AND NINETEEN SECTORS OF MEXICAN SOCIETY,[1] TO 1982

Sector[2]	Benefit
Ejidatarios	Land redistribution, some credit, and stable agricultural prices for products
Commercial farmers	Credit and (beginning with Cárdenas) exemption from the land reform laws; benefits wherein the government tacitly allows (except under Cárdenas and Echeverría) the creation of productive estates and plantations by farmers through pooling, renting, or seizing adjacent lands
Commercial cattle ranchers	Credit and (beginning with Alemán) exemption from the land reform laws; government tacitly permits growth in size as for commercial farmers
Small farmers	Exemption from land reform law; government benefits from agricultural extension
Organized laborers	Protection under the labor laws, including social security and access to housing, medical clinics, minimum salary, and the right to strike
Organized slum dwellers	Access to piped water, electricity, telephones, construction materials, paved streets, and subsidized stores (selling food, clothing, and medicine)
Middle sectors	Low inflation, subsidized food prices, and a favorable peso/dollar exchange rate permitting purchase of foreign goods and travel abroad with relative ease
Financial groups	Stable peso convertible to dollars for investment abroad with relative ease (including protection against devaluations that make dollars more costly, protection against increasing the peso cost to amortize foreign debt, and protection against foreign investors assuming more than 49 percent control in Mexican firms)
Manufacturers	Government subsidies and credits as well as benefits from tariff protection and exemption from import taxes
Official Party leaders (including governors, mayors, legislators)	Power to write and selectively enforce legislation, regulations, and tax laws as well as the position to invest with foresight in areas scheduled for public development at national, regional, and local levels (thus furthering "bossism" and patron-client relationships)
Public sector officials and advisors	Authority to develop and administer Mexico's laws, funds, permissions, and properties
Bureaucrats (including judiciary and police)	Growing supply of jobs (many permitting the collection of "tips" or bribes to supplement low wages) in the ever expanding central and decentralized governments as well as benefits from social security, housing, commissary and credit schemes
Contractors	Hired as private companies to construct public works
Teachers	Ever expanding educational system that creates teaching jobs
Students	Low admission and grading standards and fellowships as well as benefits from mobilizing to support political parties
University graduates	For graduates not going into the private sector, ever expanding pool of job opportunities in the centralized and decentralized agencies as well as opportunity to advance into politics and to become government consultants
Military	Expanding budgetary importance vis-à-vis other government priorities (at least in absolute terms), social security, housing, and a nonviolent political atmosphere
Roman Catholic Clergy	After 1938, tacit truce in the Church-state struggle
Foreign investors	Especially after 1940, political stability, joint ventures with Mexican interests (private and/or government, thereby protecting against expropriation), and free convertibility of peso to dollars

1. None of the nineteen sectors has been monolithic and benefits among them often overlap. There has been frequent tension between the government (which represents the Official Party) and one or more of the sectors, for example, organized labor in 1958 and students in 1968. Tension also has existed between the sectors, for example, organized labor and manufacturers. These implicit pacts should not be confused with the Pact of Economic Solidarity subscribed to for at least 2 years (December 1987 to December 1989) by leaders of government, labor, farm, and business organizations in order to bring inflation under control. Regardless of the explicit pact, the implicit pacts have begun to disintegrate.

2. For an alternative to my view developed here, see Frank Brandenburg, *The Making of Modern Mexico* (Englewood Cliffs, N.J.: Prentice-Hall, 1964), pp. 83–90, who delineates nine interest groups: Trade unionists, ejidatarios, civil servants, teachers, bank employees, small independent farmers, cooperativists, businessmen in commerce, and businessmen in industry. He also defines (pp. 119–140) nine political groups in three broad categories: Radical left (anarchists, communists, Trotskyites), independent left, revolutionary publics (left, center, and right within the Official Party), and conservatives (traditional and reactionary).

1988 the PRI is opening in a limited way the political system to unprecedented representation at four levels: the national Chamber of Deputies, the newly established Assembly of Representatives for the Federal District (to be elected for the first time), the state chambers of deputies, and municipal councils throughout the country.

Political Reform: The PRI as Unquestioned Power

The limited opening of the Mexican political system has been a long process involving political reform through which the PRI has sought to create an image of political fairness. Political reform was clearly necessary to overcome the negative image of voting generated by the 1946 party-registration law which limited the ability of opposition groups to gain eligibility to participate in elections. To enhance the image of democracy, presidents began to take much needed actions; for example, Adolfo Ruiz Cortines gave women the right to vote in 1954 and Luis Echeverría Alvarez gave eighteen-year-olds the same privilege in 1973.[49]

One of Mexico's most important political reforms came in 1963 when President Adolfo López Mateos (ALM) had legislation passed to allow opposition political parties to enter the national Chamber of Deputies without necessarily winning the relative majority of votes in any electoral district. ALM retained the traditional way in which candidates for the national Chamber of Deputies won their three-year terms by receiving the relative majority of votes in electoral districts (as in the U.S. process), but he supplemented that method by allowing opposition candidates to represent their party in the 210-seat Chamber of Deputies provided their legally registered party gained at least 2.5 percent of the total nationwide vote for deputies.[50]

Thus, ALM developed a "mixed system" which has existed, with revisions, to the present: "majority deputies" represent "electoral-district seats"; and "proportional-representation deputies" or "party deputies" represent "at-large seats." Each has the same rights to participate in the Chamber's debates and votes. ALM's legislation allowed only parties winning fewer than twenty electoral-district seats to win at-large seats, as follows: five seats for 2.5 percent of the total vote and one seat for each .5 percent thereafter up to a maximum of twenty seats for each minority party.

Because only the conservative Partido de Acción Nacional (PAN) surpassed the 2.5 percent floor in the 1964 election (and also won its maximum of twenty at-large seats), ironically the Official Party bent the law to abide by the "spirit of the legislation," assigning at-large seats to weak parties which gained as little as .7 percent of the vote.[51] To legalize the spirit of the 1964 law, in 1972 the electoral code was modified to reduce the floor for proportional deputies to 1.5 percent of the total votes. (This modification also raised the maximum number of at-large deputies for each party to twenty-five.)

Political reform to open the Chamber of Deputies has continued apace as opposition to the PRI has risen. In 1977 parties were permitted temporarily to apply for conditional registration, which became permanent for each party gaining 1.5 percent of the vote and continuing to win that amount. (Since 1986, initial registration of new parties requires 65,000 members nationwide, with 3,000 in at least half of the states or 300 in at least half of the electoral district; continued registration requires winning 1.5 percent of the vote.)

Regardless of the opening of the system to opposition, the PRI's critics could argue persuasively that the political reforms were merely cosmetic. In allowing opposition parties to win at-large seats, ironically the PRI no longer needed to lose many (or any) electoral-district seats. Further, by giving at-large seats to weak parties, the PRI could dilute the strength of the PAN, which since its establishment in 1939 had become the main opposition to the growing statism of the Mexican politico-economic system.

Assessing results of Mexico's political reform has grown complex since the mid-1970s. On the one hand, where opposition parties had held only 3–6 percent of the seats in the national Chamber of Deputies between 1949 and 1958, the share increased to the 16–20 percent range between 1964 and 1976 (Table 16). On the other hand, the opposition's gains in the Chamber of Deputies have won it little more than the possibility of turning that body into a national forum for debate, and it can be argued that until now even this "victory" has been severely compromised. Not only has the Chamber been a highly controlled forum for debate within the PRI, but the opposition parties have been limited as to the number of members so that they have stood no chance of winning any serious vote.

Further, by accepting entry into the Chamber of Deputies, the opposition parties gave up any immediate hope of winning many senatorial or gubernatorial positions, let alone the presidency. Opposition to the

---

[49] Daniel Levy and Gabriel Székely, *Mexico: Paradoxes of Stability and Change* (Boulder, Colo.: Westview Press, 1983), pp. 66–67.
[50] Mario Moya Palencia, *La Reforma Electoral* (México, D.F.: Ediciones Plataforma, 1964), pp. 116–118.

[51] Ibid., and Wilkie, *La Revolución Mexicana (1910–1976): Gasto Federal y Cambio Social*, p. 394.

Table 16

SEATS IN MEXICO'S CHAMBER OF DEPUTIES, 1949–85
(Electoral-District Seats plus At-Large Seats Beginning in 1964)

Year	A. Total Seats	PRI[1]	PAN	PPS	PARM	PST	PDM	PCM	PSUM	PMT	PRT	Other[3]	B. Opposition	C. %
1949	147	142	4	1									5	3
1952	162	152	5	2								3	10	6
1955	162	155	6	1									7	4
1958	162	153	6	1	1							1	9	6
1961	178	172	5	1									6	3
1964	210	175	22	11	5								38	18
1967	212	177	21	10	5								36	17
1970	213	178	20	10	5								35	16
1973	231	189	29	10	8								47	20
1976	237	195	20	12	10								42	18
1979	399	296	42	12	12	11	9	18					104	26
1982	400	299	51	10		11	12		17				101	25
1985	400	292	38	11	11	12	12		12	6	6		108	27

Header note: "Opposition Seats[2]" spans the PAN through Other[3] columns.

1. Partido Revolucionario Institucional.
2. Opposition acronym and name:

   PAN   Partido de Acción Nacional
   PARM   Partido Auténtico de la Revolución Mexicana
   PCM   Partido Comunista Mexicano
   PDM   Partido Demócrata Mexicano
   PMT   Partido Mexicano de los Trabajadores
   PPS   Partido Popular Socialista
   PRT   Partido Revolucionario de Trabajadores
   PST   Partido Socialista de los Trabajadores
   PSUM   Partido Socialista Unido de México

3. Federación de Partidos Populares Mexicanos and Partido Nacionalista Mexicano.

SOURCE: Calculated for 1949–1973, from Donald J. Mabry, "Mexico's Party Deputy System: The First Decade," *Journal of Interamerican Studies and World Affairs* 16:2 (1974), p. 228.
Calculated for 1976–1979, from Samuel Schmidt, "Democracia Mexicana: La Reforma Política de López Portillo; ¿Un Nuevo Discurso?" Serie Avances de Investigación, *Cuaderno 46* (México, D.F.: Centro de Estudios Latinoamericanos, Facultad de Ciencias Políticas y Sociales, UNAM), p. 24.
For 1982, from Kevin J. Middlebrook, "Political Liberalization in an Authoritarian Regime: The Case of Mexico," in Paul W. Drake and Eduardo Silva, *Elections and Democratization in Latin America, 1980–1985* (San Diego: Center for Iberian and Latin American Studies, University of California, 1986), p. 195.
For 1985, from M. Delal Baer, *The Mexican Midterm Elections, Report No. 3,* CSIS Latin American Election Studies Series (Washington, D.C.: Georgetown University, Center for Strategic and International Studies, July 31, 1985), Appendix.

Official Party has been confined to the Chamber of Deputies, where total membership rose from 147 in 1949 to 237 by 1976.

With regard to the size of Mexico's Chamber of Deputies, to satisfy the demands of an increasing number of PRI aspirants to power as well as the need to give the opposition a voice, in 1977 the Official Party increased the size of the Chamber to 400 members. President José López Portillo adopted the ALM system to allocate 25 percent or 100 of the seats to proportional representation among the opposition parties.

Under the complicated 1977 law designed to protect the PRI, all parties that won fewer than 60 electoral-district seats (called "uninominal seats") and that ran candidates in at least one-third of the country's electoral districts were entitled to share in the 100 at-large seats (called "plurinominal seats" or "proportional-representation seats").[52] For the proportionally allocated seats, the law divided the country into regions and voters cast their ballots for a party when they vote for a candidate. Each party is entitled to two proportional-representation deputies for each region in which it wins 1.5 percent of the vote, with the remainder of seats distributed according to the proportional strength of the contending parties.[53]

[52] Technically any party, including the PRI, could win at-large seats through proportional voting, but because the PRI won more than 60 electoral district seats, it was not eligible to win at-large seats.

[53] M. Delal Baer, "The Mexican Midterm Elections, Report No. 2," CSIS Latin American Election Studies Series, Georgetown University Center for Strategic and International Studies, Washington, D.C., June 26, 1985, p. 18.

This 1977 system of representation was also instituted (with varying proportions) in state legislatures (giving 169 opposition seats throughout Mexico) and in major city councils, with all city councils affected beginning in 1982 (yielding 1,416 opposition seats).[54]

Political Reforms of 1986 and 1987: The PRI Foresees Its Loss of Majority Status

Although the share of opposition seats in the Chamber of Deputies (which had not exceeded 20 percent prior to 1976) reached 26 percent in 1979, 25 percent in 1982, and 27 percent in 1985 (Table 16), and in spite of the gains made by the opposition to become part of the public debating process, the 1980s brought a new international context for Mexico's internal politics. The emergence of democratic regimes in South America and the extension of U.S. media coverage of Mexico–United States border issues cast into ill repute the PRI's standard operating procedures for rigging elections outside of the limited sphere of the officially approved opposition seats discussed above. Indeed, in 1985 the PRI's political repression of the opposition became more blatant than usual, regional PRI bosses ruthlessly sweeping aside rising opposition in the north.[55] Ironically, the central government may have desired to control the excesses of its party militants but could not do so without upsetting one of its most important PRI regional support bases.

Because of the rising number of complaints against the PRI's heavy-handed control of gubernatorial elections, in 1986 President Miguel de la Madrid Hurtado took additional steps to respond to criticisms about democracy in Mexico and to protect the PRI. He made major reforms in the electoral law.

First, MMH enlarged the Chamber of Deputies from 400 to 500 seats. In the new 500-seat Chamber to be elected July 6, 1988, 300 seats represent electoral districts to be decided by relative majority vote (the "uninominal seats") and 200 represent regional seats elected by proportional vote and reserved for parties winning at least 1.5 percent of the total votes cast (the "plurinominal seats"). Of the 500 total seats,

MMH guaranteed that the opposition would have at least 30 percent or 150. Further the majority party is limited to 70 percent or 350 of the 500 total seats.[56]

Second, and most important, however, MMH's 1986 legislation anticipated that in the 1988 elections the Official Party would not win enough electoral-district seats to hold a 51 percent majority in the national Chamber of Deputies. To counter this problem, the 1986 legislation provided that the party winning at least 51 percent of the national votes for deputies, or at least the most seats for federal deputy (that is, the PRI), can win up to 50 of the 200 proportional seats in order to assure that its share of seats is at least 51 percent of the total seats,[57] thus assuring continuance of the one-party system.

MMH has justified the 1986 legislation by arguing that Mexico requires a stable, efficient system dominated by one political party. In his view, Mexico's political system must avoid being overcome by the fragmentation of power that would result without strong leadership by the majority party.[58]

To offset its bad image in the north and to give representation for the first time to the millions of persons living in the Federal District, the PRI authored legislation in 1987 to inaugurate in 1988 the Assembly of Representatives of the Federal District, to be reelected at three-year intervals beginning in July 1988. The population there, more than 13 percent of all Mexicans, has been denied representation in the same way as has the population of the District of Columbia (which constitutes only about .3 percent of the U.S. population).

Establishment of the Federal District Assembly has contradictory meanings. It has 66 seats, of which 40 are relative majority seats and 26 are proportional seats.[59] Should the PRI win all of the fixed seats, the opposition could win up to 39 percent of the seats in an elected body. But because in the 1988 election the PRI expects to lose relative majority seats, it will lay claim to some proportional seats in order to protect its majority role. The Official Party no longer seeks to win all the majority seats but to make up the difference with proportional votes previously reserved for the opposition, as it will do in the Chamber of Deputies.

Inauguration of this new Assembly stems the call for converting the Federal District into a state replete with full legislature and an elected governor. (The

[54] Partido Revolucionario Institucional, Comité Ejecutivo Nacional, *Código Federal Electoral* (México, D.F.: n.p., [1987]), p. 25.

[55] On PRI election fraud in the north, see Juan Molinar, "[Regreso a Chihuahua]: Una Pequeña Historia," *Nexos* 111 (1987), pp. 19–32; and Samuel Schmidt, "Votación en la Frontera México–Estados Unidos, 1961–1982," in Samuel Schmidt, James W. Wilkie, Manuel Esparza, eds., *Estudios Cuantitativos sobre la Historia de México* (México, D.F.: Universidad Nacional Autónoma de México, 1988), pp. 23–39. See also two articles by Chandler Thompson: "How to Rig a Mexican Election: PAN Says PRI Put Out Manual," *El Paso Times*, May 20, 1988; and "PRI's Dilemma: Election Manual: Debunking Book Could Mean Admitting Fraud," *El Paso Times*, May 22, 1988.

[56] Partido Revolucionario Institucional, *Código Federal Electoral*, p. 32.

[57] Ibid., pp. 40 and 136; *Proceso*, July 18, 1988, pp. 24–25.

[58] Ibid., p. 34.

[59] *Comercio Exterior*, September 1987, p. 729; *Proceso*, January 11, 1988, pp. 28–29.

mayor of the Federal District is a PRI leader appointed by the president of Mexico.) Although the Assembly will oversee the administration of the District's budget and be able to call public officials to inform them about the development of government activities and services, it does not have the powers of a state. It has a limited role allowing it to promote, regulate, and supervise land use, housing, health, education, transport, and the food supply system.

To assure that the Assembly will remain under the control of the PRI, MMH provided that the majority party names the Assembly's seven-member Governing Commission, which controls procedures and makes all appointments to positions.

A Political Scenario for the Future

Although some observers foresee the PRI losing power through violent overthrow (which also could trigger a military coup, as could continued economic malaise), in light of the political reforms discussed above, we should examine a scenario in which the PRI must concede ever more positions to the political opposition. This conforms to the established precedent and could be expanded outside the Chamber of Deputies in order to offer positions of influence to the PRI's opposition.

One test of the PRI's willingness to open the political system further will be the results of the 1988 voting for senators, especially in the Federal District. The opposition candidate who hopes to break the PRI's stranglehold on the Senate is Porfirio Muñoz Ledo. The only other time an opposition member won a Senate seat came in 1976 in an arrangement made by Muñoz Ledo when he was president of the PRI. In that arrangement, the PRI ceded to the Partido Popular Socialista (PPS) a Senate seat from Oaxaca to end dispute over the PPS claim that it had won the governorship of Nayarit.

Regardless of the extent to which the Senate is opened to the opposition, and regardless of the fact that the opposition will not win any governorships in the 1988 elections, the opposition parties will have gained representative forums throughout Mexico from which they can pressure the PRI on many fronts. For the first time opposition parties have a real chance to build a credible image of leadership by participating in local, state, and federal assemblies, forums increasingly more open to them. Opposition parties implicitly have been given an opportunity to demonstrate their stability, maturity, statesmanship, and ability to build networks of support throughout Mexico, the requisites for offering viable political alternatives to groups traditionally committed to the PRI. The real test of the opposition will be to create permanent and cohesive networks throughout the republic—no easy task without bureaucratic patronage to dispense. If they effectively organize, they will be in a position to more fully test the PRI's power in the mid-term elections of 1991 and the presidential election of 1994. In 1989 only the gubernatorial election in Baja California will offer a real challenge to the PRI's domination of the state level.

In the meantime, both the opposition and the PRI are trapped in this system of voting which offers limited access to elected positions. The opposition may cry fraud or demand civil disobedience to protest manipulation of the election results, but it can do neither too loudly without compromising its real gains in seats within the sphere of representation to which it has acceded.

The new political equation has complicated the affairs for three major parties. Within the PRI, Salinas faces serious dilemmas because the old guard feels that the power of the Official Party has been compromised. Indeed, Fidel Velásquez, the octogenarian leader who has controlled the official labor movement for half of his life, is furious at De la Madrid, whom he believes has yielded power unnecessarily in the 1986 electoral code.

Within the Frente Democrático Nacional, the challenge will be to convert the movement into the planned social democratic party. Six groups make up the FDN (Corriente Democrático, Movimiento al Socialismo, Partido Popular Socialista, Partido Auténtico de la Revolución Mexicana, Partido Frente Cardenista de Reconstrucción Nacional, Partido Mexicano Socialista), few of which have similar goals and tactics. It is doubtful that the Partido Popular Socialista (PPS) and the Partido Frente Cardenista (PFCRN) would be willing to join the new social democratic party to unite the left, the latter merely exploiting Cuauhtémoc Cárdenas's name without his membership.

Within the PAN, views are also contradictory. Some members see the FDN as a PRI front-group intended to detract from the PAN's role as the only credible opposition (thus costing the PAN votes against the PRI if not for the PAN). Other PAN members see the Frente as a ploy to siphon support from PAN groups who favor state protection of industry.

An irony in the new equation is that as the statist-oriented FDN tries to organize a successful long-term movement, the PRI and the PAN may be forced into an implicit alliance against the Frente—the PRI of MMH and CSG is privatist oriented, as is the core of PAN.

Conclusions

In tracing the outlines of Mexican twentieth-century history through six ideological periods, we have seen the complexity of affairs. Few problems have been "solved"; rather, problems are half-resolved before new ones take priority. Mexico's experience since 1910 has involved a series of crises which are reacted to and partially resolved in ways that interact with new historical events. The ironies that one can find in this process are numerous.

The Official Party of the Revolution justifies its maintenance of power by the need to resolve crises in development, but that desire itself generated opposition which led the PRI in 1986 to foresee its eventual loss of majority status. The electoral code of that year provides the complicated mechanisms by which the PRI will try to preserve the "benefits" of majority-party rule, and the opposition will now need to seek revision of that code and to obtain ever greater representation at all electoral levels. If the opposition can defeat the PRI's policy of attempting to confine electoral challenge to the Chamber of Deputies, then Mexico can move forward gradually from "one-party democracy" to a multiparty system.

Although many positive developments have taken place in the six periods, some accumulated "non-political" problems bode ill for Mexico's development. As the Official Party attempts to privatize the economy, for example, it does so without a private banking system and with little financial liquidity. Real deposits in the government-owned banks have fallen to 53 percent of the pre-nationalization level of 1982, for example, but the PRI seemingly has difficulty giving up majority control; until it does so, it cannot generate the confidence needed to encourage the return to Mexico of the majority amount of funds which fled. CSG will have to ponder this problem and resolve it by preventing a revolt from the left wing of the PRI dominated by JLP and LEA, who would strongly protest denationalization of the banks as would the newly powerful Democratic Front.

Yet Mexico's present crisis since 1982 can be seen as a healthy one, which has provided the first real incentive to overcome the statism that could only prevail at a high cost. As long as the money flowed, implicit pacts would keep interested parties working to support the Official Party in ways that did not make economic sense. But the state structure should be dismantled in a way that would not harm Mexico's economic base and that would cushion the blow to Mexico's workers as the country shifts from an inefficient base to one that can compete in the modern world. How to manage this shift is the issue that CSG will face when inaugurated in December 1988. Iron-ically, the PRI may lose the Mexico City vote and win the election by relying on its compliant peasant base in the poor southern states.

The ironies of Mexico's "Permanent Revolution" are compounded by the traditional classification of presidents as being of the left or right. For example, Gustavo Díaz Ordaz (GDO) is seen as a rightist mainly for his attacks on the students in 1968, but, as the data given here on land reform show, he published more resolutions to distribute land to ejidatarios than any other president and he actually distributed almost as much as did Lázaro Cárdenas, the hero of the left.

Although since 1976 presidents have lost interest in land reform as they focus on industrialization and converting Mexico to an export-oriented country, the historical problem of land will linger. The expanding population will never fit on the land, but the land reform cannot easily be undone. A major test of the "Revolutionariness" of the PRI is its continued distribution of land to the peasants, its strongest supporters. Future presidents must rationalize the need for large-scale commercial agriculture to supply the majority urban population who want inexpensive food, yet must find nontraditional ways to help the peasants who live in increasingly impoverished economic conditions.

This interpretation of the six ideological phases governing Mexican history since 1910 has drawn on long-term quantitative data to suggest the nature of the contradictions and problems faced by Mexico's leaders. The themes considered here exemplify the broad range of social and economic issues that interact with political matters. It is hoped that this overarching view of the meaning of Mexico's past provides a basis for thinking about the country's alternative futures.

Postscript, October 1988, Puerto Vallarta, Jalisco

Since spring 1988 when this volume was prepared for publication, Mexico has undergone unprecedented political change while socioeconomic problems continue to multiply. Though consistent with the threat to the PRI's power as analyzed above, the far-reaching results of the July elections have been a surprise to most participants, including the PRI, PAN, FDN, and voters.

Although only one-third of the 1988 preelection polls predicted that Salinas would win the presidential election, three-quarters showed him winning only a relative majority, not the coveted absolute one. Whereas most opinion polls put CSG's victory in the

37 to 47 percent range, El Colegio de México and the UNAM Faculty of Political and Social Sciences workshop each forecast that CSG would win with 61.4 percent of the ballots.[60]

However, depth of discontent with the Official Party was so great and monitoring of voting places by the PRI's opposition so effective that when the first electoral results became known after the polls closed on July 6, the FDN realized that it could claim victory. The government, which had banned the Gallup organization from conducting exit polls on July 6 and which delayed releasing the vote results, soon had to admit not only that it won by bare relative majorities for the presidency and for the Chamber of Deputies, but also that it had to cede four seats in the 64-seat senate and recognize that it won only 39.4 percent of the vote for the Assembly of Representatives of the Federal District. As the contested vote count continued, both the FDN and the PAN rejected the PRI's claim to victory.

Four views of the presidential election results are given in Table 17. According to the opposition FDN, it won the election with 39.4 percent of the vote to 35.8 for the PRI. This view is buttressed by "military" data on the election leaked to the PMS, an ally of the FDN. (It seems that the military, in charge of transporting and guarding the votes, was privy to this "real" vote count and subsequent manipulation by the PRI.) But the Comisión Federal Electoral reported that the PRI had won 50.4 percent. When the Chamber of Deputies met in September to certify the results, the PRI majority raised the amount by .3 percent, thus giving it the 51 percent required to claim a "mandate." The PAN, which like the FDN had monitored polling places throughout Mexico, also promised to release its independent view of the results, but it did not do so. Some observers have suggested that the PAN may have won even fewer votes than the 17 percent indicated by the official results. Yet the FDN view suggests that the PAN won 4 to 5 percent more votes than the government would admit. Oddly, some PANistas continued to argue that the FDN had been created by the government in order to discredit the PAN and its role as the traditional opposition to the PRI.

With regard to the vote count, the government legally is obligated after the election to open all voting records for verification by the parties involved, but records were opened for only 55 percent of the polling places. The government promised that the records for the remaining 45 percent would be made available for inspection, but in the end did not do so because the records apparently showed that the PRI had been defeated. Thus the Official Party deputies voted in a bloc to declare Salinas president-elect of Mexico, an act which led the FDN to announce that the PRI had consummated a "technical coup d'état,"[61] not through a military coup but through an "illegitimate" action which required popular resistance. Although the PAN voted against Salinas, within two months it announced recognition of the PRI candidate as president-elect.

The basis for concluding that the PRI was defeated in the 1988 presidential election is found in Table 18 which shows that according to the verified vote Cárdenas won the election with 39 percent, the amount claimed by the FDN. Given that Salinas won only 34 percent of the verified vote, he would have had to win 67 percent of the unverified vote in 24,642 places to overcome Cárdenas's advantage. Cárdenas's verified percentage would have to be cut nearly in half in the unverified vote, an unlikely event in light of the strong trend in the verified 55 percent. The PRI claims that the unverified vote came from distant rural areas, mainly in the south, which traditionally vote for the Official Party. Although this trend may have been strong in the past, the decline in land reform (depicted in Table 2, above) means that such support must have weakened. It is doubtful that the PRI won 89.9 percent of the vote in Chiapas (Table 19), as certified by the Comisión Federal Electoral.

While the PRI won a relative majority of votes among ballots cast, other ratios were not so favorable. The share of registered voters who backed the PRI was only 25 percent. The PRI's share of voting-age population (registered or not) was perhaps as low as 18.5 percent (Table 20).

The decline in the legitimacy of the Official Party is revealed in Table 21. The percentage of registered voters favoring the current political system, since it was established implicitly in 1917 and explicitly in 1929, was over 86 percent through 1976, except in 1946 and 1952 when the share fell into the 70 percent range. The PRI vote fell to 71 percent in 1982 when the present economic crisis began, and its fortunes again declined in 1988.

---

[60] For a survey of the 1988 opinion polls leading up to the Mexican election, see "Del Impacto Político de los Sondeos de Opinión," *El Cotidiano* 25 (1988), p. 29. On the UNAM poll (conducted by only three professors for a nonexistent "workshop") and on Gallup poll results claimed to be for May 1988 but which actually may have been March (which gave CSG 56 percent, Cárdenas 23 percent, and Clouthier 19 percent), see Dan Williams, "Polls Becoming an Issue in Mexico's Campaign," *Los Angeles Times*, June 28, 1988. See also, Dan Williams, "Mexico Bans Exit Polls for Today's Election," *Los Angeles Times*, July 6, 1988, who notes that the PRI officials expected CSG to win 55 to 60 percent of the vote, with Cárdenas and Clouthier sharing 20 percent each.

[61] Marjorie Miller, "Salinas Okd as Mexico's Next President," *Los Angeles Times*, September 11, 1988.

Table 17

COMPETING VIEWS OF 1988 PRESIDENTIAL ELECTION RESULTS
(100.0 Percent = Legal Vote)[1]

View	Salinas	Cárdenas	Manuel J. Clouthier	Other[6]
Comisión Federal Electoral[2]	50.4	31.1	17.1	1.4[a]
Chamber of Deputies[3]	50.7	31.1	16.8	1.4
Democratic Front[4]	35.8	39.4	21.4	3.4
"Military"[5]	30.4	32.1	35.4	2.1[b]
PAN	--[c]	--[c]	--[c]	--[c]

1. Excludes nullified votes and votes for nonregistered candidates.
2. PRI-dominated official body, results of July 13, 1988, given in *El Cotidiano* 25 (1988), p. 16; see Table 19 below for complete data.
3. *Los Angeles Times*, September 11, 1988.
4. Frente Democrático Nacional, results of monitoring election polling places, dated July 12, 1988, supplied by Ricardo Pascoe Pierce.
5. Figures reported as leaked to PMS deputy Eduardo Valle, " 'probablemente' provenientes del ejército" (*Proceso*, August 8, 1988, p. 19), here recalculated to total 19,037,793 (omitting a reported 584,929 nullified votes and 18,000 votes for nonregistered candidates).

6. PDM's Gumersindo Magaña Negrete (GMN) and PRT's Rosario Ibarra de Piedra (RIP).

a. The Comisión Federal Electoral credited GMN with 1.0 percent and RIP with .4 percent.
b. Reputedly 1.1 percent for GMN and 1.0 percent for RIP.
c. The PAN promised to release its own monitoring of election polling places but never did so.

Table 18

PERCENTAGE OF "UNVERIFIED VOTES" NEEDED BY SALINAS TO GAIN 50.4 PERCENT AND OVERCOME "VERIFIED VOTES" WON BY CARDENAS FOR THE PRESIDENCY IN 1988

Category	Verified	Unverified	Total
Total[1]	100[a]	100[b]	100.0[c]
Salinas	34	67	50.4
Cárdenas	39	20	31.1
Clouthier	22	12	17.1
Other	5	1	2.5

1. Total polling places: 54,641 at which 19,099,157 votes were cast

a. Verification by political parties for 29,999 polling places at which 10,313,544 votes were cast.
b. Unverified vote for 24,642 polling places at which 8,785,613 votes were cast.
c. See note 1.

SOURCE: Pablo González Casanova, "La Democracia Transparente," *La Jornada*, August 3, 1988, p. 11.

It is not uncommon for some Mexican intellectuals to argue that the Official Party is now rejected by more than 80 percent of the voting-age population. Such views are based, however, on the questionable assumption that *all* persons who do not register or who vote for opposition parties or who cast invalid ballots are rejecting the whole Mexican political system. To make this argument, one adds the number of nonregistered voters (14.1 million) to the number of those registered who did not vote (18.9 million) to reach a figure of 33.0 million alienated persons among the 52.2 million of voting age, or 63.2 percent.

To the 33.0 million, one then adds 9.4 million who did not vote for Salinas, reaching 42.4 million or 81.2 percent.[62]

The argument that more than 80 percent of potential voters have rejected the PRI does not account for the long-term trend which shows that the share of the age-eligible population which votes has never exceeded 57 percent (1940). Even between 1941 and 1976, when the Official Party enjoyed steady economic growth with only two periods of serious political protest (1958–60 and 1968), the share of voters in the voting-age population averaged about 47 percent (Table 21). That figure fell to 22 percent in 1982 but increased to 36 percent in 1988, not far below the 39 percent of 1970. To buttress the argument that the PRI is not necessarily on an automatic downward spiral, its share of voters among persons registered doubled between 1982 and 1988. The decline from 1982 to 1988 of the PRI's share of the vote from 47 to 19 percent of the voting-age population (Table 20) can be attributed in part to the Official Party's need to share percentages of the vote with the opposition parties that it had stimulated following the 1976 campaign, when the PAN did not (or could not) name a candidate.

Regardless of speculation about the presidential trend in Official Party legitimacy, the 1988 election results for federal deputies proved to be disastrous for the PRI. Opposition parties won 233 fixed seats or only 47 percent. Because the PRI won 51.9 percent

[62] These calculations are based on Comisión Federal Electoral data given in *El Cotidiano* 25 (1988), p. 12. Calculations will vary depending upon the estimate used for population of voting age and even for the actual number of persons registered. If data on registration were used from MMH's *Sexto Informe de Gobierno* (p. 17), they would increase by 860,000 for 1982 and decrease 495,000 for 1988.

Table 19

VOTING FOR MEXICAN PRESIDENTIAL CANDIDATES, BY STATE, 1988
(Percent)

Totals = 100.0 Percent

State	MJC[1]	CSG[2]	CCS[3]	GMN[4]	RIP[5]	Total	Registered	Percent Voting[6]
Total	17.07	50.36	31.12	1.04	.42	19,145,012	38,074,926	50.28
Aguascalientes	28.42	50.21	18.67	2.41	.29	168,899	334,920	50.43
Baja California	24.39	36.66	37.19	.81	.95	413,953	817,466	50.64
Baja California Sur	19.00	54.02	25.87	.48	.63	85,643	150,348	56.96
Campeche	12.37	70.88	16.30	.32	.14	116,107	229,954	50.49
Coahuila	15.34	54.27	29.95	.29	.14	328,239	866,211	37.89
Colima	14.80	47.83	35.74	1.05	.58	97,316	218,028	44.63
Chiapas	3.39	89.91	6.45	.14	.11	658,195	1,189,034	55.36
Chihuahua	38.19	54.58	6.77	.27	.20	521,995	1,295,067	40.31
Distrito Federal	22.01	27.25	49.22	.79	.74	2,904,169	5,095,462	57.00
Durango	16.99	63.63	18.82	.23	.33	356,446	682,290	52.24
Guanajuato	29.93	44.03	22.01	3.80	.23	726,312	1,572,760	46.18
Guerrero	2.44	60.53	35.80	.86	.37	510,797	1,200,804	42.54
Hidalgo	5.84	64.72	28.26	.91	.28	421,893	812,252	51.94
Jalisco	30.76	42.57	23.87	2.50	.30	1,194,247	2,514,777	47.49
México	16.33	29.79	51.58	1.55	.75	2,331,479	4,190,232	55.64
Michoacán	10.28	23.21	64.16	2.11	.24	614,899	1,530,443	40.18
Morelos	7.44	33.74	57.65	.67	.51	278,208	583,597	47.67
Nayarit	5.72	56.56	36.80	.71	.20	205,214	405,300	50.63
Nuevo León	23.70	72.08	3.83	.21	.18	704,156	1,509,564	46.65
Oaxaca	4.63	63.81	30.25	.47	.83	628,155	1,364,539	46.03
Puebla	9.87	71.55	17.69	.56	.33	1,091,658	1,695,380	64.39
Querétaro	19.43	63.34	15.81	1.16	.27	238,058	409,408	58.15
Quintana Roo	9.69	65.70	24.14	.32	.15	94,322	188,191	50.12
San Luis Potosí	21.15	68.25	8.81	1.61	.18	380,418	868,279	43.81
Sinaloa	32.07	50.81	16.75	.20	.16	623,904	1,113,969	56.01
Sonora	20.85	68.59	9.98	.27	.31	410,386	899,250	45.64
Tabasco	5.25	74.30	19.94	.42	.09	268,071	634,687	42.24
Tamaulipas	9.91	59.33	30.15	.44	.18	470,309	1,120,265	41.98
Tlaxcala	5.88	60.21	31.00	2.53	.39	184,000	331,907	55.44
Veracruz	5.21	62.59	31.05	.88	.28	1,516,257	3,045,721	49.78
Yucatán	31.19	67.08	1.61	.06	.06	307,657	602,041	51.10
Zacatecas	10.77	66.17	22.31	.62	.14	293,650	602,780	48.72

1. MJC = Manuel J. Clouthier.
2. CGS = Carlos Salinas de Gortari.
3. CCS = Cuauhtémoc Cárdenas Solórzano.
4. GMG = Gumersindo Magaña Negrete.

5. RIP = Rosario Ibarra de Piedra.
6. Voters as share of registered voters.

SOURCE: Comisión Federal Electoral data, quoted in *El Cotidiano* 25 (1988), p. 16.

of the votes cast nationally for deputies,[63] however, under the 1986 election law it became eligible to receive the 27 proportional representation seats needed to maintain an absolute majority, in this case 52 percent of the seats. Of the newly won 240 opposition seats in the Chamber of Deputies, the FDN won 28 percent and the PAN 20 percent. Thus in one blow the opposition increased its number of seats in the Chamber by 78 percent (compare Tables 16 and 22).

Beyond the Chamber of Deputies, the FDN broke into the Senate, where it captured four seats. Porfirio Muñoz Ledo was elected senator from the Federal District, which now hails him as a hero as he moves about Mexico City. He is credited with having used the political experience that he developed within the PRI to out-campaign the PRI in its seat of power.

In the new Assembly of Representatives of the Federal District, inaugurated in October 1988, the PRI won only 26 of the 66-seat total, or 39.4 percent. This relative majority made it eligible to win the 8 proportional seats needed to give it the absolute majority, as required by law according to MMH's 1987 statement that one-party leadership must be maintained in Mexico.

[63] Absolute data on the number of votes for deputies (16,116,818) yield the following percentages supplied by the Chamber of Deputies: PRI, 51.93; PAN, 18.34; PPS 9.37; PMS, 4.53; PFCRN, 9.54.

Table 20

PRI LEGITIMACY, 1982 AND 1988

Category	1982	1988
	Millions	
Votes for the PRI[1]	16.75	9.64
Voting-Age Population	35.72	52.21
Registered Voters	31.53	38.07
Voters	23.59	19.15
	Percent	
PRI Vote/Voting-Age Population	46.9	23.0
PRI Vote/Registered Voters	53.1	25.3
PRI Vote/Voters	71.0	50.4

1. In 1982 includes PPS and PARM.

SOURCE: Adapted from *El Cotidiano* 25 (1988), p. 15, and *Geografía de las Elecciones Presidenciales de México, 1988* (México, D.F.: Fundación Arturo Rosenblueth, 1988), p. 6.

The opposition in the Assembly won 48 percent of the seats. But where the FDN won the major opposition role in the Chamber of Deputies and Senate, in the Assembly that role went to the PAN, causing many observers to question the vote count. The FDN victory in the Federal District (where 49 percent voted for Cárdenas, 27 percent for Salinas, and 22 percent for Clouthier) dictated odds that the FDN would be the major opposition party in the Assembly. Yet the FDN won only 21 percent of the seats in the Assembly compared with 27 percent for the PAN (Table 23).

Major PRI reactions to the rise of the FDN were at least five. First, PRI Secretary General Manuel Camacho Solís admitted that since July 6 for the first time in history the Official Party can no longer count on the necessary majority to change the constitution.[64] He has proposed to "modernize Mexican politics," code for the Salinas campaign plan to bury the idea of pure "revolutionary nationalism" which PRI reformers see as having been used by old-line party bosses to irrationally centralize political power. Further, in advancing the cause of rational decision-making by "técnicos" (as opposed to "políticos," who govern by intrigue for personal gain),[65] Camacho Solís calls for the PRI to now open a "democratic dialogue with the opposition parties," thus developing understandings and "even alliances."[66]

[64] Quoted in *El Día*, October 5, 1988.
[65] See José Martínez, "Cambiar las Reglas del Juego, Meta de la Política Moderna," *El Financiero*, October 3, 1988.
[66] Quoted in "Los Neoideólogos del PRI Proponen Hasta la Renovación Sindical, Que Fidel Pretende Parar," *Proceso*, September 12, 1988, pp. 22–23.

Table 21

MEXICO PRESIDENTIAL ELECTIONS: VOTING-AGE POPULATION,[1] REGISTRATION, AND VOTING, 1917–88

			Registered Citizens	
	A.	B.	C.	D.
		Percent of		Percent
	Voting Age	Voting Age	Percent	Voting for
Year	(Millions)	Population Voting[2,3]	Voting[2]	Official Party[4]
1917	3.2	25		97.1
1920	3.4	35		95.8
1924	3.6	44		84.1
1928	3.9	43		100.0
1929	3.9	53		93.6
1934	4.2	54		98.2
1940	4.6	57		93.9
1946	5.2	56	92[c]	77.9
1952	6.4	44	73	74.3
1958[a]	14.5	51	68	90.4
1964	18.6	50	69	89.0
1970	22.8	39	65	86.0
1976[b]	29.7	40	69	92.3
1982	35.7	22	25	71.0
1988	52.2	36	50	50.7[d]

1. Through 1973 the voting-age population is calculated as age 20 or over (according to the law only married men over 18 and single men over 21 could vote until the electoral reform of 1954 when women of the same ages as men were allowed to vote). Since 1973 the pool of eligible voters includes all persons age 18 or over. Registration and voting have been obligatory under the Constitution of 1917, but this provision has not been enforced.
2. The total votes in any year given may be only for "legal votes," that is, votes for legally registered candidates and votes not nullified because of protest markings or suspected vote fraud.
3. The percent of the citizenry voting (participation rate of voting-age population) is susceptible to change depending upon differing calculations of the number of persons eligible to vote and upon the varying inclusion of nullified votes and votes for candidates not legally registered. The average participation rate for the ten Mexican presidential elections between 1934 and 1988 is 45 percent (calculated from Col. B), which is 12 percent less than the average participation rate of 57 percent for the United States (based upon valid votes cast and counted as defined by each state) for the fourteen elections between 1932 and 1984 (calculated from data in *World Almanac, 1987*, p. 305), the U.S. high being 63 percent in 1960 and the low being 51 percent in 1948.
4. Usually for legal (i.e., valid) vote.

a. First presidential election in which women voted.
b. First presidential election in which minimum voting age became 18.
c. Prior data not available.
d. The Comisión Federal Electoral certified the total as 50.4 percent, but the Chamber of Deputies raised the total to 50.7 percent when it declared Salinas president of Mexico on September 10, 1988, thus giving him a mandate of 51 percent.

SOURCE: Cols. A–C, 1917–40, Pablo González Casanova, *Democracy in Mexico* (New York: Oxford University Press, 1970), p. 221;
1946–76, Banco Nacional de México, *México Social, 1984*, p. 399;
1982–88, *El Cotidiano* 25 (1988), p. 12.
Col. D, 1917–70, Wilkie, *Statistics and National Policy*, p. 28;
1976, Banco Nacional de México, *México Social, 1984*, p. 399;
1982–88, *El Cotidiano* 25 (1988), p. 12.

For the historical view, see Wilkie, *La Revolución Mexicana (1910–1976), Gasto Federal y Cambio Social*, p. 398; and for 1988, see *Excelsior*'s view of July 21, "Election Results According to Economic and Social Structure," translated (with maps and graphs) in *U.S.-Mexico Report* (PROFMEX, Nason House, New Mexico State University), August 1988, pp. 13–20.

Table 22

SEATS IN MEXICO'S CHAMBER OF DEPUTIES, 1988
(Number)

Type of Seat	Total	PRI	PAN	Frente Democrático Nacional[1]			
				PPS	PARM	PMS[2]	PRCRN[3]
Number of Electoral-District Seats	300[a]	233	38	1	6	0	22
Number of At-Large Seats	200[b]	27	63	32	25	19	34
Total Seats	500	260	101[c]	33[c]	31[c]	19[c]	56[c]
Percent	100	52	20	7	6	4	11

1. The FDN (see Table 23) also includes Corriente Democrática and Movimiento al Socialismo, groups not registered as political parties; each group retains its identity, with PMS as ally.
2. Partido Mexicano Socialista, registered in June 1987.
3. Partido Frente Cardenista de Reconstrucción Nacional, registered in September 1987.

a. Three hundred seats elected by relative majority vote.
b. Two hundred seats elected by proportional share of votes received by each party winning 1.5 percent of the votes cast for deputies.
c. Total opposition seats = 240 (48 percent): 139 for FDN (28 percent) and 101 for PAN (20 percent).

SOURCE: México, Cámara de Diputados, "Relación de Diputados Electos de Mayoría Relativa y de Representación Proporcional Integrantes de la 'LIV Legislatura,'" Mexico City, n.d.

Table 23

SEATS IN FEDERAL DISTRICT ASSEMBLY OF REPRESENTATIVES,[1] 1988
(Includes Majority and Proportional Seats)

Party	Seats	Percent
PRI	34[a]	51.5
PAN	18	27.3
FDN[2]	14	21.2[b]
PARM[3]	2	3.0
PFCRN[4]	3	4.5
PPS[5]	3	4.5
FDN-coalition	3	4.5
PMS[6] (FDN ally)	3	4.5

1. Ostensible seats, not yet confirmed by the Assembly, which has control over its 66-seat membership.
2. Frente Democrático Nacional, led by Cuauhtémoc Cárdenas and Porfirio Muñoz Ledo of the Corriente Democrática and Ricardo Pascoe Pierce and Adolfo Gilly of the Movimiento al Socialismo.
3. Partido Auténtico de la Revolución Mexicana, led by Carlos Cantú Rosas.
4. Partido Frente Cardenista de Reconstrucción Nacional, led by Rafael Aguilar Talamantes to capitalize on Cárdenas's name. Cárdenas is not a member.
5. Partido Popular Socialista, led by Jorge Cruickshank García.
6. Partido Mexicano Socialista, led by Heberto Castillo, Pablo Gómez, and Gilberto Rincón Gallardo.

a. The PRI won only 26 majority seats; with this relative majority, it was awarded 8 proportional seats to gain the absolute majority required by law.
b. Total does not add to 21.2 owing to rounding of the five subtotals.

SOURCE: El Día, October 3, 1988.

Second, presidential confidant Enrique González Pedrero stated:

Since July 6 the transition toward full political democracy has begun. . . . The PRI has ceased being the only agglutinating force holding together all political parties.[67]

Third, an unnamed old-line PRIista was quoted as criticizing the whole concept of the PRI having granted proportional representation seats in the Chamber of Deputies since 1964:[68]

In all countries of the world which engage in electoral voting, those who obtain the majority of votes win and do not go about giving consolation prizes to those who lose, in our case gift seats.

Let us suppose that for the same congressional post Juan, Alberto, and Pedro enter into competition. Only one wins and the votes for the other two are lost, as in the lottery. Their votes are not transferred later to others in the losing party in order to make a deputy.

This unnamed PRIista concluded by noting that the "popular will is indivisible" and cannot be apportioned to reward losers, "in many cases even including persons who did not take part in the election."

[67] Quoted in ibid.
[68] Quoted by Hesiquio Aguilar, "Con la Reforma Política al PRI le Salió el Tiro por la Culata," Impacto, September 22, 1988, p. 9.

Fourth, Fidel Velázquez, effective head of the PRI's Confederación de Trabajadores de México (CTM) since 1941, said:[69]

instead of fighting the opposition, the PRI has ceded power step-by-step, each negotiation leading to the opposition's benefit; members of the PRI have been uselessly sacrificed [in the elections], among them some members of the CTM in order to give more power to the opposition. The labor movement is not in accord with these tactics because they lead to defeat and failure.

Further, in reacting to the FDN's unprecedented September 1 demonstration that interrupted MMH during his sixth presidential address, Fidel publicly called demonstration leader Porfirio Muñoz Ledo an uncivilized leader and, specifically, an "hijo de puta."[70]

Fifth, PRI president Jorge de la Vega, noted for his caution and blandness, startled the nation in a speech September 16 when he made thinly veiled threats against the FDN, which, ironically, he labeled with the following adjectives: foul-mouthed, calumnious, peurile, immoral, perverse, lying, fascist, simplistic, disruptive, destabilizing, intransigent, dogmatic, degrading, offensive, insolent, insensible, strident, provocative, reactionary, and utopian.[71]

Confronted by this harsh reaction in the PRI, Salinas faces at least three wings. Emerging at the center, Salinas and Camacho Solís had to convince the PRI right wing, led by spokesmen such as Fidel Velázquez, to allow PML to be seated in the Senate; and they have to take into account the PRI's left wing, now called the Corriente Crítica, made up of former collaborators of the Corriente Democrática who did not leave the Official Party to join the FDN and its proposed new Partido de la Revolución Democrática (PRD).

The task of Salinas will be to mediate among the wings of the PRI and to end the monopoly of his own monetarist group which governed with exclusivity under MMH, who brought him to power. One of Salinas's proposed plans for "modernizing the PRI" is to end the party's corporate basis and institute geographic representation. PRI leaders would be chosen to represent states, cities, towns, and places rather than organizations such as the National Confederation of Peasants and the CTM. Clearly this would make the PRI more accountable to the various regions of Mexico. The 88-year old Fidel Velázquez will present a problem to the PRI if it tries to eliminate

the CTM as one of the pillars of the Official Party; indeed his followers have threatened to break with the PRI to form a party of the proletariat,[72] should Salinas further weaken the role of the state or further damage the Official Party by "surrendering" to the opposition such major posts as governorships.

In light of these problems, and the Official Party's historical justification of its one-party rule as required to manage successive crises in the six ideological stages of Mexico's national development, I have joked that perhaps the most to which Salinas can aspire politically is to reconstitute the PRI with a new title such as Partido de la Crisis Permanente (PCP). A PCP could attempt to resolve the crises within the Official Party as well as in the nation.

The big opposition parties have also been affected by the July 6 election results. The PAN must reconcile itself to the fact that it is no longer the major opposition party, which can benefit from votes by citizens who merely want to vote against the PRI.

To challenge the PRI and to maintain its position vis-à-vis the PAN, the FDN must establish itself under one banner as the PRD; otherwise it will lose state elections. (By late 1988 the FDN was still not able to follow up its July 6 triumph, for example, losing the struggle to win governorships in Tabasco and Veracruz.) The PPS and PFCRN have now stated that they will not join the PRD, making state victories problematic even if the FDN were not opposed vehemently by Fidel Velázquez and other old guard PRIistas. To complicate matters for the Cárdenas-led PRD, the PFCRN will confuse voters by appearing to be the Cárdenas party.

To win federal elections, the opposition parties will have to unite to wrest control from the Federal Election Commission. The Official Party–government bloc has dominated the Commission for 33 of its 43 years of existence, as is shown in Table 24. Although the PRI theoretically played a minority role for eight years from 1979 to 1987, the PRI was always easily able to retain control by winning the support of a divided opposition. With MMH's realization in 1987 that its days were numbered as the unquestioned power, the PRI-government bloc was given a strong majority position.

Although the 1987 election code attempted to modernize electoral practices by providing public funds to all political parties, the code did not live up to the myth created about the benefits to opposition parties. According to the myth propagated by MMH, under the code

[69] Quoted in *Tiempo*, September 20, 1988, p. 19.
[70] Quoted in *Mexico Journal*, September 19, 1988, p. 11.
[71] Quoted in Fernando Heftye, "La Fanciscana Actitud de De la Vega Se Torna Violenta," *Impacto*, September 22, 1988, p. 55.

[72] Salvador Corro, "La Estructura Infiltrada por Reacciones: Si Desvía el Rumbo, la CTM hará Otro Partido: [Arturo Romo] Gutiérrez," *Proceso*, October 24, 1988, pp. 20–21.

Table 24

MEMBERSHIP OF MEXICO'S COMISION FEDERAL ELECTORAL, SINCE 1946

Category	1946–50	1951–72	1973–78	1979–82	1982–84	1985–87	1987–
Government Members	4[a]	3[d]	3[d]	4[g]	4[g]	4[g]	3[h]
PRI Members	1[b]	1[b]	1[b]	1[b]	1[b]	1[b]	16[i]
Total PRI-Government	5	4	4	5	5	5	19
Opposition Members	1[c]	2[e]	3[f]	6[f]	6[f]	8[f]	12[i]

a. Secretary of Interior, one other cabinet member, one senator, and one deputy.
b. Named by the PRI.
c. Named by one opposition party.
d. Secretary of Interior, one senator, one deputy.
e. Named by two opposition parties.
f. All definitively registered parties given representation.
g. Notary, presumably voting with PRI.
h. Notary eliminated.
i. Each party entitled to one member for each 1.5 percent of the vote received in previous presidential election, up to a maximum of 16 representatives.

SOURCE: Juan Molinar, "La Asfixia Electoral," *Nexos* 123 (1988), p. 40.

each party, regardless of size, was given an equal amount of free air time on all radio and television stations in the nation—this year more than 51 hours per party. Each party also received federal funds in proportion to its electoral support in previous elections.[73]

The reality of the electoral code for the 1988 elections is quite different.[74] True, opposition parties were given access to radio and television but only in officially approved time slots, usually at undesirable hours. The parties received the right to use the mail and telegraph without charge, but not the expensive phone and telex services required to run an effective campaign. The funds provided to each party depend on the average cost of electing a federal deputy, but in the last election (1985) did not take into account inflation (over 600 percent). Thus the PPS and PFCRN each received about 15,000 dollars monthly in public funds, the PARM about 9,000 dollars. (The PAN refused any cash subsidy, but used its tax-free right to raffle an auto.) Such small amounts of funds could not have provided prime-time television even if the opposition were permitted access.

Mexico City television, which has only seven full-service channels, gave complete coverage only to the PRI. Two of the channels are run outright by the government and five are run by Televisa, a private company which is closely identified with government policy. (The Instituto Politécnico Nacional runs a limited educational channel.) The government channels and Televisa gave the PRI complete, live campaign coverage but covered the opposition parties by interviewing only their leaders, thus avoiding the projection of any crowd scenes not supporting the PRI.

Televisa's support of the PRI became so one-sided that its programming ethics were the subject of public censure. For example, immediately after the election Televisa politically edited its serial "Senda de Gloria" (a historical drama on the Revolution from 1917 to 1938), censoring it to omit mention of Lázaro Cárdenas. According to the historian who coauthored the serial, the omission of references to Cárdenas cost the entire serial not only the resolution of the historical themes taken up from the outset, but also its dramatic conclusion.[75]

To protest Televisa's openly biased news program "24 Horas," the PAN not only called for a national viewers' boycott, but was also instrumental in the launching by the Comisión Federal Electoral of an investigation of Televisa's news programming.[76]

[73] The myth was developed for U.S. consumption by Mark Edward Moran, a Washington lobbyist representing the office of the president of Mexico, in an Op-Ed article, "Rise of Opposition Doesn't Spell the End of Mexico's No. 1 Party," *Los Angeles Times*, September 23, 1988.

[74] On the reality of public funding of elections in Mexico, see Miguel Cabildo, Gerardo Galarza, and Rodrigo Vera, "La Oposición o el Arte de Hacer Política sin Recursos Económicos," *Proceso*, October 31, 1988, pp. 6–11.

[75] See historian Fausto Zerón Medina's letters of complaint directed to Miguel Alemán Velasco, president of Televisa, and the sponsors of "Senda de Gloria" for whom he coauthored the teleplay (*Proceso*, August 8, 1988, p. 24). See also Carlos Marín, "Los Autores de 'Senda de Gloria' Repudian la Mutilación de Su Obra," ibid., pp. 20–27.

[76] On unfair television coverage, see Pascual Salanueva Camargo, "Denuncia de la Comisión Federal Contra . . . Televisa por Difamación y Calumnia," *La Jornada*, July 13, 1988.

The PRI's use of television in the presidential campaign was unprecedented and took advantage of the fact that the country has an estimated 20 million television sets that now reach two-thirds of the population. Televisa not only gave 90 percent of its news coverage to CSG, but it donated time for more than thirty CSG "dialogues" with citizens who phoned in to discuss issues or make complaints.[77] Speaking by telephone in a controlled setting, CSG exuded warmth and genuine concern in his conversations with callers; perhaps selected for their nonpartisan tone, many of them openly criticized the government. In my view, CSG was at his best in these television dialogues, which presented him from a low camera angle which enlarged his presence on the screen. Certainly CSG's small stature did not help him on the campaign trail.

CSG's preference for using television during the campaign can be understood in light of the difficulties of traveling among the people, which he tried to confine to lightning-like visits. Too often for comfort he was greeted by either small crowds or open hostility. For example, in Coahuila picket sticks were hurled at him by angry peasants and in Yucatán water balloons were dropped on him from a movie theater. In Morelos sugarcane workers beat angrily on his bus.[78] Such incidents had never happened in the previous ten presidential campaign tours managed by the Official Party, dating back to 1934 when Lázaro Cárdenas initiated travel to every corner of the republic. Television did not show CSG's problems en route, but rather focused on places where he was well received.

Newspaper treatment of the 1988 election campaign was somewhat more fair than television coverage, especially in reporting the size of Cuauhtémoc's crowds, but it had grave limits stemming from the PRI's tradition of buying newspaper coverage. According to one keen U.S. observer:

Reporters receive free room and board on the campaign trail; telephone service is gratis. Traditionally in Mexico, reporters are paid extra money by the government ministries that they cover, and the same holds true for the PRI campaign. . . . Over the course of the eight-month campaign, the sum of such payments runs into thousands of dollars, reporters say.

Opposition campaigns receive front-page coverage in most newspapers, although the placement of stories on the page reflects a clear bias toward the PRI. First, all opposition parties are treated as equally inferior. The miniscule campaign of the right-wing Mexican Democratic Party is often given the same weight as Cárdenas's surprisingly strong campaign.

Moreover, exceptional displays of support for the opposition are often belittled in the press. A recent unprecedented turnout of supporters of Clouthier . . . along 10 miles of Insurgents Avenue in Mexico City was generally scorned by the capital's newspapers.[79]

Beyond propaganda, the Official Party has an advantage over the opposition parties that no electoral code can offset. Government welfare programs are routinely carried out under the PRI's red, white, and green emblem, making it difficult to tell where the government ends and the PRI begins. For example, *tortiobonos* (government coupons permitting consumers to buy two pounds of tortillas at about one-seventh their regular price) are distributed by PRI membership recruiters, as are cards enabling parents to obtain free milk for their children.[80]

The election on July 6 was itself uneventful, much to the surprise of U.S. observers who flocked to Mexico to watch the proceedings. What the observers saw was citizens voting peacefully in secret balloting. They did not realize that the real action takes place after the election when the vote totals are released and public comment begins in the press.

The one event that jarred the campaign process was the murder of two FDN campaign functionaries. Because the murders remain unsolved, three theories, in the form of questions, have emerged in the FDN about the cause of the deaths. Did PRI right-wing thugs commit the murders to create an incident (perhaps involving a warning)? Were the murders nonpolitical revenge killings resulting from local hatreds in Michoacán? Or, in light of the crime wave sweeping Mexico since 1982, were the killings part of an ordinary robbery that was aborted?[81]

Indeed the problem of street crime had become so apparent during the MMH presidency that it was an issue in the presidential campaign. To overcome police inability to cope with crime and the rise of gangs, President-elect CSG is contemplating the creation of a federalized national police force made up of 45,000 agents, 15,000 from police groups to be abolished and 30,000 from the Mexican army.[82] In

[77] On CSG's use of television, see John Ross, "Mexico: PRI Candidate Salinas Plays Populist, Proves Media Mastery," *Latinamerica Press* (Lima), June 30, 1988.
[78] Ibid.

[79] Dan Williams, "Mexicans Fear 'Alchemy' May Mar Presidential Vote," *Los Angeles Times*, June 26, 1988.
[80] Dan Williams, "Campaign Tactics Under Fire in Mexico: Ruling Party Uses Government Resources, Cut-Rate Tortillas," *Los Angeles Times*, September 28, 1987.
[81] On the murders of Francisco Xavier Ovando and Román Gil Hernández, see *Proceso*, July 11, 1988, pp. 24–26.
[82] On the idea for a new national security corps, see *El Financiero*, October 4, 1988, p. 6. The problem of creating such a corps, of course, is that it could foster a police-state mentality; see Hesiquio Aguilar, "Mejorar la Seguridad sin Caer en un Estado-Policía: Ignacio Morales Lechua," *Impacto*, October 6, 1988, p. 9. Meanwhile the government of MMH is organizing citizens' security committees to intervene directly by working with police to plan for patrols, crime prevention, and elimination of prostitution, according to the *Mexico City News*, October 10, 1988.

recognizing that many of the currently employed police are simply criminals with badges who rob and kill each other as well as innocent citizens, the new government seems to realize that it must find new ways to protect the personal safety of the population,[83] a problem that has grown as the economy has faltered in the 1980s.

As president, Salinas must confront the continued decline in real minimum wages, depicted in Figure 8, which suggests the collapse in the standard of living for so many Mexicans. Through 1981 the minimum wage was fixed in January after which it declined throughout the year. To overcome the consequent problem of decline in worker purchasing power by mid-year, beginning in 1983 the government began to adjust the wage twice yearly, but inflation since 1986 has required readjustments from three to five times yearly. Despite five adjustments in 1987, the real wage still lost 14 percent in value between January and December (Table 25).

MMH attempted without much success to overcome a parallel collapse in capacity for economic production which is portrayed for Latin America in the data on investment of funds per worker (Table 26). Between 1981 and 1986, Mexico's capacity for economic production fell by 55.5 percent, the fifth worst case in Latin America after Chile, Bolivia, Argentina, and Costa Rica. Although Chile suffered the worst decline, 67.5 percent, it did so over three years and subsequently has begun to recover; Venezuela suffered the worst decline in one year (1983), 52.8 percent; and, like Mexico, it has failed to begin real recovery. In Latin America investment per worker had been rising for two decades prior to the foreign debt crisis of the 1980s; however, since 1981 the region's role has evolved from recipient of net financial transfers from abroad to sender of financial resources.

Mexico's shift in net financial transfers from abroad came in 1982, as can be seen in Table 27. From 1977 through 1981, the country received about 23.2 billion dollars in net funds, "windfall" mainly from sales of oil at high prices and borrowing to expand extraction of the black gold. Since 1982, the country has sent 48.9 billion dollars out of the country, mainly in government service of the foreign debt and private capital flight. Whereas net transfers added 6 percent to the GDP in 1977, after 1984 they subtracted almost 6 percent. The six years of net transfers out of the country between 1977 and 1987 were made at the expense of investment in Mexico's productive plant. The resulting time lag needed to recover from this long-term decline in investment has created a gap in research and the ability to complete in technological development that will take years to overcome. To resolve Mexico's economic problems, MMH continued to borrow abroad. By 1987 the foreign debt rose to 93.2 billion dollars in standard terms of 1980 (Table 6, part 2), an increase of 18 percent. MMH was able to reduce the total to 81.4 billion by the time he left office, but he did so at the high cost of slicing development funds for industry and agriculture as well as for social services.

Foreign debt interest payments by the Mexican central government, parastate agencies, and the private sector are also shown in Table 27. While they totaled 42.2 billion under JLP, they rose to 57.3 billion for the years of MMH. Under JLP the interest payments were offset by the positive flow of net transfers. Under MMH the payments constituted a serious drain on a situation that was already very serious.

The problem of the public debt is not only serious with regard to the funds that leave Mexico, but it is also serious because the public sector borrows internally to help service the debt. Hence the interest and amortization payments on the domestic and foreign debt absorb an increasing share of Mexico's GDP, as is evident in Table 28. Public sector payments as a share of GDP, which did not surpass 11 percent between 1971 and 1981, averaged 21.3 percent after the onset of the crisis. They reached an astounding 27.7 percent of GDP in 1986, the last year for which data are available. Whereas the central government used to account for less than half of the total public sector debt service in GDP, since the crisis it has accounted for up to 81 percent. Why?

Because there is little discretionary funding in the parastate agencies (which in any case collect and spend their own funds), the president of Mexico must rely on the Secretary of the Treasury to collect funds which he can then allocate flexibly to the central government or to cover deficits and debts in the parastate sector. As the central government has had to

---

[83] The presidential campaign of PRT's Rosario Ibarra de Piedra did much to focus on human rights problems in Mexico, especially the inability to account for 547 "disappeared persons" since 1968. Because of her success in locating 148 persons during the last ten years who were once counted as disappeared, she will not participate in the building of the PRD but will concentrate on locating persons and freeing political prisoners (*El Universal*, October 8, 1988, p. 12). On the 1987 sworn account by Mexican Army deserter Zacarías Osorio Cruz about his membership in a military death team that he claims killed hundreds of disappeared prisoners between 1978 and 1983, see John Ross, "The Heart of Evil," *Mexico Journal*, September 19, 1988, pp. 23–26. Osorio Cruz apparently worked at times under General José Hernández Toledo (earlier the military commander of the Federal District at the time of the 1968 Tlatelolco massacre and later head of the anti-guerrilla campaign in Guerrero during the mid-1970s). According to Antonio Hernández, who coordinates the PRT hunt for political prisoners, the government illegally seized several categories of persons: PRI political opponents, people within the PRI-run structure whose knowledge of certain events necessitates their "disappearance," and drug dealers who are often subjected to extortion in return for their freedom.

Table 25

INDEX OF REAL MINIMUM SALARY DECLINE, 1977–89
(1978 = 100)

Year/Month	Index	Year/Month	Index	Year/Month	Index
1977	101.6	1981	92.9	1985	65.2
January	109.1	January	102.1	January	71.3
February	107.5	February	100.1	February	69.0
March	106.3	March	98.3	March	66.4
April	104.3	April	96.5	April	64.2
May	103.6	May	95.6	May	62.5
June	102.7	June	94.1	June	71.1
July	101.5	July	92.5	July	69.8
August	99.2	August	90.9	August	66.9
September	97.7	September	88.9	September	64.6
October	97.5	October	87.0	October	62.0
November	95.8	November	85.3	November	59.2
December	93.8	December	83.0	December	55.6
1978	100.2	1982	92.9	1986	58.4
January	105.9	January	106.8	January	67.0
February	106.0	February	103.5	February	64.6
March	105.0	March	110.7	March	61.3
April	103.6	April	105.6	April	57.6
May	101.9	May	100.6	May	54.0
June	100.0	June	97.2	June	62.8
July	98.5	July	93.0	July	60.0
August	97.9	August	83.7	August	56.3
September	97.9	September	80.0	September	53.2
October	96.6	October	76.6	October	53.5
November	94.9	November	82.0	November	57.3
December	93.5	December	74.8	December	53.0
1979	98.8	1983	72.5	1987	55.3
January	104.5	January	86.0	January	60.7
February	103.9	February	82.5	February	58.5
March	103.2	March	79.0	March	53.0
April	102.2	April	74.1	April	58.6
May	101.2	May	70.7	May	54.6
June	100.5	June	73.9	June	51.0
July	99.6	July	73.9	July	58.2
August	97.5	August	70.9	August	54.1
September	95.9	September	68.9	September	51.0
October	93.6	October	66.6	October	58.9
November	92.9	November	63.1	November	55.1
December	91.4	December	60.5	December	52.2
1980	91.9	1984	66.0	1988	49.2
January	103.7	January	73.7	January	57.6
February	101.5	February	70.4	February	53.2
March	99.2	March	67.4	March	52.4
April	97.2	April	64.5	April	50.8
May	95.0	May	62.4	May	49.8
June	92.4	June	68.1	June	48.6
July	89.0	July	69.5	July	47.6
August	87.3	August	67.5	August	47.3
September	86.6	September	65.9	September	46.9
October	85.3	October	63.4	October	46.3
November	84.1	November	61.1	November	45.6
December	81.6	December	58.1	December	44.5
				1989[a]	45.2

a. January–October, 1989.

SOURCE: Comisión Nacional de Salarios Mínimos.

Figure 8

INDEX OF REAL MINIMUM WAGES, 1977–88
(1978 = 100)

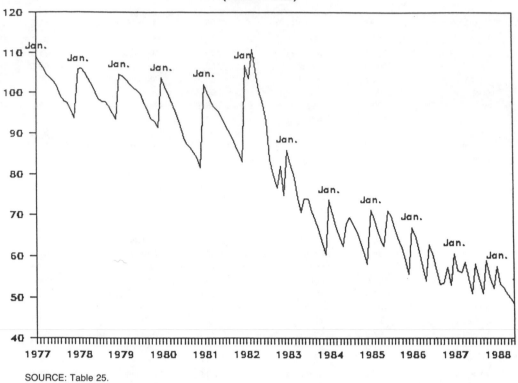

SOURCE: Table 25.

increase its efforts to cover the debt, less is left to meet the demands of society for economic services (including credit) and public services.

The grave situation into which Mexico has entered is depicted in the share of the central government actual expenditure devoted to servicing the debt (Table 29). Since 1986 the central government has actually spent more than 60 percent of its outlay for one purpose: to service the debt. This means that the ability of the government to solve problems in Mexico and to start new programs is near zero. The present situation contrasts starkly with data for other years, shown in Table 29 and Figure 9. After Díaz reached 32 percent in 1900–01, the share devoted to amortization and interest declined to 3.6 percent in 1931, during the trough of the depression. During World War II the share rose to 22.5 in 1942, but it did not reach that level on a regular basis until the 1960s. When López Mateos paid off loans early in the 1960s, debt service declined to 11.3 by 1976. The share increased to 43.4 percent by the time JLP left office; and the stage was set for the debt service to swallow the bulk of central government expenditure under MMH. (See Fig. 10.)

A developing country where the private sector has neither a tradition of social conscience nor the funds to make up for the fact that the central government has lost its flexibility, Mexico now must find its way on an uncharted path. The social needs for education and public health have increased with Mexico's rapidly expanding population even as budgets have been cut in these areas to service especially the foreign debt, 49 percent of which is its direct responsibility (Table 6, Part II). Deficit spending will not solve Mexico's problem; it is already included in the expenditure data discussed here.

To put the best face on a bad financial situation and to convince domestic and foreign interest groups that the government is resolving economic problems, the government has taken the debt figures out of its analyses. By not providing the data in a usable way to the public, the government has been able to shift the focus from the time series presented in Tables 28 and 29.

To show itself in the best possible light, as having worked to successfully reduce deficit spending, the government has developed three views of the

Table 26

INVESMENT PER WORKER IN LATIN AMERICA,[1] 1960–87
(1980 = 100.0)[2]

Country	1960	1970	1980	1981	1982	1983	1984	1985	1986	1987	Worst Decline[4] Percent	Number of Years
Argentina	55.6	76.8	100.0	75.7	60.1	53.1	46.9	36.9	43.1	49.5	63.1	5
Bolivia	60.5	108.4	100.0	111.9	63.8	62.6	54.3	70.3	40.8	46.3	63.5	5
Brazil	33.4	56.4	100.0	84.2	75.8	56.8	55.5	63.1	76.3	76.0		
Chile	47.4	97.0	100.0	119.2	40.4	32.5	55.8	50.9	56.7	69.7	72.7	2
Colombia	63.8	78.4	100.0	110.3	113.2	107.9	98.9	87.0	89.1	94.3		
Costa Rica	39.2	60.0	100.0	60.6	43.9	56.9	61.4	64.3	71.4	66.1	56.1	2
Dominican Rep.	20.5	52.5	100.0	86.2	77.4	76.6	68.5	69.1	68.6	83.0		
Ecuador	33.2	48.1	100.0	84.0	91.9	61.3	58.7	60.5	59.4	58.8		
El Salvador	97.7	93.7	100.0	93.2	81.2	72.1	72.0	65.9	77.6	73.7		
Guatemala	50.4	74.9	100.0	112.0	88.0	71.0	73.1	57.1	55.0	63.4		
Haiti	26.2	35.9	100.0	98.7	90.2	93.1	95.5	104.3	93.6	90.1		
Honduras	39.1	72.6	100.0	80.7	46.4	54.2	73.7	70.4	63.0	60.0		
Mexico	36.8	67.2	100.0	111.2	81.6	57.7	59.3	64.4	49.6	50.3	55.4	5
Nicaragua	75.8	130.5	100.0	147.2	116.9	122.3	118.8	113.8	108.2	98.5	33.1	6
Panama	33.9	88.1	100.0	109.4	98.8	76.1	65.8	68.3	74.7	67.0		
Paraguay	14.0	26.6	100.0	113.6	91.6	72.8	71.7	70.3	70.8	70.4		
Peru	54.9	59.5	100.0	117.1	105.7	63.8	55.9	46.1	57.2	56.8		
Uruguay	48.5	43.3	100.0	90.5	73.5	46.2	46.6	37.7	37.2	46.3		
Venezuela	67.8	102.3	100.0	96.8	105.6	49.8	59.3	58.1	60.1	59.2	52.8	1
Latin America[3]	43.1	67.3	100.0	95.8	80.4	58.9	58.7	60.4	62.0	63.3	41.3	4

1. Gross domestic investment divided by labor force, excluding Cuba.
2. Calculated in constant 1986 dollars.
3. Total Latin America equals 1,639 dollars in 1980; totals include Barbados, Guyana, Jamaica, Suriname, Trinidad and Tobago.

4. Calculated here for change from highest to lowest year.

SOURCE: John Elac, General Studies Division, Inter-American Development Bank, quoted in *IDB Monthly News*, October 1988.

Table 27

MEXICO FOREIGN DEBT, INTEREST,
AND NET TRANSFERS ABROAD,[1]
1977–88

Year	A. Net Change in Debt	B. Interest (Millions of Dollars)	C. Net Transfers[2]	D. Net Transfers/GDP (Percent)[3]
1977	2,436	1,980	456	− .1
1978	4,802	2,949	1,853	− 1.8
1979	7,276	4,907	2,369	− 1.8
1980	12,056	7,390	4,666	− 2.5
1981	26,572	12,757	13,815	− 5.8
1982	7,674	12,203	− 4,529	2.8
1983	2,452	10,103	− 7,651	5.3
1984	2,241	11,716	− 9,475	6.6
1985	581	10,156	− 9,575	6.1
1986	2,009	8,342	− 6,333	6.5
1987	4,551	8,116	− 3,565	5.5
1988	1,343	8,895	− 7,552	6.4

1. Public and private payments.
2. A minus sign indicates transfers abroad (A less B).
3. A minus sign indicates contribution of net transfers to GDP.

SOURCE: Adapted from Banco Nacional de México, *Review of the Economic Situation of Mexico*, July 1988, p. 295, and since 1982 calculated from data in *El Mercado de Valores*, May 1, 1989, pp. 7–8.

Table 28

**PUBLIC SECTOR DEBT SERVICE[1]
AS SHARE OF GDP, 1978–86**

Year	Public Sector Percent	Central Government Percent
1978	11.1	4.2
1979	10.2	4.5
1980	10.4	3.7
1981	11.3	5.2
1982	21.4	15.1
1983	20.8	13.0
1984	18.4	11.1
1985	18.0	11.9
1986	27.7	22.0

1. Actual consolidated expenditure by the central government and parastate agencies to cover amortization and interest payments on the
domestic and foreign debts.

SOURCE: Calculated from unrevised data in Miguel de la Madrid Hurtado,
Sexto Informe de Gobierno, 1988; [Tomo] Estadístico (México, D.F.,
1988), pp. 43 and 55.

deficit (Table 30). Whereas the "financial deficit" includes the debt, the "primary economic deficit" and
the "operational deficit" do not. Government reports
emphasize the primary deficit, much to the conster-
nation of the *Mexico Journal*, which has written:

The earthquakes of 1985 and the oil shock of 1986
have come to plague De la Madrid's hopes for recovery.
The latter cost Mexico the equivalent of 7 percent of GDP
in export income. But funny accounting prevailed and the
primary surplus was close to 1.6 percent of GDP. Meanwhile reserves increased by nearly a billion dollars in borrowed money.[84]

Thus MMH claimed that he reduced the primary
deficit from 7 percent in 1982 to a 5 percent surplus
in 1987.[85] However, if we use the data with the debt
included, the financial deficit shown in Table 30, as
we must if we want clarity, it is clear that the deficit
that counts was 17 percent in that year.

To offset government data presented in the best
light, the Private Sector Economic Studies Center
has made independent analyses. One 1988 study is
summarized by the *Mexico Journal*:[86]

Between 1982 and 1988, public investment went from
21 percent of the Gross Domestic Product (GDP) to 5 percent. Worse, investment in basic infrastructure slipped from

[84] Cindy Anders, "Pomp and Circumstance," *Mexico Journal*,
September 12, 1988, p. 20. Compare the data on primary surplus
given in Table 30, which shows an average surplus of 2.7 for 1985
and 1986.
[85] Miguel de la Madrid Hurtado, *Sexto Informe de Gobierno*,
1988, p. 24.
[86] September 19, 1988, p. 13.

5.5 percent to 2 percent of GDP. The figures, brandished
by the Private Sector Economic Studies Center, show that
public investment in real terms plummeted almost 40 percent from the level reached in the Lopez Portillo administration. This year's 5 percent is the lowest state investment
figure in the past 20 years.
Private economists say this means a severe limit will
be placed on economic growth in the near and medium
term. . . .
One result of reduced investment is greatly reduced
employment. Another is the visible boom in the underground economy, which is now—private economists calculate—equivalent to 30 percent of the GDP. This boom has
prevented a serious social problem in Mexico, the center
commented. Mexico only has the capacity to employ 43
percent of its working-age population, the center believes.
This makes nonsense of all official unemployment figures
and dangerous nonsense of the practice of driving the underemployed off the streets.

With imports now flowing into Mexico to provide inexpensive consumer goods under the GATT
as well as part of the Pacto de Solidaridad Económica
(PSE), Mexican industry must respond. It must compete internally with the foreign goods as well as expand exports based upon the country's comparative
advantage in wages and energy costs; otherwise the
nation faces loss of scarce financial reserves.

The level of reserves, shown in Table 31, had
doubled between 1971 and 1978 and more than doubled again by 1982 to reach 5 billion dollars. In Mexico's economic crisis of 1982 the reserves fell to a low
of 1.7 billion. With devaluation after 1982, the
reserves reached 12.5 billion by the end of 1987 (16.5
billion in April 1988) before heading below 5 billion
by early 1989.

Pressure on Mexico's reserves comes from two
other sources as well. First, the peso has been progressively overvalued; it has been held without devaluation at less than 2,300 to the dollar as part of
the PSE. This overvaluation has hurt exports from
Mexico, but it has kept consumer prices low for the
Mexican middle class. For a time the overvaluation
provided some incentive to keep their money in Mexico, but by fall 1988 an overvaluation estimated by
some observers to be 40 percent suggested that Salinas would have to devalue soon after inauguration.

Second, the volatility of oil prices has continued
to cause Mexico problems. We can assess the price
that Mexico receives for its oil by examining the average price per barrel paid by the United States (Table
32). The price rose from 13 dollars in 1977 to a peak
of 33 dollars in 1981. The fall to 28 dollars in 1982
triggered the crisis in which Mexico still lives, but
prices held at about 25 dollars through 1985. Collapse
to less than 12 dollars came in 1986 and 1988; in 1987
the price reached 16 dollars, a level at which Mexico
now hopes it might peg its prices if Iran and Iraq can

Table 29

DEBT SERVICE AS SHARE OF MEXICAN CENTRAL GOVERNMENT ACTUAL GROSS EXPENDITURE, 1900–88

PART I. Yearly

Year	Percent	Year	Percent	Year	Percent
1900–01	32.3	1937	9.4	1963	17.1
1901–10	~	1938	11.2	1964	24.4
1910–11	27.8	1939	14.5	1965	26.9
1911–12	25.5	1940	12.5	1966	21.5
1912–13	23.8	1941	12.1	1967	28.9
1913–16	~	1942	22.5	1968	21.7
1917	.2	1943	16.6	1969	20.4
1918	4.0	1944	19.1	1970	21.3
1919	5.1	1945	16.9	1971	17.9
1920	4.7	1946	14.9	1972	14.4
1921	3.0	1947	15.6	1973	12.3
1922	7.1	1948	16.0	1974	13.4
1923	16.5	1949	14.2	1975	11.8
1924	7.5	1950	16.0	1976	11.3
1925	6.9	1951	16.5	1977	16.4
1926	13.8	1952	13.8	1978	22.4
1927	16.7	1953	14.7	1979	22.2
1928	13.5	1954	13.3	1980	16.9
1929	7.0	1955	20.1	1981	20.0
1930	4.6	1956	16.0	1982	43.4
1931	3.6	1957	17.6	1983	41.5
1932	5.9	1958	15.6	1984	39.6
1933	10.5	1959	22.0	1985	41.8
1934	14.0	1960	27.3	1986	60.1
1935	7.7	1961	36.2	1987	68.0
1936	7.3	1962	27.2	1988	63.6[a]

1. Includes amortization and interest payments on the foreign and domestic debt of the central government; excludes "off-budget" categories which arise from time to time; for example, from 1938 to 1947 projected and actual budgets excluded foreign loans for road building (see SALA, 24, p. 864).

a. Actual expenditure January–July, 1988; according to the budget, the projected share for 1988 was 63.6 percent so at mid-year plans were still on target.

PART II. Average by President[1]

President[2]	Average Percent	President[2]	Average Percent
Díaz (2)	30.1[a]	Cárdenas (6)	10.9
Madero (1)	25.5	Avila Camacho (6)	17.0
Madero/Huerta (1)	23.8	Alemán (6)	15.4
Carranza (4)[b]	3.5	Ruiz Cortines (6)	16.2
Obregón (4)	8.5	López Mateos (6)	25.7
Calles (4)	12.7	Díaz Ordaz (6)	23.5
Portes Gil (1)	7.0	Echeverría (6)	13.5
Ortiz Rubio (3)	4.7	López Portillo (6)	23.6
Rodríguez (2)	12.3	De la Madrid (6)	52.4[c]

1. Amortization + interest on the foreign and domestic debt of the central government. Excludes service on the debt of the parastate sector.
2. Number in parentheses is the number of years in average.

a. Sample years for Díaz, 1900/1901 and 1910/1911.
b. Includes 1920 interim government of Adolfo de la Huerta, president for seven months.
c. Includes projected (not actual) percent for 1988.

SOURCE: James W. Wilkie, *La Revolución Mexicana (1910–1976)* (México, D.F.: Fondo de Cultura Económica, 1978), pp. 142 and 368; and since 1977, calculated from data in Miguel de la Madrid, *Quinto* and *Sexto Informe de Gobierno, Tomo Estadístico*, p. 103 and p. 55, respectively.

Figure 9

**DEBT SERVICE AS SHARE OF MEXICAN CENTRAL GOVERNMENT
ACTUAL GROSS EXPENDITURE, 1900–86**

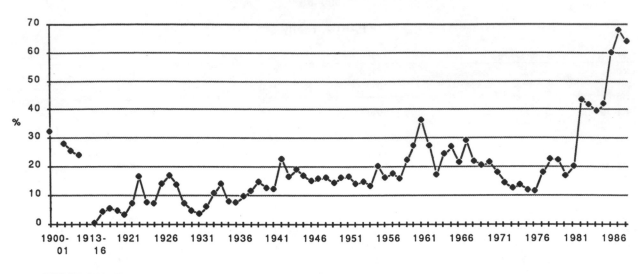

SOURCE: Table 29

agree on OPEC quotas. In the meantime, Mexico is concerned about reports that international oil prices could fall to 5 dollars or lower per barrel.[87]

To help Mexico survive the OPEC oil price crisis and to reduce the outflow of Mexico's reserves until its foreign debt can be renegotiated, the U.S. government provided a 3.5 billion dollar bridge loan in October 1988. The loan is also intended to help Mexico recover from the economic damage caused by September's Hurricane Gilbert, which hit the usually dry Monterrey area as well as the regions where most storms strike, Yucatán and the Gulf coast. Moreover, the United States made the loan to facilitate CSG's taking office on December 1, 1988, thus assuring the continued restructuring of the economy and dismantling of the parastate sector. Indeed, as a condition of the loan CSG agreed to reaffirm and to extend the reforms already under way in Mexico.[88]

As Salinas prepares to take office in December, no doubt he will reflect on the many ways in which Mexico is influenced by world economic affairs, especially the twin problems of oil prices and debt, but he will also have to consider the extent to which domestic politics will let him continue to deemphasize the parastate sector. He will face tough negotiating in the Chamber of Deputies to go as far as he might like.

The parastate sector makes expenditures important to the economy and its continued contraction has major implications for the central government. Parastate expenditure in 1986 was already down to 18.9 percent of GDP compared with its 1981 high of 22.2 percent (Table 33). At the same time, the central government's share of GDP went from its previous high of 34.7 in 1982 to 36.7 in 1986. As the parastate agencies decline, it appears that the importance of the central government will rise. Whereas as late as 1980 the two shared the same importance in GDP, today the central government expends twice as much as the agencies. Consolidated expenditure fell from 52.2 percent of GDP in 1982 to 43.4 by 1988.

Ironically, the present restructuring of the Mexican economy and the reduction of the role of the parastate sector may well give the central government the expenditure power that it originally sought to recapture from the decentralized agencies in the 1960s. Where the original ideas that presidents developed to foster recentralization failed because the central government could never figure out how to control the agencies, most of which collect and spend their own income according to their special role, the selling of agencies may accomplish recentralization of government power. Rather than living up to the theory that they would pay taxes to help national development, in reality most parastate agencies have operated inefficiently and at a financial loss. Few have ever been efficient enough or rich enough to be able to pay taxes or share profits with the central government.

[87]Art Pine, "Impact of OPEC Action . . . ," *Los Angeles Times*, November 26, 1988.
[88]Walter S. Mossberg and Peter Truell, "U.S. Will Lend Mexico Up to 3.5 Billion," *Wall Street Journal*, October 18, 1988.

Figure 10

AVERAGE CENTRAL GOVERNMENT SHARES OF ACTUAL OUTLAY FOR PUBLIC DEBT SERVICE, 1900–88

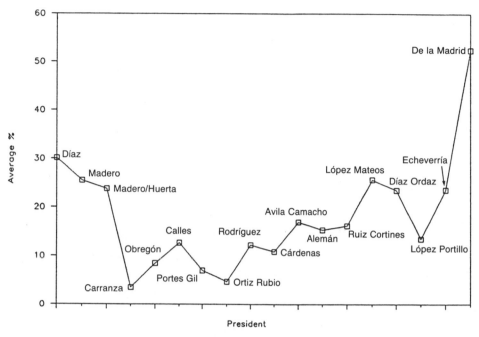

SOURCE: Table 1.

Table 30

THREE VIEWS OF MEXICO'S DEFICIT, 1965–88
(% of GDP; Minus = Surplus)

Year	Financial[1]	Primary Economic[2]	Operational (Real Deficit)[3]
1965	.8	0	.5
1966	1.2	.2	.8
1967	2.2	.9	1.9
1968	2.0	.8	1.5
1969	2.1	.7	.1
1970	3.6	1.4	2.7
1971	2.4	.5	1.4
1972	4.7	2.3	3.3
1973	6.6	3.6	2.6
1974	6.9	3.8	3.1
1975	9.6	6.2	6.8
1976	9.5	4.7	4.4
1977	6.4	2.2	2.8
1978	6.4	2.3	3.6
1979	7.3	2.7	4.0
1980	7.5	3.0	3.8
1981	14.1	8.0	9.9
1982	16.9	7.3	5.5
1983	8.6	− 4.2	− 1.1
1984	8.5	− 4.8	0
1985	9.6	− 3.4	.1
1986	16.0	− 1.6	1.9
1987	15.8	− 4.7	− 1.4
1988	10.8	− 7.4	2.8

1. Financial deficit indicates the total financing needed to cover gap between outlay and income of the public sector. (The public sector includes the central government plus parastate agencies.)
2. The primary economic deficit (financial deficit less interest payments on debts contracted in past) indicates the autonomous financial effort made each year to overcome budgetary problems caused by the disequilibria of expenditures in previous years.
3. The operational deficit (financial deficit less the inflationary component of interest payments on the debt) indicates the real change in public indebtedness each year.

SOURCE: Nacional Financiera, *El Mercado de Valores*, January 1, 1989.

Table 31

MEXICO FOREIGN RESERVES, 1950–88
(Year-End)

Year	Billions of Dollars
1950	.3
1951	.3
1952	.3
1953	.3
1954	.2
1955	.4
1956	.5
1957	.5
1958	.4
1959	.5
1960	.4
1961	.4
1962	.4
1963	.5
1964	.6
1965	.6
1966	.6
1967	.6
1968	.7
1969	.7
1970	.8
1971	1.0
1972	1.2
1973	1.4
1974	1.4
1975	1.6
1976	1.4
1977	1.9
1978	2.2
1979	3.1
1980	3.9
1981	5.0
1982	1.7
1983	4.7
1984	8.0
1985	4.9
1986	5.7
1987	12.5
1988	5.3

1. Foreign exchange + SDRs + Mexico's reserve position in the International Monetary Fund + gold as valued by the Bank of Mexico.
SOURCE: International Monetary Fund, *International Financial Statistics—Yearbooks, 1980* and *1988.*

Table 32

U.S. CRUDE OIL PRICE IMPORT COSTS, 1973–88[a]

Year	Mexico	Venezuela[1]	OPEC[2]
1973	——[b]	5.39	5.43
1974	——[b]	10.71	11.33
1975	11.44	11.04	11.34
1976	12.22	11.32	12.23
1977	13.42	12.68	13.29
1978	13.24	12.45	13.30
1979	20.29	17.37	19.91
1980	31.11	24.78	32.25
1981	33.13	28.86	35.11
1982	28.07	23.77	33.45
1983	25.19	21.48	28.45
1984	26.37	24.16	27.59
1985	25.33	23.64	25.66
1986	11.84	10.92	12.21
1987	16.36	15.08	16.43
1988	12.18	12.97	13.46

1. Included in OPEC.
2. Includes Venezuela.
a. U.S. average per barrel, FOB at country of origin.
b. Not applicable.

SOURCE: U.S. Energy Information Agency, *Monthly Energy Review*, April 1989, p. 92.

They have required subsidies and now assumption of some of their foreign debt payments by the central government.

The ability of Mexico to overcome its economic slowdown and to begin to resolve social problems caused by deferred social expenditure since 1982 depends greatly upon how much discretionary funding remains in the central government budget after payment of amortization and interest on the foreign and domestic public debt. It also depends importantly on the real value of the Mexican foreign debt and the liquidity of the country's banking system.

With respect to payments on the debt, the Mexican presidency has been caught in a "Catch 22" situation because, on the one hand, it would like to show the international banking community that the service on the foreign debt is excessive in relation to the country's capacity for repayment. On the other hand, for domestic political purposes the government has sought to understate the importance of all public debt payments. Under President Miguel de la Madrid domestic political considerations won out and Mexico lost much of its negotiating power with the international community, including the U.S. Treasury Department.

Thus, the government has presented the share of foreign debt payments in relation to GDP rather than to central government expenditure on foreign and domestic debt. Foreign debt payments are seen, then, to be only 6 percent of GDP, which sounds manageable.

Also the government has downplayed the share of expenditure on all of the debt by removing it from its presentations on public expenditure, further obfuscating the issues. Hence, few observers inside or outside Mexico have been fully aware of the internal impact of the country's entire debt problem.

To help resolve the debt problems, CSG plans to reform the giant and corrupt PEMEX enterprise in order to gain control over discretionary funding. Although PEMEX was able to end central government subsidies to it and also to pay taxes and rents to the central government since the oil boom of the late 1970s, PEMEX could have generated much more for the national treasury and for central government discretionary funding had it been run honestly and efficiently.

PEMEX corruption at all levels and especially the nefarious union veto power over management decisions, control over assignment of workers (including bribery and sale of jobs), and control of contracts (re-

Table 33

CENTRAL GOVERNMENT AND PARASTATE AGENCY ACTUAL GROSS EXPENDITURE SHARE OF GDP, 1978–88

PART I. Absolute Terms, 1978–86 (Millions of Current Pesos)

	A.	B.	C.	D.
Year	GDP	Consolidated Expenditures[1]	Central Government Expenditures[2]	Parastate Expenditures[2,3]
1978	2,337,398	861,879	434,689	480,077
1979	3,067,526	1,141,594	626,000	587,330
1980	4,276,490	1,711,745	933,534	905,486
1981	5,874,386	2,644,620	1,532,735	1,304,912
1982	9,417,089	4,911,702	3,269,769	1,990,249
1983	17,141,694	8,393,270	5,367,456	3,734,332
1984	28,748,889	13,348,463	8,065,349	6,335,816
1985	45,588,462	20,123,962	13,020,464	8,666,247
1986	77,778,086	40,832,582	28,574,614	14,706,665

PART II. Percentage Terms, 1978–88

	E. Consolidated/GDP	F. Central/GDP[4]	G. Parastate/GDP[5]	H. Net Transfers/GDP[6]
1978	36.9	18.6	20.5	2.2
1979	37.2	20.4	19.1	2.3
1980	40.0	21.8	21.2	3.0
1981	45.0	26.1	22.2	3.3
1982	52.2	34.7	21.1	3.6
1983	49.0	31.3	21.8	4.1
1984	46.4	28.1	22.0	3.7
1985	44.1	28.6	19.0	3.5
1986	52.5	36.7	18.9	3.1
1987	49.3	~	~	~
1988	43.4	~	~	~

1. Public sector expenditure equals central government plus parastate agency outlays, excluding net transfers between the central and parastate subsectors and thus here avoiding double-counting of expenditures.
2. Included in col. B; data in cols. C and D include some double-counted transfer of funds between the two subsectors.
3. Excludes "off-budget" agencies which have never been brought under budgetary control; for example, in 1988: Teléfonos de México, the Departamento del Distrito Federal, and the Mexico City Metro. Expenditure by off budget agencies was 6.1 percent of GDP in 1988 (down from 7.6 in 1987), according to *El Mercado de Valores*, May 15, 1989, p. 9.
4. This series offers alternative data to that given in SALA, 24–3405. (The SALA total for 1981 should have been 26.5 percent.)
5. This series offers alternative data to that given in SALA, 24–3406. (The SALA total for 1981 should have been 20.6 percent.)
6. Net transfers between the central government and parastate agencies (cols. F plus G substracted from col. E) which are not counted in cols. B and E.

SOURCE: Calculated from data in De la Madrid Hurtado, *Sexto Informe de Gobierno; [Tomo] Estadístico*, pp. 55 and 56; and *El Mercado de Valores*, May 15, 1989, p. 9.

duced from 50 percent to 2 percent under MMH) by the infamous PEMEX union leader Joaquín Hernández Galicia ("La Quina") has had grave consequences for Mexico. "La Quina's" power not only damaged the government's ability to marshall national resources but also hurt Mexico's image abroad.

Foreign bankers, IMF officials, and U.S. Treasury Secretaries James A. Baker III and Nicholas F. Brady have argued that Third World debtors including Mexico would never clean up rampant corruption like that of PEMEX if debt relief were to come prematurely.

In this difficult situation, the value of Mexico's foreign debt began to fall in the secondary market, that is, the free market or market of real value. Real value stood at 83 percent of book value by December 1984, as shown in Table 34 and Figure 11. Within a year it fell to 70 percent where it held until February 1986 when it fell to 64 percent and to about 58 percent one month later. Although it remained at about 58 percent until mid-1987, it continued downward to reach 50 percent by year's end. After hitting 48 percent in February 1988, it continued downward, reaching 43 percent by the end of 1988.

Table 34

MEXICO FOREIGN DEBT: REAL PERCENT OF BOOK VALUE IN THE SECONDARY MARKET,[1] 1984–89

Sample Date	Percent	Sample Date	Percent
12/84	83	12/87	50
12/85	70	2/88	48
2/86	64	5/88	53
3/86	58	8/88	47
5/87	59	11/88	43
8/87	48	12/88	43
11/87	53	6/89	43

1. The secondary market is the free market, the primary market for "fixed-value" loans guaranteed by the government not being viable for Mexican foreign debt. Theoretically, government-backed loans should retain 100 percent of their value, no secondary market being operable.

SOURCE: SALA, 26–2809, Merrill Lynch, December 1988, and *El Financiero*, June 13, 1989.

Figure 11

MEXICO FOREIGN DEBT: REAL PERCENT OF BOOK VALUE ON THE SECONDARY MARKET, 1984–88

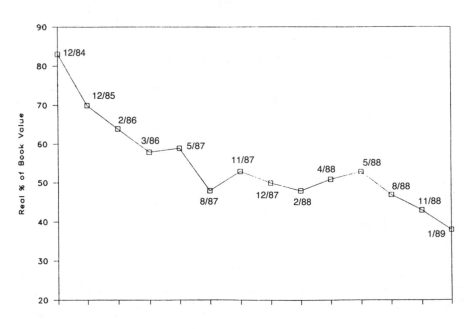

SOURCE: Table 34.

Figure 12

INDEX OF MEXICO COMMERCIAL BANKING DEPOSITS, 1982–88

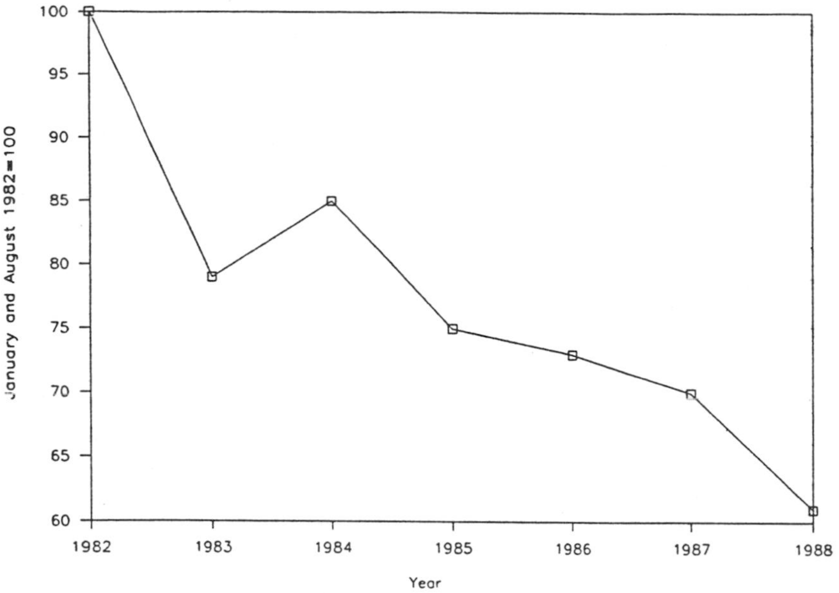

SOURCE: Table 13.

Given the reality of the declining free market value of the Mexican foreign debt (of which only about 27 percent is private as shown in Table 6, Part III) and the country's increasing share of outlay to support that burden, in my view we can juxtapose these two trends and suggest that to reduce the burden for Mexico and to prevent the real value of the debt from falling further for foreign bankers, a viable solution would be to apply the vaunted Reagan/Bush free-market philosophy. By officially recognizing that the debt is worth less than half of its book value, Mexico's interest payments could be cut in half, leaving it funds to undertake economic and social recovery. And the foreign bankers could even see gains in the real value of the Mexican debt held by them.

Such a proposal to revalue Mexico's foreign debt by relying on the free market to set the debt's worth is congruent with the historical moment, and it could be combined with negotiation to set the total at 50 percent contingent upon implementing a grace period of up to ten years during which Mexico would not have to make payments on some or all of the debt service.

But a foreign solution will provide only part of the answer to Mexico's debt problems. Mexico may want to take the domestic action of fully denationalizing the commercial banking system because the partially denationalized system does not have the confidence of the private sector. Since 1982 all deposits have fallen in real terms by almost 40 percent, as is shown in Table 13 and Figure 12. Mexico can-

not effectively undertake modernization and privatization of its economy with a statist-oriented banking system which is unable to provide liquidity for the private sector, the banks serving as a collector of deposits which it channels to the state and to pay Mexico's debt. Full denationalization would play an important role in encouraging the return of funds to Mexico, funds needed for internal development. Denationalization need not mean full deregulation.

Regardless of how the debt problem is resolved, if Mexico is to undertake effective national development it must become fully aware of its three interrelated expenditure and credit problems: lack of discretionary funds available to the central government, unreal value of the debt, and illiquidity of the partially nationalized banking system.[89]

Given the ironies and complexities of society and economy outlined in this study, Mexico's politicians face formidable tasks as they seek to extricate Mexico from its crisis of the 1980s. It is hoped that this work delineates some of the issues and provides the data for further analysis.

[89] See James W. Wilkie, "La Problemática Mexicana: Retrospectiva y Prospectiva," *Revista Mexicana de Sociología* 2/1989, pp. 481–506, who through the use of statistics examines the banking and debt problems and through oral interviews with first-class passengers on Delta airline flights between Los Angeles and Mexico City during 1988 identifies new trends in Mexico's economic efficiency. See also James W. Wilkie, "Del Crecimiento al Estancamiento Económico en México," *El Economista Mexicano* 20:4/5 (1989), pp. 61–98.

2

The Development of Engineering Expertise for Social and Economic Modernization in Mexico since 1929

DAVID E. LOREY

Since the institutional consolidation of the Mexican Revolution in 1929, Mexican leaders have attempted to mold a modern Mexico by two principal means: rapid economic growth and government-sponsored social reform. The development of professional expertise in a wide variety of areas, from primary school teaching to computer engineering, has been considered central to these paths to modernity. At the same time, Mexicans from widely divergent backgrounds have come to see professional careers as a way to take part in the modern Mexico promised by the country's leaders. Pablo González Casanova, the Mexican sociologist and former rector of the Universidad Nacional Autónoma de México (UNAM), voiced this idea in 1962: "In today's Mexico which is being industrialized and urbanized there is permanent social mobility. The peasants of yesterday are today's workers, and the workers' children can be professionals."[1] The Mexican university system has been tailored to the demands of both the development of professional expertise and the satisfaction of the popular desire for upward mobility.

Mexico's desire for rapid economic growth dates back to the nineteenth century and was given special impetus during the administration of the dictator Porfirio Díaz (1876–1911). The push for social development ranging from land reform to health care for all Mexicans began with the Revolution of 1910, which plunged the country into civil war (until 1919) and a period marked by military rebellions (until 1929). When the Revolution was consolidated in 1929 into an Official Party to forestall further violence, Mexico's leaders faced the need to construct a higher education system that would provide:

1. technical expertise for the modernization of society and economy, and
2. inexpensive higher educational opportunities to Mexicans of all backgrounds.

Scholars have tended to focus on the second of these two higher education aims and the problems that have accompanied attempts to achieve it, emphasizing the process by which the public university system has rapidly expanded its enrollment. Much study has been devoted to the history of student agitation for universal and free education and particularly to the struggle over university "autonomy": in 1929 the students won the autonomy of the university from direct political intervention—the National University became the National Autonomous University.[2]

In this study, I explore the successes and failures of the Mexican system in relation to the first goal of providing technical expertise for the modernization effort, defining advances Mexico has made since 1929 and outlining gaps that remain through an analysis of the engineering fields. I have chosen to focus on engineers because of the close connection between engineers and the creation and maintenance of social and economic infrastructure, from potable water systems and improvements in agricultural techniques to multilane freeways and modern telecommunications networks. Mexican engineers form a key link between public policy and economic and social change.[3]

AUTHOR'S NOTE: Special thanks to Ing. José Arreola C. for his comments on an earlier draft, and to Enrique Ochoa for support in Los Angeles.

[1] González Casanova (1962). There is much evidence that this hope has been seriously undermined since González Casanova wrote these words; see González's own later comments (1965) on social mobility.

[2] On student unrest and university autonomy see Levy (1980) and Mabry (1982).

[3] For a general discussion of twentieth-century development in the professional fields see Lorey (1988).

I analyze the development of engineering expertise in the context of the institutionalized Mexican Revolution to answer three general questions:

1. How have the modernization environments created by Mexican presidents and ruling coalitions affected the training of engineers?
2. Have social and economic modernization been equally provided for in terms of engineers in diverse fields and specialties?
3. How are the two goals of the higher education system related to the modernization effort?[4]

Methodological focus here is two-pronged. On the one hand, the length of professional education requires the application of time lag in analyzing data such as those presented here. What light does adjusting the data for the six-year difference between entrance and graduation shed on the scholarly periodization of the Mexican Revolution since 1929? On the other hand, a priori definitions of Mexican needs for engineering have only limited utility. How can we define which engineering fields Mexico has developed successfully, which in excess, and which it has failed to develop sufficiently?

The study is organized into five parts. First, I introduce the basic trends in the production of engineers. Second, I use a time lag adjustment to fit the trends in production of engineers to the pattern of twentieth-century presidential administrations. Third, I discuss the correlations between long-term modernization strategy and production of engineering specialties. Fourth, I offer a case study of sanitary engineering and related professional fields to define one important area of technical expertise needed in order to improve water service and eliminate water-borne disease. Fifth, I address the debate over the goals of Mexican public university education with reference to engineering education. I concentrate here on the 1929–85 period because it was in the early 1930s that professional education in general, and technical and engineering expertise in particular, took a prominent place in the Mexican modernization effort as defined by presidents, their ruling coalitions, and the dominant party.

Three appendixes provide background for the study. Appendix A contains discussions of the data base and interpretation of the three series of data used in the analysis. Comprehensive data in tabular form are presented in Appendix B. Appendix C provides the breakdown of the engineering field categories used in the text and figures.

Engineering Expertise, 1929–85

The most dramatic change in the education of engineers since the 1930s has been the explosive absolute growth shown in Figure 1. Figure 1 presents data on students in all engineering fields who have:

1. received a Mexican degree (*titulados*);
2. completed course work in Mexico but left the university without completing the required thesis or project for the degree (*egresados*);
3. registered a degree with the Mexican government (*registrados*).[5]

Engineering degrees have also constituted an important part of all professional careers since 1929. Engineers are shown as a percentage of all degrees granted, egresados, and degrees registered in Figure 2. Engineering was very important in relative terms from the late 1930s to about 1950, and reached another peak of relative importance in the 1960s. As measured by egresados and registrados, there has been a decline in engineering's relative share of professional careers since the late 1960s. Because the engineering fields grew so rapidly in relative terms until the 1960s, we can conclude that much of the post-1940 growth in professionalism apparent in the EAP (economically active population) census data (from under one percent to more than 7 percent between 1940 and 1980) took place in this career area.[6]

It is important to assess the amount of change in relative proportions of engineering fields during this period. Although experts in engineering fields all contribute to modernization, they do so in different ways. Have the classic fields of agricultural, chemical, civil, electrical, mechanical, and extractive engineer-

---

[4] I use the term "modernization" throughout this study to paraphrase Mexican goals. Although the term "modernization," like "development," has become a much debated concept in the recent literature, it has been the concept chosen by Mexican leaders themselves since at least 1929 to characterize their aims for Mexican society. For these leaders, modernization has meant sustained economic growth and thoroughgoing social change to directly benefit the Mexican masses. In that Mexico has been characterized by a high degree of political consensus since 1929, the goal of a "modern Mexico" in this sense can be said to be a goal shared by the majority of the Mexican people. In this study, I test the performance of the Mexican system against Mexican goals. For an idea of what modernization has meant at different times to different Mexican leaders, see Secretaría de Programación y Presupuesto (1985), especially vol. 1, pp. 15–134.

[5] For further definition and discussion of these three indicators see Appendix A. The figures generally represent only the numerically most important fields and those fields that have experienced marked growth in the period under discussion.

[6] A sign of the gradually increasing importance of engineering fields in Mexico is the acceptance of engineering degrees in the hierarchy of political power. Mexico has not yet had an engineer-president as have Colombia and Peru in the last few decades. But, whereas before 1930 it was rare to find engineers in positions of power, now it is a more common occurrence (see Camp 1980).

Figure 1

ENGINEERING TITULADOS, EGRESADOS, AND REGISTRADOS, 1929–85

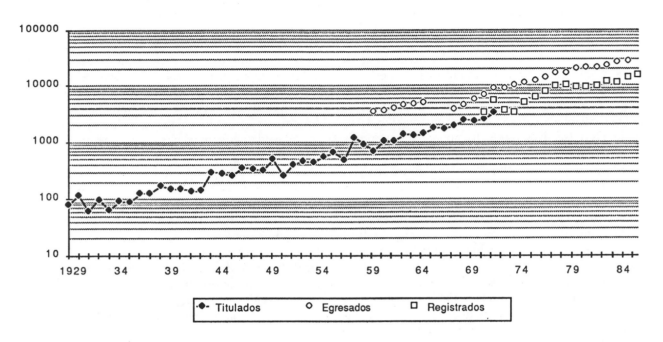

SOURCE: Appendix B, table 1.

Figure 2

**ENGINEERING TITULADOS, EGRESADOS, AND REGISTRADOS
AS PERCENTAGE OF TOTAL TITULADOS, EGRESADOS, AND REGISTRADOS, 1929–85**

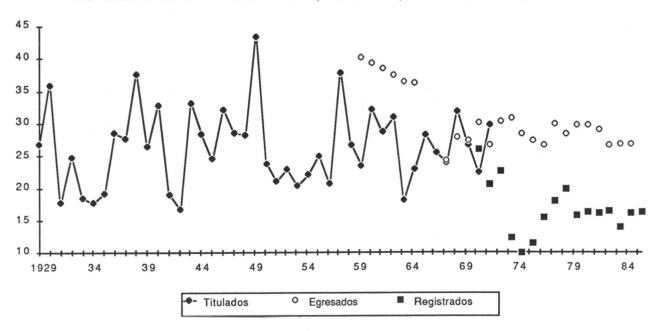

SOURCE: Appendix B, table 1.

ing changed in relation to new engineering fields such as industrial and computer engineering? The absolute and relative growth and decline in specific engineering fields in the period are portrayed in Figures 3–6 (titulados), Figures 7 and 8 (egresados), and Figures 9 and 10 (registrados).[7]

Titulados data for the 1929–38 period (Fig. 3) show prominently a large and growing "other" category, which indicates increasing diversity in engineering fields away from the three classic fields of agricultural, chemical, and civil engineering tabulated by the DGE (see References for abbreviations) in this early period.[8] Data for the 1939–71 period are more specific in relation to this large, undefined area of rapid growth.

Absolute data for the 1939–71 period (Fig. 5) show rapid growth in civil and mechanical-electrical engineering fields, with somewhat slower growth in chemical engineering. Agricultural engineering and veterinary medicine experience two peaks of development, one in the mid-1940s, and another, higher one in the late 1950s. The smaller fields of extractive, petroleum, and topographic-hydraulic engineering show marked growth during the period, with a particularly sharp rise in the number of degrees in petroleum engineering.

In relative terms (Figs. 4, 6, 7), degrees granted in civil engineering, which is the most prestigious of the "traditional" engineering fields, hold their own during the 1939–71 period, as do degrees in agricultural engineering, veterinary medicine, and extractive engineering (including petroleum engineering). The peaks in agricultural engineering and veterinary medicine in the late 1940s and late 1950s are of equal magnitude. Since 1960 degrees in mechanical and electrical engineering have grown rapidly at the expense of other fields. The percent share of degrees in chemistry rises during the 1950s but later falls to pre-1950s levels. Extractive engineering declines while petroleum engineering experiences a gradual rise. Topographic-hydraulic engineering, through 1949 representing an average of 8.1 percent of all degrees, falls off rapidly after that year, to between 1 and 2 percent in the late 1960s. The growth of the "other" category, 1939–71, indicates a growing diversity in engineering

preparations through 1955, but a decreasing diversity thereafter.[9]

The detailed data on egresados (Figs. 7, 8) present a more complex picture. There is a strong surge in the absolute number of egresados in agricultural engineering after 1979, as well as steady, rapid growth of the dynamic industrial engineering field. Chemical engineering peaks in the 1970s, while electrical engineering reaches a plateau in the same decade.

In relative terms, there are dramatic drops in the importance of traditional fields, including civil, mechanical and mechanical-electrical, chemical (which, although retaining its share through 1979, falls off quickly thereafter), and extractive engineering in the 1967–84 period. At the same time, there is a surge in the agricultural and veterinary medicine areas, which grow steadily from 13 percent of total egresados in 1967 to 38 percent in 1984. Another significant increase is apparent in the new industrial engineering field, the importance of which doubles from the beginning of the period to the end. Some of the older, smaller fields remain stagnant, such as topographic-hydraulic, or fall sharply, such as textile, while the newer field of computer engineering shows rapid growth after 1975.

Finally, indexes of changes in registered degrees (Figs. 9, 10) reinforce the trends apparent in the other series. All fields show growth in the period under review. Agricultural engineering and veterinary medicine show particularly rapid growth in registrations in the years from 1970 to 1986, although the growth in the latter field is the greater of the two. The most dramatic growth, however, is in industrial engineering registrations. Figure 10 shows that in relative terms (here shown using an index of percentage shares of the sample fields), industrial engineering has grown at the expense of all other registered fields.

In summary, these interrelated time series illustrate three important changes in the period from 1929 to 1985. First, there has been a long-term decline in the importance of the classical engineering fields, with the exception of the remarkable rise in the importance of agricultural engineering and its allied field of veterinary medicine. Second, rapid growth has been experienced in new engineering fields closely related to Mexico's push for economic modernization, and especially the development of industry. Particularly striking is the rise of the new field of industrial engineering which appears destined to

---

[7] Data on registered degrees (registrados) have been presented here using indexes with a base year of 1980 to facilitate comparison with the series on titulados and egresados. Registrados data are not comprehensive and a few fields and specialties are used here as indicators of each category (see Appendix C); thus the presentation of percentage share data could lead to inexact comparisons with the percentage share data for the other series.

[8] The agricultural engineering category includes veterinary medicine in all three series (see Appendix C).

[9] The "other" category is estimated in the 1963–71 period to make it consistent with previous years. As no clear trend is apparent previous to this period, a flat average for each year has been used.

Figure 3

ENGINEERING TITULADOS, FOUR FIELDS, 1929–38

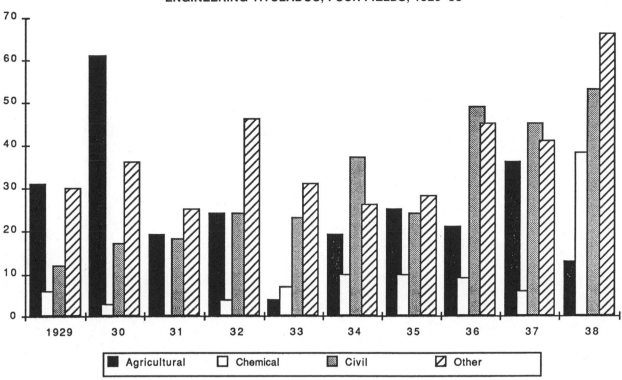

SOURCE: Appendix B, table 2.

Figure 4

ENGINEERING TITULADOS, PERCENTAGE SHARE, FOUR FIELDS, 1929–38

(%)

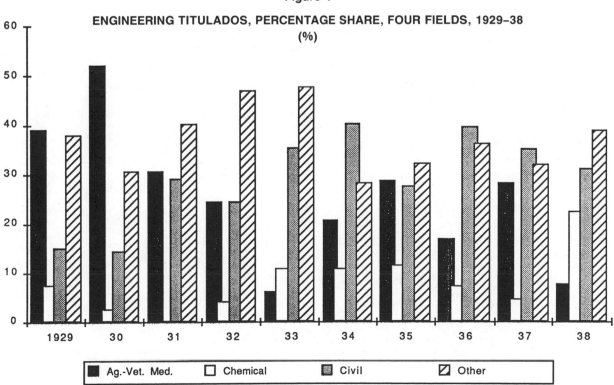

SOURCE: Appendix B, table 2.

Figure 5

ENGINEERING TITULADOS, BY FIELD, 1939–71

PART I

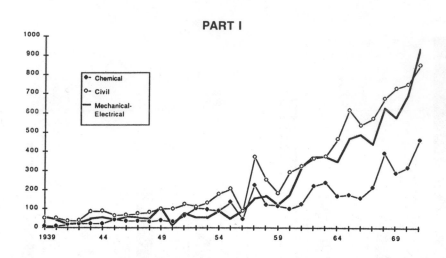

PART II

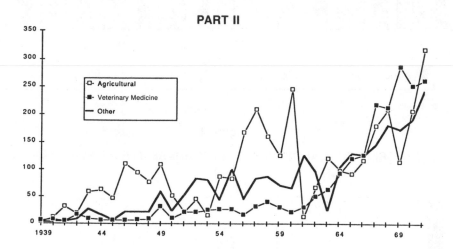

PART III

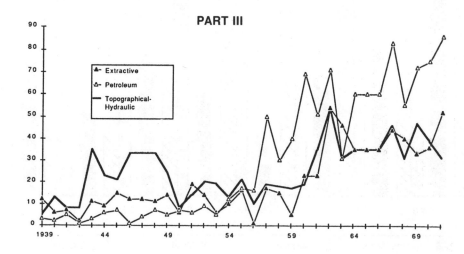

SOURCE: Appendix B, table 3.

Figure 6

ENGINEERING TITULADOS, PERCENTAGE SHARE, BY FIELD, 1939–71

(%)

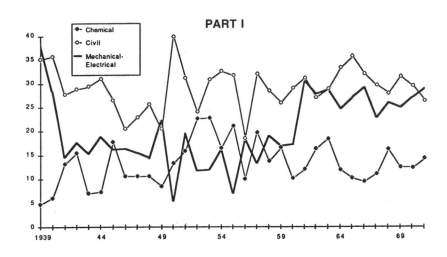

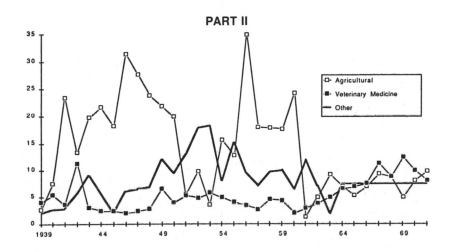

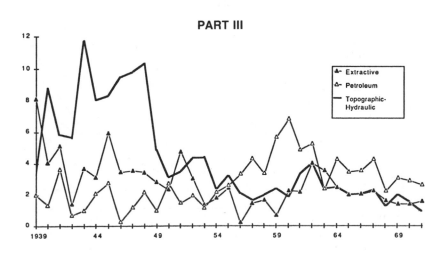

SOURCE: Appendix B, table 3.

Figure 7

ENGINEERING EGRESADOS, BY FIELD, 1967–84

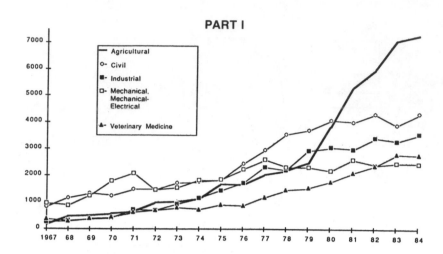

PART I

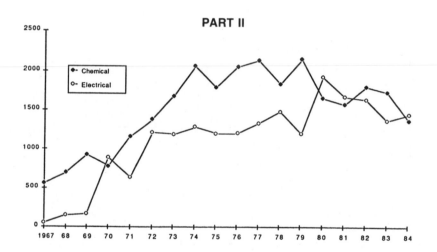

PART II

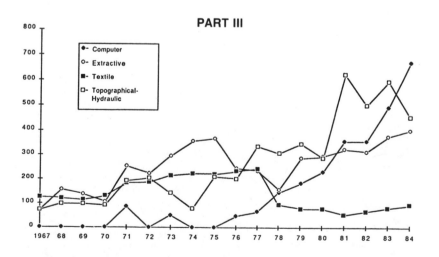

PART III

SOURCE: Appendix B, table 4.

Figure 8

ENGINEERING EGRESADOS, PERCENTAGE SHARE, BY FIELD, 1967–84
(%)

PART I

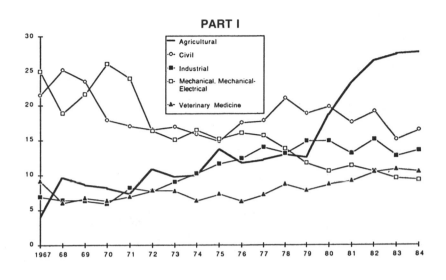

PART II

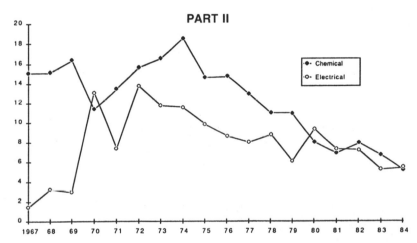

PART III

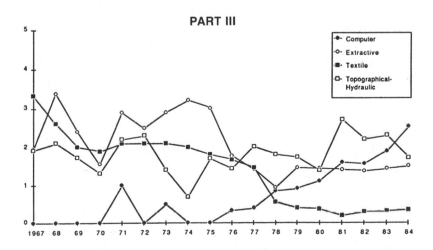

SOURCE: Appendix B, table 4.

Figure 9

INDEX OF ENGINEERING REGISTRADOS, 1970–85

(1980 = 100)

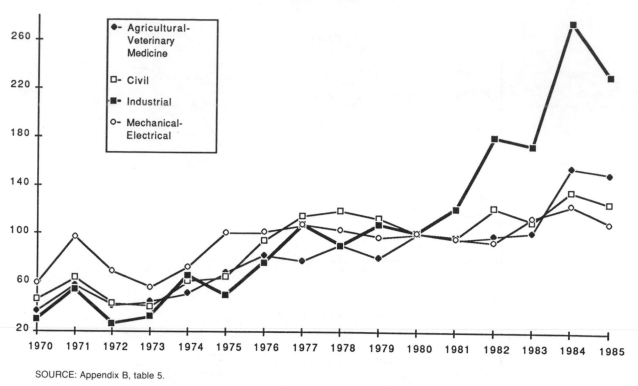

SOURCE: Appendix B, table 5.

Figure 10

INDEX OF ENGINEERING REGISTRADOS, PERCENTAGE SHARE, BY FIELD, 1970–86

(%)

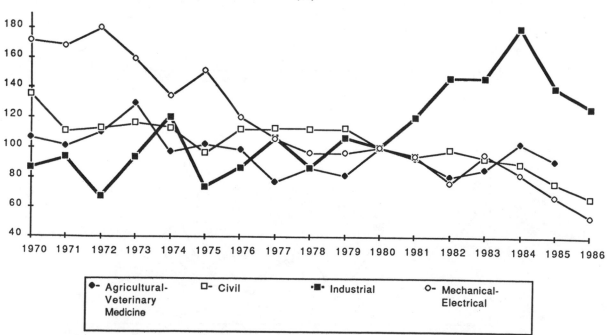

SOURCE: Appendix B, table 6.

become a "classic" engineering field in Mexico in the future. Industrial engineering, as well as computer engineering, has been able to cut into the dominance of traditional specialties even during a period of rapid growth in the agricultural engineering–veterinary medicine area. The new electronic engineering component of the electrical engineering category has slowed the decline of the traditional electrical engineering field. Third, while the data show moderate long-term growth in diversity, diversity has not been one of the most important products of the rapid growth in all engineering fields.

The Time Lag Factor

Clearly, a Mexican student, stimulated perhaps by presidential rhetoric, but more likely by the expectation of real employment opportunities, cannot decide overnight to become an industrial engineer rather than a lawyer. There is a significant length of time between choice of professional field and employment in the engineering fields.[10] In order to place the evolution of engineering fields in the context of twentieth-century modernization strategies, it is necessary to apply a time lag factor to the data discussed above.

The appropriate time lag for the comparison of engineering training and Mexican modernization paths is best chosen by consulting data on average time of enrollment in engineering fields. Garza (1986) has shown that the average engineering career at UNAM—from the time of first matriculation to the award of the degree—lasts 8.6 years (with a standard deviation of 3.2 years), compared with an overall licentiate average of 7.8 years (with an average standard deviation of 3.2 years). At the same time, Garza shows that the average degree rate (that is, the percentage of those matriculating in a given year who eventually receive the degree) has been only 35 percent in engineering fields, compared with 40 percent overall at UNAM. The average figure of 35 percent in engineering fields obscures an important change over time in university efficiency. The average degree rate in engineering has seen continuous decline over

the 1955–71 period examined by Garza, from a high in 1955–59 of 50 percent to a low in 1971 of only 20 percent.[11]

From this information two important trends can be derived: (1) students frequently work (and most undoubtedly work in the area of their degree field) while completing work for the degree, thereby lengthening their program of study, and (2) the number of egresados who decide to work without achieving the final degree, or for some other reason leave the university after completion of course work, is growing (as is also shown in the large gaps between egresado and titulado data graphed above and discussed in Appendix A).

I estimate here that the typical engineering preparation from time of choice, after *preparatoria*, to time of completion of university course work (estimated time from entrance to possible employment, not to granting of degree) lasts six years. This six-year time lag factor takes into account the long preparation time from entrance to degree, the fact that the degree is frequently never achieved, and the fact that many engineering students work in their fields beginning early in their university careers.

While it is true that some selection is necessary before entering one of three preparatory tracks, it is possible to change careers within a fairly broad range upon entering the university. The establishment of a common body of first-year course work (*tronco común*) has also apparently made changes between careers more common. Also, switching among engineering fields is not overly difficult, and among specialties even less so. At the same time, if UNAM and the Instituto Politécnico Nacional (IPN) are not representative of all Mexican universities (and clearly they are not), it is likely that matriculation to degree time is shorter at other universities, particularly at private ones.[12]

It would take at least six years, then, for the effects of governmental modernizing initiatives to be

---

[10] There remain important reasons for choosing a traditional career over a new career. Employment in many new fields is uncertain at best, and often little prestige is attached to these professions, but these careers still provide a good measure of prestige, independent of whether the profession is ever practiced. While it is frequently commented that Mexico produces far too many lawyers, for example, the strength of this traditional field reflects rather well the lack of career opportunities in new fields. For an in-depth discussion of these matters, see ECLA (1967). These two factors—employment opportunities and lingering prestige—produce another time lag effect in the stimulation of new professions that is not considered here.

[11] Here we see one of the many problems with working primarily with statistics on university enrollment. University enrollment has been increasing dramatically since the 1960s throughout Latin America; Mexico has frequently had one of the two or three highest rates of increase in Latin America (see IDB-SPTF, 1967, p. 34 and subsequent years). Garza's data show, however, that fewer and fewer of those who matriculate at UNAM actually complete their degree goal (Garza 1986:table 2). Many university students drop out after the first year, or as soon as they can find employment (see ECLA 1967). At the graduate level, about 90 percent of those who enter never finish degree work.

[12] If licentiate studies at the University of the Americas-Puebla, which last no more than 4 to 4.5 years, are representative of other small, private universities in Mexico, then private universities are important despite their small enrollments. The efficiency rate (graduates divided by entrants) at the University of the Americas is 70 to 80 percent, much higher than the 35 to 40 percent at UNAM or IPN.

felt in the engineering fields. Conveniently for analysis, six years is the length of Mexican presidential administrations. In Figures 11–14, I have moved a sampling of the data on the engineering fields discussed above back by six-year periods in an attempt to gauge the power of government modernization policy to stimulate the engineering fields. These graphs indicate the number and relative importance of persons entering the engineering fields who would eventually graduate with the licentiate degree, would leave with the diploma of egresado, or would register their degree with the DGP. Among other advantages, this approach allows discussion of the early 1930s, for which data are available only in highly aggregate form.

General stimulation of all engineering fields created peaks of development in the early 1930s and late 1940s. A low plateau between 1944 and 1950 was followed by another peak in the mid-1950s which lasted into the early 1960s. Egresados and registrados percentage shares indicate growth in the early 1970s, after some decline in the late 1960s.

Figures 12–14 use agricultural and industrial engineering sample fields. Time lag–adjusted titulados data (Fig. 12) indicate strong stimulation of agricultural engineering in the mid-1930s, a drop to a low in 1947, another dramatic rise in the early 1950s, a drop by the late 1950s, and a slow climb during the 1960s. Data on egresados (Fig. 13) indicate that the slow climb in agricultural engineering of the 1960s gave way to a sudden rise in the mid-1970s. Industrial engineering, which had been growing steadily through the 1960s, was curbed in the 1970s by the growth of agricultural engineering. Data on registered degrees (Fig. 14) show a rise in industrial engineering between 1974 and 1978.[13]

Engineering Expertise and the Institutionalized Revolution

Use of a six-year time lag factor to place engineering field shifts, 1929–85, in the context of the sexennial progression of presidential administrations allows analysis of the effect of modernizing ideology on the development of engineering expertise. Does the development of the different engineering specialties fit into James W. Wilkie's stages of revolutionary ideology?[14] Wilkie has defined five ideological periods

between 1930 and 1976 by analyzing projected and actual expenditures in social, economic, and administrative areas: (1) a social revolution during the presidency of Lázaro Cárdenas (1935–40); (2) an economic revolution during the presidencies of Manuel Avila Camacho (1941–46), Miguel Alemán (1947–52), and Adolfo Ruiz Cortines (1953–58); (3) a balanced revolution during the administrations of Adolfo López Mateos (1959–64) and Gustavo Díaz Ordaz (1965–70); (4) a statist revolution under Luis Echeverría Alvarez (1971–76) and José López Portillo (1977–82); and (5) a restructured revolution under Miguel de la Madrid Hurtado (1983–88), who sought to reduce the state's role and to open Mexico to world trade.

The data in Figures 12–14 can be used to place the development of the sample field of agricultural engineering in the context of modernization strategy. Agricultural engineering was greatly stimulated during the Cárdenas administration. A decline occurred under president Avila Camacho (1941–46), followed by a dramatic rise during the administration of president Alemán (1947–52). The data show that both Cárdenas and Alemán, generally considered at opposite poles of Mexican development ideology, fostered the development of agricultural expertise. Agricultural engineering declined in importance during the administration of Ruiz Cortines (1953–58), and then slowly gained during the 1960s with president López Mateos's (1959–64) "balanced revolution" ideology. Under president Echeverría (1971–76), who adopted Cárdenas's rhetoric on agricultural development, agricultural engineering was stimulated to new heights.[15]

As Figures 12–14 show, engineering fields were dominated by more typically "social" concerns in the 1930s, evidenced by the strength of agricultural engineering training. A period characterized by a marked increase in industry-related specialties followed after 1940. In the 1960s, the data indicate a balance between industrial and agricultural fields in terms of percentage share distribution of the fields. In more recent years, we find the remarkable rebirth of agricultural engineering in the Echeverría years and the appearance of the dynamic industrial engineering field.[16]

Along with these basic correlations, it should be noted that industry-related engineering fields were already receiving strong stimulus in the 1930s and that

---

[13] The importance of agricultural engineering appears depressed compared with egresados data. But the registrados indicator does not reflect the rapid growth in diversity in the agricultural engineering area during the 1970s and thus shows a plateau rather than growth during the decade.

[14] See Wilkie (1978), with epilogue on Mexico since 1963, and Chapter 1 in this volume.

[15] Agricultural policy is considered one of the prime indicators of presidential social concern. The debate over whether or not agricultural policy really holds the key to social development in Mexico, particularly in the 1980s, is not discussed here.

[16] We will have to wait until the 1990s to analyze the effects of López Portillo's Staple Foods Program and Global Development Plan and to assess de la Madrid's "industrial reconversion" policies.

Figure 11

**ENGINEERING TITULADOS, EGRESADOS, AND REGISTRADOS,
1929–85, ADJUSTED FOR SIX-YEAR TIME LAG**

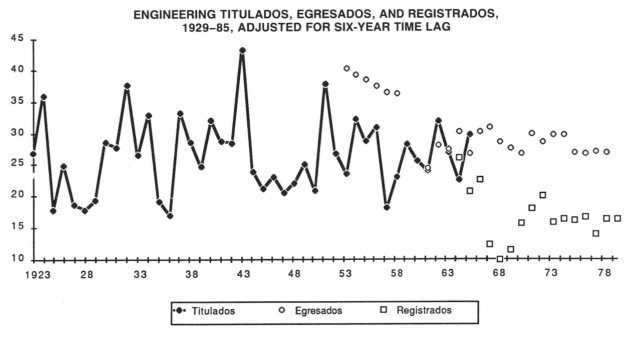

SOURCE: Appendix B, table 1.

Figure 12

**ENGINEERING TITULADOS, PERCENTAGE SHARE, SELECTED FIELDS,
1939–71, ADJUSTED FOR SIX-YEAR TIME LAG**

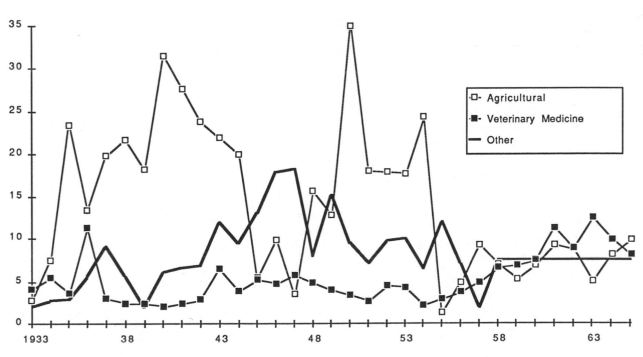

SOURCE: Appendix B, table 3.

Figure 13

**ENGINEERING EGRESADOS, PERCENTAGE SHARE, SELECTED FIELDS,
1967–84, ADJUSTED FOR SIX-YEAR TIME LAG**

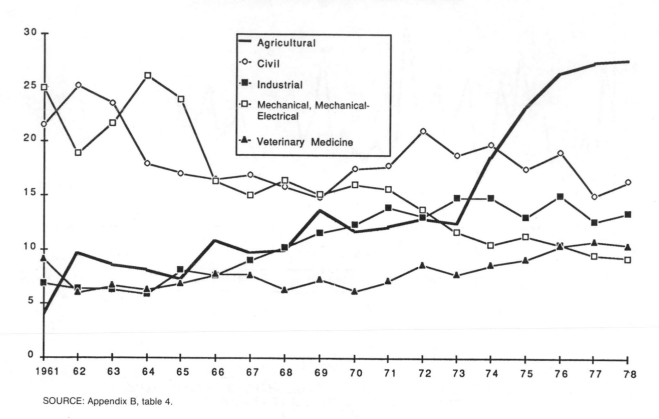

SOURCE: Appendix B, table 4.

Figure 14

**INDEX OF ENGINEERING REGISTRADOS, PERCENTAGE SHARE, SELECTED FIELDS,
1970–85, ADJUSTED FOR SIX-YEAR TIME LAG**

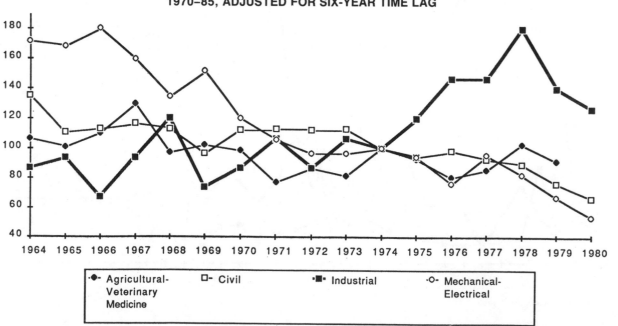

SOURCE: Appendix B, table 6.

the "balanced" revolutionary ideology of the late 1950s and early 1960s (beginning with president López Mateos) is not as well reflected in these data as in Wilkie's data on federal expenditure. In general, we see in the data presented with the time lag the early appearance and strong long-term performance of indicators of "economic" emphasis. Although Wilkie sets the economic period from 1940 to 1960, he suggests that it began in the late 1930s under Cárdenas. My data on the production of engineers confirm this view. The data indicate that the economic phase of the Revolution had already begun in the 1930s under Cárdenas with the creation of industrial and economic infrastructure specialties such as mechanical-electrical and civil engineering.

The evidence of the engineering fields indicates that not only did "economic" revolution follow "social" revolution, but also that much of the human resources for economic revolution were created during the earlier "social" phase.[17] The economic revolution begun during the 1940s was, then, in part a response to trends set in motion in society and economy in the 1930s. Presidents Avila Camacho and Alemán recognized and legitimated social and economic priorities and decisions about the path to a modern Mexico made in the 1930s. The development of engineering expertise implies a continuum that links Cárdenas's social revolution with later modernization policies emphasizing economic development.

That this long-term continuum linking implicit modernization strategies of presidents during the 1930s and 1940s has continued into more recent administrations is revealed in the character of the new industrial engineering field. The course makeup of this field explains its rapid growth since the late 1950s. Programs in industrial engineering are actually an agglomeration of several distinct fields, most of them not historically areas of engineering expertise. The course work in a typical program in the field includes, for example, 20 percent of credits in business skills such as accounting, administration, finance, and computer systems and software. This percentage compares with roughly 2 to 3 percent of credits in such areas in the fields of civil or mechanical engineering. An industrial engineering education also typically includes 2 percent legal training and 7 percent foreign language study (generally English).[18]

Industrial engineering, then, is the engineering field least concerned with technical engineering skills. It is, in fact, more akin to a degree in business than a degree in engineering. Industrial engineers are frequently employed by industries and businesses as "todólogos," professionals who can do a bit of everything (from the Spanish *todo*—everything). The development of the field attests to two realities: (1) Mexican presidential administrations continue to emphasize financial and industrial routes to a modern Mexico, and (2) highly specialized engineers are not being produced for other sectors of society and economy that need development. The growth in the industrial engineering field fits well with the extremely rapid growth in business preparations since 1940 in Mexico, which I have discussed elsewhere.[19]

Three interrelated conclusions are possible at this point (1) the career path decisions of engineers have been in line with presidential modernization ideology; this is evident in the time lag–adjusted data; (2) the expenditure of government funds in particular areas appears to be more important than verbal rhetoric in influencing the choice of engineering fields by university students; this conclusion is supported by the impetus given to agricultural engineering by both Cárdenas and Alemán, whose explicit modernization rhetoric was, of course, very different; (3) real employment opportunities provided by public and private investment coincident with long-term government modernization strategy have been a direct stimulus to the development of engineering expertise in Mexico.

Measuring Need for Professional Expertise: The Case of Sanitary Engineering and Related Fields

Has the development of the engineering profession, guided by government modernization strategy, coincided with Mexico's needs? Perhaps the greatest difficulty in drawing far-reaching conclusions from the data presented here is that we have no commonly accepted method for defining needs for professional skills. It is extremely difficult to define a priori how many engineers should be educated in Mexico, or in what proportion to other areas of professional expertise such as business management or the health professions. It is equally difficult to define the most desirable distribution among specific engineering fields in Mexico.

The statistical evidence analyzed above shows that thousands of engineers leave the Mexican educa-

[17] This conclusion is compatible with analyses of the "social" revolutionary period of the 1930s under Cárdenas; see, for example, Glade (1963), Mosk (1950), and Reynolds (1967). This is not to assert that development has been cumulative (see Wilkie 1978:29). General development "environments," like those defined by Wilkie, are generally more important than specific development policies; see Latapí's analysis (1980) of the direct effect of Echeverría's policies.

[18] Data from survey of course catalogs of Mexican universities.

[19] Lorey (1988).

tional system every year. Mexico appears to have the purely numerical critical mass of engineers to avoid the near-term effects of a "dynamic shortage" in engineering expertise—a situation wherein technological and industrial modernization stagnate because of lack of human capital.[20] Also, other sources indicate that the Mexican system cannot employ all the engineers it produces, especially those trained in the more traditional fields. In fact, the general oversupply of professional expertise has resulted in a serious devaluation of educational achievement: and many Mexican engineers currently work below the level of their professional training.[21]

Yet it is relatively easy to define areas of engineering expertise that are needed in Mexico by analyzing certain gaps in social infrastructure development. Data on water service and quality, as measured by the presence of drainage systems, incidence of water-borne diseases, and government expenditure on drainage, reveal areas of basic social infrastructure that clearly need much development in Mexico. It is common knowledge that sewerage and water supply systems are constructed with "ad hoc" or "informal" expertise in many parts of Mexico, where such systems are built at all. Lines for the two services are sometimes laid in the same trench, with obvious health risks if effluents of the two systems mix.

The data in Table 1 show clearly that Mexico has historically suffered, and continues to suffer, from a lack of water supply and waste management modernization. While falling steadily over the period, the percentage of Mexicans living without drainage of sewage remains somewhere between 45 and 50 percent.[22] Water service in rapidly growing Mexico City actually declined in coverage between 1940 and 1960. Water service to populations of other rapidly growing urban areas has increased at a rate less than that for rural areas.[23]

Data on deaths from diarrhea and enteritis show only a slow decline in death rates in the years from 1940 to 1970, and the national-level figures hide large differences between Mexico's developed and less developed regions. In terms of water-borne diseases as a cause of death, Mexico lags behind all the more highly developed Latin American countries, with

which it is usually ranked on other criteria. Only those Latin American countries generally considered least developed—El Salvador and Paraguay, for example—have higher rates of death by these causes than Mexico.[24]

Data on government expenditure for water system improvement (included in Table 1) show that, regardless of government rhetoric,[25] potable water supply and drainage have not been aspects of modernization in which the government has seen it worthwhile to develop programs and spend money. As a consequence, government employment in these fields has not drawn engineering students to related engineering specialties. Government employment is crucial for modernization of water and waste systems, of course, since water supply, sanitation, and pollution control works, like social infrastructure in general, are generally not the result of private sector initiative.

Over the period examined here, engineers in sanitation, water system development, waste treatment, and related fields have constituted a tiny fraction of total engineers. While civil, agricultural, and chemical engineers are currently educated in many specialties and subspecialties, none of them are experts in sanitation, potable water supply, or waste treatment in urban or rural areas. No Mexican university produces licentiate level egresados or titulados in sanitary engineering, water supply, or waste management, according to the ANUIES data base.[26]

With regard to the number of experts produced in some allied fields, it is possible to suggest basic dimensions. In 1984, the most recent year for which data are available, Mexican universities produced 36 egresados in municipal engineering, 23 in public health, and 2 in environmental engineering. Several licentiate programs with focuses in "urbanism" have not yet produced egresados. At the master's level that year, Mexico produced 155 egresados in public health (of which 132 were in the general field of public health, and 9 in parasitology and water-related sicknesses), 17 in urban and regional planning, 11 in urban construction, and 10 in "control systems" for environmental pollution. These 254 egresados represent one quarter of one percent of the total licentiate

[20] For discussion of this factor see Thomas (1972:218–230).
[21] See Carnoy (1977) for a general discussion of educational devaluation and Davis (1967) for a discussion of the Mexican case.
[22] Data for 1980 are not strictly comparable as they refer to housing units, rather than population, without drainage. Living quarters without drainage systems or running water are generally also the most crowded; thus the 1980 percentages are probably much higher than shown and the percentage changes showing improvement therefore less impressive than indicated.
[23] Calculated from Wilkie (1978:263 and 374–375).

[24] SALA, 24–708. Diarrhea and enteritis are not the only water-borne causes of death, but the most easily identifiable. The World Health Organization includes a separate category for "causes of perinatal mortality" in its statistics on causes of death. Many Mexican children undoubtedly die of water-borne infections.
[25] See Wilkie (1978:200–201).
[26] Arce Gurza (1982:Appendix III) lists two specialties—civil sanitary and municipal sanitary—which do not appear in the ANUIES data. If these programs existed in the early 1980s, they may have been short-lived, or may have not yet produced egresados.

Table 1

MEXICO POTABLE WATER AND DRAINAGE AND DISEASE INDICATORS, 1940–80

	PART I. Percent					PART II. Index (1970 = 100)					PART III. PC[1]			
A. Population without Drainage (%)	86.5	79.7	71.5	58.8	42.8[a]	147.1	135.5	121.6	100.0	72.8	−7.9	−10.3	−17.8	−27.2
B. Distrito Federal without Drainage (%)	25.4	27	30.2	22.6	13.8[a]	112.4	119.5	133.6	100.0	61.1	6.3	11.9	−25.2	−38.9
C. Government Expenditure for Potable Water and Drainage (% of Budget)	.2	.3	.4	.2	.3@	100.0	150.0	200.0	100.0	150.0	50.0	33.3	−50.0	50.0
D. Death by Diarrhea and Enteritis (% of All Deaths)	21	17.2	14.9	14.3	8.8	146.9	120.3	104.2	100.0	61.5	−18.1	−13.4	−4.0	−38.5

1. Calculated from Part II.

a. Percentage of houses without drainage.

SOURCE: A, Wilkie (1978); DGE, X Census.
B, Wilkie (1978); DGE, X Census.
C, Wilkie (1978).
D, INEGI-EHM.

and graduate egresados in 1984.[27] There exists one doctorate degree program in sanitary engineering which has not yet produced an egresado.

Taken together, data on this important area of Mexico's social infrastructure and data on engineers in related fields reflect the general lack of response to the immense health side effects and environmental impact of modernization strategies which have brought rapid industrializaton and urbanization to Mexico. This neglect is especially troublesome in the high plateau area where both population and industry are concentrated. Mexico City, soon to be the most populous city in the world, continues to dump its daily tons of sewage untreated into nearby streams. Pollutants disposed of in Mexico City have been found in fruits and vegetables grown hundreds of miles away and trucked into the metropolis. While industrialists and agriculturalists complain that these streams are increasingly unfit for secondary agricultural or industrial usages, they continue to be used for household purposes, including cooking, by many Mexicans downstream.

An ironic proposal designed to slow the growth of Mexico City and to end its water problems has been made. It would require fewer (not more) sanitary engineers. Alan Riding (1984) suggests that if water quality is further neglected, Mexico City might become less attractive to migrants. But neglect has not solved the problem and the long-term solution involves the decentralized development of potable water systems and other social infrastructure in the provinces. Because the states have limited funds, such decentralization will not take place without central government support. Development of a potable water supply and water treatment facilities requires a massive contribution from a central government that has long monopolized the states' monies in order to meet the housing and communication needs of the capital, a process which has in turn drawn millions of migrants to Mexico City from less favored provinces. Ironically, the de la Madrid administration has asked the state governments, which lack the resources to build their own roads and potable water supply systems, to contribute more funds to higher education in an effort to decentralize professional training.[28]

Because the education of engineers has responded primarily to the stimulus of modernization strategies geared to the Mexican economy, the development of fields in civil and topographic-hydraulic engineering has been devoted predominantly to economic infrastructure, highways, and irrigation systems, rather than development of urban or rural housing, water supply, or sewerage. The high incidence of water-borne infections demonstrates the neglect of basic social improvements. Because government investment emphasis has been on breaking bottlenecks that limit economic growth, development of engineering fields has favored industrial and economic applications, rather than the modernization of social infrastructure.[29]

[27] Although civil engineers may comprise the bulk of water system constructors or consultants, and this field shows a high degree of development in the data above, it is clear from data on water and health that civil engineers in general have not been directed toward this apsect of basic social infrastructure development.

[28] For a discussion of regional differences in intestinal parasites found in children in Mexico, see Cruz López et al. (n.d.).
[29] See Hellman (1983:71–72) on bottlenecks; and Wilkie (1978: 189–207 and 354–356) on the importance of social expenditure in areas other than education.

Engineering Expertise and the Mexican University System

Although the preceding sections suggest that government modernization strategy is the main determinant in the development of engineering fields, the Mexican university system, even if it is a passive element in this development, also has contributed to the trends and distortions discussed above. The distortions are directly related to the two competing goals of the university described at the outset—the growth pattern of the higher education system has, for many reasons, damaged its ability to produce high-quality graduates.[30]

The rapid growth of the university system since the early 1960s is generally attributed to Mexico's historically rapid population growth and the increase in the number of secondary school graduates resulting from the expansion of the educational system at lower levels. The reality is, however, that public university policy, particularly the university's insistence on low- or no-cost education, has been the main cause of rapid growth in enrollment. Rapid growth, then, does not by itself explain the university's current problems. The undirected nature of that growth and the emphasis of the public university on efficiency, that is, on the lowering of per-student costs, rather than on the effectiveness of university education, have made a large student body difficult to manage.

Undirected growth in university enrollment in Mexico has made human resource planning to meet Mexican social needs extremely difficult. UNAM rector Jorge Carpizo has commented that "it is as if the university were content to merely distribute diplomas without wondering what types of graduates are needed by society."[31] In the engineering fields, government preference for expenditure in economic areas has led to high production of fields related to economic growth, and is reflected as well in the weaker growth in fields related to social needs. While some traditional economic fields have declined in importance, their place has been largely taken by the newer industrial engineering field. The emphasis of government modernization strategy has swelled the enrollment in economic fields beyond available employment opportunities. The university has been unwilling to curb this trend and the government has

supported this enrollment policy because the university has provided an escape valve for unemployed youth.[32]

Emphasis on efficiency rather than effectiveness has had a negative effect on the quality of education received by engineers. Measured by overall teacher-student ratios and the ratio of full-time to part-time professors, quality at Mexican universities has improved since the late 1960s. I suggest, however, that the quality of education has not improved at the rate that demand for high-quality graduates has grown, and that this slow rate of improvement explains much of the public university system's current malaise.

At the large public universities such as UNAM and IPN, which train most engineers, teacher-student ratios were about 1 : 80 in 1985 and the ratio of full-time to part-time (hourly) faculty was half the national average—almost 90 percent of the professors at UNAM are employed on an hourly basis.[33] With the financial crisis from 1982 to the present, university funds, particularly for teacher salaries, have been cut drastically while growth in enrollment has not diminished. Minimal entrance requirements and low examination and other degree criteria have exacerbated a crisis in quality that is recognized throughout the Mexican educational system.[34] Alonso Fernández, rector of UNAM, for example, has remarked: "Many people think that a 'university for the masses' is a positive thing. But its only accomplishment is to train a gigantic mass of mediocre graduates."[35]

In relation to the engineering fields, low standards for educational achievement have intensified the historical lack of communication and exchange between public and private sector employers and the university.[36] The public university system does not provide industry or administration with engineers and technicians with appropriate levels of expertise or in needed areas. One common complaint is that Mexico has produced too many engineers and not enough technicians in engineering fields; ideally, numerous technicians should be educated to support

---

[32] That it is possible to affect these ratios was shown in the restricted admission of medical students in the late 1970s.

[33] See, for example, ANUIES-AE, various years, and ANUIES-ESM, 1970–76.

[34] It has also been recognized for many years. See Silva Herzog (1974:186–187).

[35] Quoted in Jacobsen (1987:A100).

[36] See Wichtrich (1979) for the comments of a U.S. businessman. See *La Jornada*, August 26, 1987, p. 9, for business views of attitudes toward private initiative in Mexican college textbooks. In 1987 CANACO (the Mexican National Chamber of Commerce) called for more private sector influence in the National Commission on Free Textbooks, an organization that provides many texts to the universities. See Vernon (1964) for a general discussion of linkages between industry and public policy.

---

[30] Some of the following distortions are recognized by some sectors of the university system (see the unprecedented self-critique in UNAM 1986).

[31] Quoted in Castañeda (1987:A106).

each engineer. Senior engineers comment that while there are enough secondary technical schools, their programs encourage graduates to enter the university and become engineers. At the other end of the educational spectrum, training of unskilled and semi-skilled workers in an attempt to equip them with technical skills has proven difficult because of the common lack of basic, particularly quantitative, skills.[37] The result in engineering fields has been the employment of many engineers, particularly engineering egresados as technicians, which satisfies neither engineers nor employers.

As quality at public universities has failed to keep pace with change in economy and society, two systems have developed, with government support, to keep alive the goal of providing Mexico with highly trained engineers. These alternatives are the education of engineers abroad (particularly in the United States) and the development of private university programs in dynamic engineering specialties. Available evidence indicates that while Mexican students in the United States are not numerous,[38] professionals trained abroad may, along with those educated privately, make up the elite sectors in the professions and in the public and private sectors of the economy.[39] This tendency is a strong force if training abroad is at the graduate level, and is particularly relevant in the private sector. Entry-level exams for both public and private sector corporations seem to be slanted toward Mexican students educated privately and abroad.[40] The encouragement of alternate systems is clearly in direct conflict with the aim of providing social mobility for Mexico's less-favored social sectors by way of a public university education.

The pattern of growth in the public university system has severely damaged the popular hope of professional employment for all, especially in engineering and technical fields, which had been hailed as the professional preparations par excellence in the 1930s.[41] The engineering students who are best prepared at entry, who can afford to devote themselves to full-time study, and who eventually earn the degree come from predominantly middle- and upper-class backgrounds. And even among these social sectors, discontent over the increasing lack of mobility provided by the university system is growing.[42] University leaders have been unable to direct this discontent toward reform of the system that might mean better study and employment opportunities for future generations.[43]

A combination of problems related to providing higher education opportunities at artificially low costs, then, has swamped the public university system and hindered its ability to produce the highly trained engineers needed for modernization. At the same time, these problems have diminished the system's capacity to create opportunities for social mobility for less-favored Mexicans. The inability of the government and the university to reform the public education system has created two ironic developments: (1) although the university is open to all, high-level employment opportunities in the engineering fields are increasingly available only to students able to pay for private or foreign education; (2) a market saturation has stimulated continued growth in traditional engineering fields because these fields offer graduates the advantage of prestige; the growth in traditional fields has in turn slowed the development of other fields and of diversity.

Conclusion

The Mexican government has subsidized economic growth and particularly industrial development since before 1940, but has not supported with meaningful investments in social infrastructure the development of the complex engineering expertise

---

[37] Data from interviews and conversations with senior- and lower-level engineers in the public and private sectors. Llinas Zárate (1987) states that 81 percent of technical school graduates go on to the university. Legally mandated training of workers by business was president López Portillo's (1977–82) response to the inability of the secondary education system to produce the technicians and lower-level personnel needed by business and industry. This training requirement has been shirked by an estimated 117,000 small- and medium-sized firms (*La Jornada*, September 15, 1987).

[38] Mexican students abroad generally represent less than one quarter of one percent of egresados in Mexico. Business, engineering, and physical and life sciences are the most important fields studied by Mexican students in the United States. See Lorey (1988).

[39] Private universities such as the Universidad Iberoamericana also appear to be becoming important centers for training Mexican political elites (see *Proceso*, March 31, 1986).

[40] See Cleaves (1985:122–130).

[41] Data on income indicate that professional fields continue to offer the hope of a higher salary, so the main pull factor has not changed; see, for example, BANAMEX (1983) for data on income and expenditure by level of academic achievement.

[42] The fading of popular hope, and the popular function, of the university is not admitted by all. Jorge Carpizo, rector of UNAM, said at a 1987 graduation ceremony (Lind 1987): "The UNAM is at the service of all sectors of the nation, transcending regional and sectorial limitations. . . . The UNAM makes no distinction of class or economic status. The university came into being in a poor country and has been a . . . canal of social ascension." For a different view of the historical representation of non–middle class sectors in UNAM, see Lewis (1958). Interestingly, Carpizo's words show that he is able to recognize the failure to achieve the first goal of the university system but not the distortions introduced by historical adherence to the second goal (quoted in Jacobsen 1987:A100).

[43] See *Voices of Mexico*, June–August 1986.

profile necessary for the social modernization of the country. The basic social improvements promised by the Revolution have not appeared automatically as products of "Mexican miracle" economic growth, and have lagged far behind improvements in economic infrastructure.

The university system reflects this bias and has developed problems of its own that have made it difficult to respond to historical needs for professional skills. According to many public and private sector managers and senior engineers, engineering expertise is not even being provided for the sustained and competitive development of the Mexican economy, even though this has been the emphasis of government budgets since the 1930s. Because the increasing diversity of modern engineering training worldwide, in both "social" and "economic" fields, is not well reflected in the Mexican system, Mexico is in danger of falling further behind the demands of its modernization goals.[44]

[44] See Clark (1987) on the problems of rapidly growing complexity in the modern university and university and government options for responding to this complexity.

The most significant finding of this study is that the Mexican government has the ability to stimulate the growth of professional fields in line with its modernization goals. By directly or indirectly expanding employment in fields important to the modernization effort, particularly through its control of the public sector wage structure, the Mexican government can direct student career decisions toward fields of needed professional expertise.

Mexican society may have gained historically from opening wide the university's doors in pursuit of the second goal of the higher education system, but must now allocate resources to meet the pressing need for high-level expertise for modernization. This study indicates that to achieve its modernization aims Mexico must expand the basic strategy adopted by its leaders since at least the 1930s and coordinate government and university policy with the country's specific needs for highly qualified professionals.

APPENDIX A

Construction of the Time Series and Notes on Their Interpretation

The major part of scholarly work on higher education in Mexico that attempts to quantify aspects of historical changes in the system has relied on enrollment statistics, which are easily found and are generally consistent over long periods of time. The three series I use here are superior to data on enrollment in several important ways, three of which are particularly significant in the context of the education of engineers.

First, differential dropout rates among professional fields mean that the field distribution of matriculated students in many cases differs from that of students who actually leave the system, either as egresados or titulados. This difference is particularly great between first-year students and leaving students and thus can be used to show how expectations for employment opportunities change during the course of professional education.[1] Enrollment statistics, though, are not the best gauge of available engineering expertise.

Second, dropout rates at public universities are much higher than those at private universities, and thus the importance of the public university system is overrepresented in enrollment data. As noted in the text, graduates of private universities may also be relatively more important for other reasons. Thus there is a double devaluation of the real role of the private university in the Mexican system inherent in the use of aggregate enrollment figures for public and private universities.

Third, the three series used here are far more accurate on a purely numerical level as to the availability of engineers and real employment opportunities than enrollment data. If only 26 percent of engineering students who entered UNAM in 1973 actually received degrees,[2] studies that attempt to measure supply and demand for human resources using undeflated enrollment figures may be off by almost 75 percent on the supply side. Likewise, demand calculations that do not take into account the difference in training level between engineering egresados and

[1] See UNESCO-SY and Urquidi and Lajou Vargas (1967:39, 46).

[2] Garza (1986).

titulados can be very misleading. Enrollment figures will remain most useful for quantifying the growth in enrollment rather than in trying to measure the effects of that growth in the higher education system and in society.

Mexican decennial censuses provide information on the development of professional fields, but only in very general terms. The censuses supply rough numbers of "technical and professional" employment positions (categorized by self-definition of census informants), but little information about the employment of engineers and less about the development of specific engineering fields. Further, census-taking techniques, particularly definition of employment categories, have changed numerous times since 1900.

For detailed coverage of shifts in the development of various engineering areas, we must consult data on professional education that can be disaggregated to reflect engineering field choices and the availability of particular areas of engineering expertise. The longest consistent series of such data—"professional degrees granted"[3]—is found in the *Anuario Estadístico* and *Compendio Estadístico* of Mexico's Dirección General de Estadística (DGE) and runs from 1900 to 1971.[4] The number of degrees granted in the various engineering fields by Mexican universities included in these statistical compilations gives a good indication of engineering expertise availability. Categories used by the DGE have not changed for the period 1900 to 1971, however, and thus do not reflect well shifts within or away from the traditional professional fields.

A second series useful in gauging the supply of engineers in Mexican society is constructed from the data on egresados of professional fields provided in the statistical yearbooks of ANUIES (Asociación Nacional de Universidades e Institutos de Enseñanza Superior). An egresado has finished all the necessary course work and has only to complete the final requirement, in the engineering fields generally a project involving practical application of engineering skills, to earn the degree. The number of egresados, then, indicates the number of relatively highly skilled persons available for employment in the engineering fields.[5] This series runs from 1967 to the present and

includes very detailed categories of engineering fields, thereby avoiding the problem of nonrepresentation of new fields.[6]

I have supplemented these two series with a third one, constructed from unpublished data on degrees registered with the DGP before employment begins. In practice, an employer may or may not require registration. The number of registrados represents some percentage of professionals practicing their profession or expecting employment in that field. Since professionals in certain fields can and do practice their professions without registration, these data also give an indication of differential demand for the various professions.[7]

These three series represent three different methods for tracking engineers and other professionals over time. The numbers of titulados and registrados represent conservative estimates of the historical production of professionals, and the egresados a more liberal gauge. The DGE has generally opted for the most restrictive measures and began using registrados instead of titulados in the *Anuario Estadístico* after 1971.[8] ANUIES, however, has increasingly employed the more open-ended definition of professional preparation represented by egresados. Although ANUIES included titulados data together with those for egresados in 1967–71, more recent publications provide only data on egresados.

These three indicators present different but complementary aspects of evolving engineering training and the supply of engineers in Mexico. They are intended as estimates of the number of persons employed or available for employment in a given engineering area. The data do not allow us to deduce the exact number of persons actually practicing a given engineering specialty at a certain level at a given time. But the numbers of titulados, egresados, and registrados are accurate gauges of the long-term trends in the development of engineering skills. Together, they provide a way to assess historical preparedness in the

---

[3] *Títulos expedidos* or *títulos otorgados.*

[4] The data are for the entire period 1900–27 and yearly from 1928 to 1971; thus, trends in the pre-1928 period are not discernible.

[5] Management views engineering egresados and titulados as more or less equals. The required final project is considered important in terms of practical experience, but is not seen as constituting a quantum leap in level of preparation. Another advantage to a firm of hiring an egresado is that egresados cannot demand the pay of titulados.

[6] Egresados have grown at the same rate as entering university students; thus, this indicator also gives an idea of the explosion in university enrollment without the disadvantages associated with the use of enrollment statistics.

[7] It should also be noted, however, that certain professionals, notably those in health and teaching professions, will almost always register their degrees. These individuals frequently work directly for government agencies in which proof of registration is required and verified.

[8] Data on degrees registered for the periods 1945–75 and 1945–76 were provided by the DGP for the DGE's *Anuario Estadístico* of 1975 and 1976. But these data are not consistent, the totals given for the second period being less than for the first period. The DGP has updated its files since the publication of these volumes; data used here are derived directly from unpublished DGP data.

engineering fields for the demands of a modernizing Mexico.[9]

Equally as important as their role in indicating available skills, these three indicators reflect the employment expectations of college students in Mexico. Because there is almost no formal career counseling in Mexican universities, these indicators represent a direct link between what I have termed "government modernization strategy," as expressed in government rhetoric and expenditure, and the career choices of students.

Numerical relationships among the three indicators can be calculated where data exist in overlapping years; the nature of these relationships is useful in data analysis. The data on egresados and titulados discussed in the text and shown graphically demonstrate, for example, that for every three engineering egresados in 1970, one person received an engineering degree. The absolute data on degrees registered with the DGP show a ratio of ten engineering egresados to one engineering registrado in 1980.

While such ratios give an idea of the relationships among the three categories at a given point in time, use of the ratios to extrapolate either forward or backward in time is misleading. The fact is that there is no way to determine with accuracy how many egresados become titulados, and how many then register their degrees with the DGP. Moreover, there is evidence that these ratios have changed over time—the number of egresados relative to both titulados and registrados has been increasing, although data on this trend are sketchy. Also, it is clear that the ratio differs from institution to institution, and especially between public and private schools. For all these reasons, attention must be focused on the implications of the relationships among the different data sets and historical changes in them rather than on the absolute data.[10]

It is important to explain why such differences exist between the three indicators. Engineers themselves suggest the following reasons:[11]

1. The registration process is difficult and time-consuming, often taking up to a year. While the university usually handles some part of the process, students are responsible for beginning it and seeing it through to completion.

2. Students find employment (within or outside their university career field) while still in school. They intend to finish their university work but never do.[12] If they do complete the degree, they may have no reason to register, as they are already employed.

3. There is often no need for the formal degree nor to register the degree in order to find employment. It is clear that in certain professions, especially business and engineering, a formal degree, much less a properly registered degree, is not required for employment.

4. Some egresados are women who leave the university to marry (although most engineering students are men). Employment opportunities are still quite limited for Mexican women and it is not considered failure, or bad form, to leave with the egresado diploma in order to marry or have children.[13]

In sum, it appears that many engineers are able to develop a marketable skill without earning the formal degree. That skill may not be directly related to the career area—simple matriculation at a university is a marketable status. Since public university education is essentially free, secondary school graduates are implicitly encouraged to continue their job search as college students at the large public universities.

But all egresados have not necessarily found work. Rather, the extra time spent completing the thesis or preparing for the professional examination for the degree is not perceived as making a great difference in one's ability to find employment. Arce Gurza (1982:257) sees this aspect of engineering education as one of the key points of difference between the older, classical professions and engineering, and one of the goals of university technical training: "the students acquire remunerative abilities which serve them in case they are obliged to interrupt the course of study before its conclusion."[14] The growing prac-

---

[9] Data have been adjusted to show one level of professional training only: the licentiate. The licentiate degree should not be confused with the United States bachelor's degree (B.A.). The licentiate degree represents a much greater degree of specialization and is better compared with European first-professional degrees (see de Grandpré [1969] for information on cross-national comparisons of degrees). The licentiate level is by far the most important numerically in Mexico, although with regard to engineering expertise in the broadest sense, technical education at the lower "vocation" level is also important; see discussion of this level below. All three statistical series used here refer to both public and private universities. All three have been adjusted to make them consistent over time and to facilitate comparisons among them.

[10] See Lorey (1988, Appendix B) for some calculated ratios between egresados, titulados, and registrados.

[11] Data from interviews and from questionnaires on professional career patterns.

[12] Cf. ECLA (1968) and Latapí (1980).

[13] For the graduate level, Malo, Garst, and Garza (1981) found that the three most important motives given by graduate egresados of UNAM for not finishing degree work were (1) not enough time to finish (42.1 percent); (2) process for presenting professional exam or project too complicated (8.1 percent); and (3) degree not necessary for work (7.4 percent); other reasons accounted for 30.3 percent.

[14] See also Arce Gurza (1982:259–260) for discussion of how this advantage (to the student) of engineering education was incorporated into a progressive degree structure in certain specialties.

tice of hiring in Mexico based on job entry examinations, in both public and private sectors, makes a degree increasingly less important in obtaining certain kinds of work (especially in business and engineering fields, where such exams are most common).[15]

At the same time, it is clear that egresados represent an intermediate level of professional training. In many engineering fields, egresados fill the demand for middle-level expertise while titulados or persons with graduate education hold more demanding and more rewarding positions. Blanca Petricioli and Clark Reynolds point out in regard to the training of Mexican economists, for example, that egresados frequently make up the pool of secretaries, clerks, compilers of data, and other auxiliary workers for both private firms and government agencies. More qualified titulados are the source of the Mexican system's professional economists. This difference in employment level is also true for engineering titulados and egresados; egresados frequently are taken on by public and private sector firms as technicians rather than as full engineers.[16]

---

[15] For a discussion of the growing importance of such exams, see Cleaves (1985:122–130). Many private and public sector corporations also provide training programs designed to make up for deficiencies in university background of new employees. IBM of Mexico, in offering training program grants in 1987, made demands that Mexican universities have not been able to make: that students have a grade point average of 8.0 (scale of 10) and be available for full-time study. IBM offered the program equally to both egresados and titulados, seeing no important qualitative difference between the two in terms of trainability.

[16] Reynolds and Petricioli (1967) suggest that it would be both beneficial and cost effective to invest in upgrading economics egresados to titulados, as there is a need for more highly trained economists while at the same time a surplus of egresados for low-paying auxiliary roles. Davis (1967), however, in regard to training of engineering technicians, sees a growing demand for auxiliary-level technicians in the industrial sector and suggests that technical training be expanded at the middle, rather than at the upper, level.

(Appendix B on overleaf)

APPENDIX B

The Time Series Data

Table 1

ENGINEERING TITULADOS, EGRESADOS, AND REGISTRADOS, 1929–85

Year	A. Titulados	Percent of Total Titulados	B. Egresados	Percent of Total Egresados	C. Registrados	Percent of Total Registrados
1929	79	26.7				
1930	117	35.8				
1931	62	17.7				
1932	98	24.7				
1933	65	18.5				
1934	92	17.7				
1935	87	19.1				
1936	124	28.5				
1937	128	27.6				
1938	170	37.4				
1939	148*	26.5*				
1940	148	32.7				
1941	137	18.9				
1942	142	16.8				
1943	299	33.1				
1944	287	28.3				
1945	253	24.5				
1946	348	32.0				
1947	337	28.5				
1948	320	28.2				
1949	495	43.2				
1950	256	23.7				
1951	401	21.0				
1952	461	22.9				
1953	434	20.4				
1954	554	21.9				
1955	651	24.8				
1956	480	20.7				
1957	1,164	37.7				
1958	894	26.5				
1959	705	23.4	3,377	40.1		
1960	1,013	32.1	3,631	39.2		
1961	1,048	28.6	4,012	38.3		
1962	1,349	30.8	4,443	37.3		
1963	1,305*	18.1*	4,771	36.3		
1964	1,406	22.9	5,023	36.1		
1965	1,731	28.1	*	*		
1966	1,689	25.4				
1967	1,948	23.9	3,729	24.1		
1968	2,429	31.8	4,595	27.9		
1969	2,324	26.7	5,674	27.3		
1970	2,564	22.3	6,877	30.0	3,248	25.9
1971	3,253	29.6	8,675	26.6	5,404	20.5
1972			8,846	30.1	3,570	22.4
1973			10,168	30.7	3,274	12.2
1974			11,114	28.4	5,046	9.8
1975			12,226	27.3	6,245	11.3
1976			13,903	26.6	7,882	15.4
1977			16,543	29.8	9,509	17.9
1978			16,794	28.3	9,919	19.9
1979			19,716	29.6	9,362	15.7

Table 1 (Continued)

Year	A. Titulados	A. Percent of Total Titulados	B. Egresados	B. Percent of Total Egresados	C. Registrados	C. Percent of Total Registrados
1980			20,581	29.6	9,390	16.2
1981			20,995	26.7	9,588	16.0
1982			22,687	26.5	11,528	16.4
1983			25,900	26.8	11,112	13.8
1984			26,435	26.8	14,121	16.1
1985					15,420	16.2

SOURCE: A: 1929–38, DGE-AE; 1939–63, DGE-CE; 1964–70, SEP-EPM; 1971, ANUIES-AE.
B: 1959–64, Urquidi and Lajous (1967); 1967–75, ANUIES-ESM; 1976–84, ANUIES-AE.
C: DGP, unpublished data.

Table 2

DEGREES GRANTED, THREE FIELDS, 1928–38

PART I. Absolute Data

Year	All	Civil	Chemical	Agricultural-Veterinary	Other
1928	134	38	10	32	54
1929	79	12	6	31	30
1930	117	17	3	61	36
1931	62	18	0	19	25
1932	98	24	4	24	46
1933	65	23	7	4	31
1934	92	37	10	19	26
1935	87	24	10	25	28
1936	124	49	9	21	45
1937	128	45	6	36	41
1938	170	53	38	13	66

PART II. Percentage Data

Year	Civil	Chemical	Agricultural-Veterinary	Other
1928	28.4	7.5	23.9	40.3
1929	15.2	7.6	39.2	38.0
1930	14.5	2.6	52.1	30.8
1931	29.0	0	30.6	40.3
1932	24.5	4.1	24.5	46.9
1933	35.4	10.8	6.2	47.7
1934	40.2	10.9	20.7	28.3
1935	27.6	11.5	28.7	32.2
1936	39.5	7.3	16.9	36.3
1937	35.2	4.7	28.1	32.0
1938	31.2	22.4	7.6	38.8

SOURCE: DGE-AE.

Table 3

ENGINEERING TITULADOS, EIGHT FIELDS,[1] 1939–71

PART I. Absolute Data

Year	Agricultural	Civil	Mechanical-Electrical	Chemical	Extractive	Veterinary	Topographical-Hydraulic	Petroleum	Other
1939	4	52	56	7	12	6	5	3	3
1940	11	53	42	9	6	8	13	2	4
1941	32	38	20	18	7	5	8	5	4
1942	19	41	25	22	2	16	8	1	8
1943	59	88	46	21	11	9	35	3	27
1944	62	89	54	21	9	7	23	6	16
1945	46	67	41	45	15	6	21	7	5
1946	109	71	57	37	12	7	33	1	21
1947	93	77	52	36	12	8	33	4	22
1948	76	82	46	34	11	9	33	7	22
1949	108	101	110	42	14	32	24	5	59
1950	51	102	14	34	6	10	8	7	24
1951	22	125	78	64	19	21	14	6	52
1952	45	111	54	104	14	22	20	9	82
1953	15	134	52	99	6	25	19	5	79
1954	86	181	90	91	10	27	13	12	44
1955	83	207	46	137	16	26	21	17	98
1956	167	89	88	48	1	16	10	16	45
1957	209	373	155	228	17	31	19	50	82
1958	159	254	169	123	15	40	18	30	86
1959	124	183	119	117	5	30	17	40	70
1960	245	294	174	103	23	21	19	69	65
1961	13	327	319	126	23	30	35	51	124
1962	66	365	374	221	54	50	54	71	94
1963	119	377	373	240	46	63	31	31	25
1964	97	468	347	168	35	92	35	60	104@
1965	91	618	468	177	35	119	35	60	128@
1966	116	542	491	159	35	126	35	60	125@
1967	179	577	442	215	44	218	46	83	144@
1968	209	679	629	393	40	213	31	55	180@
1969	114	733	578	289	33	286	47	72	172@
1970	206	755	694	318	36	251	39	75	190@
1971	317	858	941	466	52	261	31	86	241@

Table 3 (Continued)

PART II. Percentage Data

Year	Agricultural	Civil	Mechanical-Electrical	Chemical	Extractive	Veterinary Medicine	Topographical-Hydraulic	Petroleum	Other	Agricultural & Veterinary	Extractive & Petroleum
1939	2.7	35.1	37.8	4.7	8.1	4.1	3.4	2.0	2.0	6.8	10.1
1940	7.4	35.8	28.4	6.1	4.1	5.4	8.8	1.4	2.7	12.8	5.4
1941	23.4	27.7	14.6	13.1	5.1	3.6	5.8	3.6	2.9	27.0	8.8
1942	13.4	28.9	17.6	15.5	1.4	11.3	5.6	.7	5.6	24.6	2.1
1943	19.7	29.4	15.4	7.0	3.7	3.0	11.7	1.0	9.0	22.7	4.7
1944	21.6	31.0	18.8	7.3	3.1	2.4	8.0	2.1	5.6	24.0	5.2
1945	18.2	26.5	16.2	17.8	5.9	2.4	8.3	2.8	2.0	20.6	8.7
1946	31.3	20.4	16.4	10.6	3.4	2.0	9.5	.3	6.0	33.3	3.7
1947	27.6	22.8	15.4	10.7	3.6	2.4	9.8	1.2	6.5	30.0	4.7
1948	23.8	25.6	14.4	10.6	3.4	2.8	10.3	2.2	6.9	26.6	5.6
1949	21.8	20.4	22.2	8.5	2.8	6.5	4.8	1.0	11.9	28.3	3.8
1950	19.9	39.8	5.5	13.3	2.3	3.9	3.1	2.7	9.4	23.8	5.1
1951	5.5	31.2	19.5	16.0	4.7	5.2	3.5	1.5	13.0	10.7	6.2
1952	9.8	24.1	11.7	22.6	3.0	4.8	4.3	2.0	17.8	14.5	5.0
1953	3.5	30.9	12.0	22.8	1.4	5.8	4.4	1.2	18.2	9.2	2.5
1954	15.5	32.7	16.2	16.4	1.8	4.9	2.3	2.2	7.9	20.4	4.0
1955	12.7	31.8	7.1	21.0	2.5	4.0	3.2	2.6	15.1	16.7	5.1
1956	34.8	18.5	18.3	10.0	.2	3.3	2.1	3.3	9.4	38.1	3.5
1957	18.0	32.0	13.3	19.6	1.5	2.7	1.6	4.3	7.0	20.6	5.8
1958	17.8	28.4	18.9	13.8	1.7	4.5	2.0	3.4	9.6	22.3	5.0
1959	17.6	26.0	16.9	16.6	.7	4.3	2.4	5.7	9.9	21.8	6.4
1960	24.2	29.0	17.2	10.2	2.3	2.1	1.9	6.8	6.4	26.3	9.1
1961	1.2	31.2	30.4	12.0	2.2	2.9	3.3	4.9	11.8	4.1	7.1
1962	4.9	27.1	27.7	16.4	4.0	3.7	4.0	5.3	7.0	8.6	9.3
1963	9.1	28.9	28.6	18.4	3.5	4.8	2.4	2.4	1.9	13.9	5.9
1964	6.9	33.3	24.7	11.9	2.5	6.5	2.5	4.3	7.4	13.4	6.8
1965	5.3	35.7	27.0	10.2	2.0	6.9	2.0	3.5	7.4	12.1	5.5
1966	6.9	32.1	29.1	9.4	2.1	7.5	2.1	3.6	7.4	14.3	5.6
1967	9.2	29.6	22.7	11.0	2.3	11.2	2.4	4.3	7.4	20.4	6.5
1968	8.6	28.0	25.9	16.2	1.6	8.8	1.3	2.3	7.4	17.4	3.9
1969	4.9	31.5	24.9	12.4	1.4	12.3	2.0	3.1	7.4	17.2	4.5
1970	8.0	29.4	27.1	12.4	1.4	9.8	1.5	2.9	7.4	17.8	4.3
1971	9.7	26.4	28.9	14.3	1.6	8.0	1.0	2.6	7.4	17.8	4.2

1. For degrees included in fields, see Appendix C.

SOURCE: DGE-CE; ANUIES-ESM; SEP-EPM.

Table 4

ENGINEERING EGRESADOS, FOURTEEN FIELDS,[1] 1967–84

PART I. Absolute Data

Year	Agri-cultural	Extractive	Indus-trial	Mechanical & Mechanical-Electrical	Chemical	Topo-graphical-Hydraulic	Veterinary Medicine	Civil	Elec-trical	Computer	Architec-tural	Geo-graphical	Biochem-ical	Textile	Other
1967	144	73	255	930	562	72	338	803	54	0	105	24	26	124	219
1968	441	155	291	864	695	97	276	1,153	150	0	131	2	62	120	158
1969	484	137	357	1,224	928	98	378	1,332	168	0	157	5	62	114	230
1970	555	107	404	1,791	780	91	429	1,229	893	0	256	40	66	130	106
1971[a]	625	252	703	2,073	1,162	191	599	1,475	642	87	304	43	78	182	347
1972[b]	955	221	672	1,442	1,380	203	681	1,460	1,212	0	283	97	44	186	200@
1973[c]	986	295	915	1,525	1,678	142	773	1,718	1,190	51	397	92	163	214	200@
1974[d]	1,100	356	1,134	1,823	2,056	78	700	1,756	1,278	0	400	156	33	222	200@
1975[e]	1,663	367	1,418	1,846	1,785	208	880	1,809	1,198	0	489	159	61	220	200@
1976	1,627	245	1,714	2,226	2,048	200	853	2,431	1,201	47	345	270	207	232	257
1977	2,012	234	2,305	2,582	2,129	333	1,178	2,936	1,324	66	505	176	266	242	255
1978	2,162	157	2,193	2,300	1,835	304	1,454	3,529	1,473	144	538	247	101	94	263
1979	2,449	287	2,920	2,291	2,147	343	1,532	3,687	1,194	182	1,775	325	211	78	295
1980	3,824	295	3,045	2,159	1,648	285	1,765	4,069	1,918	230	310	381	246	77	329
1981	5,312	321	2,972	2,577	1,565	623	2,083	4,003	1,669	356	328	319	318	54	344
1982	6,001	312	3,403	2,379	1,798	500	2,350	4,314	1,630	354	382	297	264	68	468
1983	7,084	374	3,280	2,457	1,726	595	2,786	3,899	1,360	491	393	320	269	82	764
1984	7,306	399	3,558	2,436	1363	452	2,757	4,332	1,442	670	648	292	238	94	448

PART II. Percentage Data

Year	Agri-cultural	Extractive	Indus-trial	Mechanical & Mechanical-Electrical	Chemical	Topo-graphical-Hydraulic	Veterinary Medicine	Civil	Elec-trical	Computer	Architec-tural	Geo-graphical	Biochem-ical	Textile	Other
1967	3.9	2.0	6.8	24.9	15.1	1.9	9.1	21.5	1.4	0	2.8	.6	.7	3.3	5.9
1968	9.6	3.4	6.3	18.8	15.1	2.1	6.0	25.1	3.3	0	2.9	0	1.3	2.6	3.4
1969	8.5	2.4	6.3	21.6	16.4	1.7	6.7	23.5	3.0	0	2.8	.1	1.1	2.0	4.1
1970	8.1	1.6	5.9	26.0	11.3	1.3	6.2	17.9	13.0	0	3.7	.6	1.0	1.9	1.5
1971	7.2	2.9	8.1	23.9	13.4	2.2	6.9	17.0	7.4	1.0	3.5	.5	.9	2.1	4.0
1972	10.8	2.5	7.6	16.3	15.6	2.3	7.7	16.5	13.7	0	3.2	1.1	.5	2.1	2.3
1973	9.7	2.9	9.0	15.0	16.5	1.4	7.6	16.9	11.7	.5	3.9	.9	1.6	2.1	2.0
1974	9.9	3.2	10.2	16.4	18.5	.7	6.3	15.8	11.5	0	3.6	1.4	.3	2.0	1.8
1975	13.6	3.0	11.6	15.1	14.6	1.7	7.2	14.8	9.8	0	.4	1.3	.5	1.8	1.6
1976	11.7	1.8	12.3	16.0	14.7	1.4	6.1	17.5	8.6	.3	2.5	1.9	1.5	1.7	1.8
1977	12.2	1.4	13.9	15.6	12.9	2.0	7.1	17.7	8.0	.4	3.1	1.1	1.6	1.5	1.5
1978	12.9	.9	13.1	13.7	10.9	1.8	8.7	21.0	8.8	.9	3.2	1.5	.6	.6	1.6
1979	12.4	1.5	14.8	11.6	10.9	1.7	7.8	18.7	6.1	.9	.9	1.6	1.1	.4	1.5
1980	18.6	1.4	14.8	10.5	8.0	1.4	8.6	19.8	9.3	1.1	1.5	1.9	1.2	.4	1.6
1981	23.3	1.4	13.0	11.3	6.9	2.7	9.1	17.5	7.3	1.6	1.4	1.4	1.4	.2	1.5
1982	26.5	1.4	15.0	10.5	7.9	2.2	10.4	19.0	7.2	1.6	1.7	1.3	1.2	.3	2.1
1983	27.4	1.4	12.7	9.5	6.7	2.3	10.8	15.1	5.3	1.9	1.5	1.2	1.0	.3	3.
1984	27.6	1.5	13.5	9.2	5.2	1.7	10.4	16.4	5.5	2.5	2.5	1.1	.9	.4	1.7

1. For degrees included in fields, see Appendix C.

a. 14.7 percent of data estimated.
b. 15.9 percent of data estimated.
c. 15.4 percent of data estimated.
d. 15.8 percent of data estimated.
e. 18.7 percent of data estimated.

SOURCE: ANUIES-ESM; ANUIES-AE; unpublished data.

Table 5

INDEX OF ENGINEERING REGISTRADOS, NINE FIELDS,[1] 1970–85
(1980 = 100)

Year	Civil	Chemical	Agricultural	Extractive	Veterinary Medicine	Mechanical-Electrical	Mechanical	Electrical & Electronic	Industrial	Agricultural Eng. & Vet. Medicine
1970	46.8	40.6	30.8	20.7	42.3	59.5	28.8	25.9	29.5	36.6
1971	63.8	61.7	46.0	113.8	69.0	97.3	65.5	50.5	54.0	57.5
1972	43.0	41.8	39.4	89.7	43.6	68.7	34.8	30.7	26.6	41.5
1973	40.7	40.6	36.4	58.6	53.5	55.8	27.5	25.9	32.4	44.9
1974	61.0	56.6	61.1	175.9	42.5	72.5	63.6	51.2	65.5	51.8
1975	64.2	87.1	85.9	120.7	50.5	100.8	65.2	48.3	49.6	68.2
1976	94.5	96.0	99.5	137.9	65.4	101.1	80.3	58.5	76.3	82.4
1977	114.5	105.7	102.0	193.1	53.3	107.3	119.4	92.7	107.2	77.7
1978	118.9	109.8	85.4	144.8	97.1	102.7	108.6	81.6	89.9	91.2
1979	112.7	100.4	75.3	144.8	85.9	96.8	115.1	88.9	107.2	80.6
1980	100.0	100.0	100.0	100.0	100.0	100.0	100.0	100.0	100.0	100.0
1981	96.8	79.8	73.7	141.4	116.5	96.3	83.8	91.7	120.9	95.1
1982	121.0	87.0	69.2	113.8	127.3	93.6	121.6	129.9	179.9	98.2
1983	109.8	84.2	44.9	241.4	157.7	113.9	107.0	114.8	172.7	101.3
1984	135.3	105.3	79.8	248.3	230.4	123.7	174.7	148.2	275.5	155.1
1985	125.4	101.8	80.3	189.7	220.3	109.0	146.9	139.9	230.9	150.3

1. For degrees included in fields, see Appendix C.

SOURCE: DGP, unpublished data.

Table 6

INDEX OF ENGINEERING REGISTRADOS, PERCENTAGE DATA, NINE FIELDS,[1] 1970–85
(1980 = 100)

Year	Civil	Chemical	Agricultural	Petroleum	Veterinary	Mechanical	Mechanical-Electrical	Electrical & Electronic	Industrial	Agricultural-Vet. Medicine
1970	135.2	116.4	90.5	66.7	122.4	82.5	171.4	75.0	86.7	106.4
1971	110.5	106.8	81.0	200.0	120.7	112.5	167.9	87.5	93.3	100.8
1972	113.0	109.6	104.8	233.3	115.5	90.0	179.8	81.3	66.7	110.1
1973	116.0	116.4	104.8	166.7	153.4	77.5	159.5	75.0	93.3	129.1
1974	113.0	104.1	114.3	333.3	79.3	117.5	134.5	95.3	120.0	96.8
1975	96.3	130.1	128.6	200.0	75.9	97.5	151.2	73.4	73.3	102.2
1976	112.3	113.7	119.0	133.3	77.6	95.0	120.2	70.3	86.7	98.3
1977	113.0	104.1	100.0	200.0	53.4	117.5	106.0	92.2	106.7	76.7
1978	112.3	104.1	81.0	133.3	91.4	102.5	96.4	78.1	86.7	86.2
1979	113.0	100.0	76.2	133.3	86.2	115.0	96.4	89.1	106.7	81.2
1980	100.0	100.0	100.0	100.0	100.0	100.0	100.0	100.0	100.0	100.0
1981	94.4	78.1	71.4	133.3	113.8	80.0	94.0	90.6	120.0	92.6
1982	98.1	69.9	57.1	100.0	103.4	97.5	76.2	106.3	146.7	80.3
1983	92.6	71.2	38.1	200.0	132.8	90.0	95.2	96.9	146.7	85.4
1984	89.5	69.9	52.4	166.7	153.4	115.0	82.1	98.4	180.0	102.9
1985	75.9	61.6	47.6	133.3	134.5	87.5	66.7	85.9	140.0	91.1

1. For degrees included in fields, see Appendix C.

SOURCE: DGP, unpublished data.

APPENDIX C

Engineering Fields and Specialties

Titulados (Degrees Granted)[1]

Agricultural Engineering
  Agricultural
  Zoological
  Veterinary Medicine
Chemical Engineering
  Cemical
Civil Engineering
  Civil
Electrical, Mechanical, and Mechanical-Electrical
Engineering[2]
  Electrical
  Mechanical
  Mechanical-Electrical
Extractive Engineering
  Extractive
  Petroleum
  Mining
  Metallurgy
Other Engineering
  Other

Egresados[3]

Agricultural Engineering
  Agricultural (27 specialties). Most numerous spe-
    cialties: agronomy, plant biology, animal hus-
    bandry, parasitology, soils, production
  Fruticulture
  Forestry and Forest Development
  Rural Development
  Agroindustry

Agrochemistry
  Zoological Engineering (3 specialties)
  Veterinary Medicine
Chemical Engineering
  Chemical
  Industrial Chemical
  Administration
Civil Engineering
  Civil (8 specialties). Most numerous specialties:
    community development, structural, roads
  Municipal
  Construction
Computer Engineering
  Computer Systems
  Systems Administration
  Cibernetics and Computer Science
  Computers
Electrical and Electronic Engineering
  Electrical (6 specialties)
  Electronic
  Communications and Electronics
Extractive Engineering
  Petroleum
  Mining and Metallurgy
  Chemical—specialty in metallurgy and petroleum
Industrial Engineering
  Industrial (13 specialties). Most numerous special-
    ties: industrial, production, mechanical, electri-
    cal and electronic, chemical
Mechanical and Mechanical-Electrical Engineering
  Mechanical (2 specialties)
  Electromechanical (4 specialties)
Other Engineering
  Architectural
  Textile
  Wood
  Food Sciences
  Earth Sciences (geophysical, geographic, geologic,
    geochemical engineering)
  Aeronautic

[1] Basic field definitions for titulados are those of DGE-AE and DGE-CE; these sources do not generally indicate the specific makeup of these fields. The DGE organized engineering fields into the "classic" engineering groupings: agricultural, chemical, civil, electrical, mechanical, extractive. I include specialties when data from other sources have been incorporated to supplement the basic series.

[2] Electrical, mechanical, and mechanical-electrical engineering are combined here for several reasons. Much older data combine the three groups under one heading and separate fields cannot be disaggregated. Of the classic engineering fields, these three involve similar training. The fields are also closely related in modern practice in Mexico.

[3] The most numerous subfields are listed for each category. When the number of specialties is supplied in parentheses, quantity indicates highest number of specialties in recent years *that have produced egresados*. I also include cross-over degrees regardless of numerical importance (veterinary medicine under agricultural engineering, for example). Degree-program names vary from university to university; I have used the most common designations.

Registrados (Registered Degrees)[4]

Agricultural Engineering
  Agronomy
  Veterinary Medicine
Chemical Engineering
  Chemical
Civil Engineering
  Civil
Electrical and Electronic Engineering
  Electrical
  Communications and Electronics

Extractive Engineering
  Petroleum
  Mining and Metallurgy
Industrial Engineering
  Industrial
Mechanical
  Mechanical
Mechanical-Electrical Engineering
  Mechanical-Electrical

[4] Registrados fields represent only the most numerous specialty in each discipline, and thus are not comprehensive. For this reason, an index has been employed in the figures and Appendix B in order to show the relative growth of the different fields and for contrast with the other two series.

REFERENCES

Statistical Sources

ANUIES-AE   Asociación Nacional de Universidades e Institutos de Enseñanza Superior, *Anuario Estadístico*

ANUIES-ESM   Asociación Nacional de Universidades e Institutos de Enseñanza Superior, *La Enseñanza Superior en México* and *La Educación Superior en México*

DGE-AE   Dirección General de Estadística, *Anuario Estadístico*

DGE-CE   Dirección General de Estadística, *Compendio Estadístico*

DGP   Dirección General de Profesiones, unpublished data

IDB-SPTF   Inter-American Development Bank, Social Progress Trust Fund, *Socio-Economic Progress in Latin America* (1961–71)

INEGI-EHM   Instituto Nacional de Estadística, Geografía e Informática, *Estadísticas Históricas de México*

SALA   *Statistical Abstract of Latin America*, various. Los Angeles: UCLA Latin American Center Publications, University of California. Citations to SALA are given in abbreviated form. For example, SALA, 26–3400, refers to volume 26, table 3400.

SEP-EPM   Secretaría de Educación Pública, *La Educación Pública en México 1964/1970* (México, D.F., 1970).

UNESCO-SY   UNESCO *Statistical Yearbook*, 1984.

Other Sources

Arce Gurza, Francisco
  1982 "El Inicio de una Nueva Era, 1910–1945." In *Historia de las Profesiones en México*. México, D.F.: El Colegio de México.

BANAMEX (El Banco Nacional de México)
  1983 *Como Es México*. México, D.F.: BANAMEX.

Bazant, Mílada
  1982 "La República Restaurada y el Porfiriato." In *Historia de las Profesiones en México*. México, D.F.: El Colegio de México.

Camp, Roderic
  1980 *Mexico's Leaders: Their Education and Recruitment*. Tucson: University of Arizona Press.

Carnoy, Martin
  1977 *Education and Employment: A Critical Appraisal*. Paris: UNESCO, International Institute for Educational Planning.

Castañeda, María
  1987 "Mexico." *Journal of Higher Education*. Special report on the problems of exploding university enrollment. September.

Clark, Burton R.
  1987 "The Problem of Complexity in Modern Higher Education." Working Paper No. 9. Los Angeles: Comparative Higher Education Research Group, UCLA Graduate School of Education.

Cleaves, Peter S.
  1985 *Las Profesiones y el Estado: El Caso de México*. México, D.F.: El Colegio de México.

Cruz López, Antonio, Rodolfo Cortés Riveroll, and Francisco de Ita Crisanto
  n.d. "Parasitosis Intestinales en el Estado de Puebla." *Elementos* 12, Año 3, vol. 2. México, D.F.

Davis, Russell G.
  1967 *Scientific, Engineering and Technical Education in Mexico*. New York: Education and World Affairs.

de Grandpré, Marcel
  1969 *Glossaire international: Thèmes d'usage courant en matière de certificats d'études secondaires et de diplômes et l'enseignement supérieur dans quarante-cinq pays*. New York: UNESCO

ECLA
  1967 *Education, Human Resources, and Development in Latin America*. New York: United Nations.

Garza, Graciela
    1986 *La titulación en la UNAM.* México, D.F.: UNAM.
Glade, William P., Jr., and Charles W. Anderson
    1963 *The Political Economy of Mexico.* Madison: University of Wisconsin Press.
González Casanova, Pablo
    1962 "México: El Ciclo de una Revolución Agraria." *Cuadernos Americanos* 120:1 (January-February).
    1965 *Democracia en México.* México, D.F.: Ediciones Era.
Haber, Stephen
    1982 "Modernization and Change in Mexican Communities, 1930-1970." In James W. Wilkie and Stephen Haber, eds., *Statistical Abstract of Latin America,* volume 22. Los Angeles: UCLA Latin American Center Publications, University of California. Pp. 633-654.
Hellman, Judith Adler
    1983 *Mexico in Crisis.* New York and London: Holmes and Meier.
Institute of International Education
    1966 *La Agricultura y la Universidad.* Buenos Aires: Institute of International Education, Council of Higher Education in the American Republics.
Jacobsen, John
    1987 "Introduction." *Journal of Higher Education.* Special report on the problems of exploding university enrollment. September.
Latapí, Pablo
    1980 *Análisis de un Sexenio de Educación en México, 1970-1976.* México, D.F.: Editorial Nueva Imagen.
Lerner, Victoria
    1979 *La Educación Socialista.* México, D.F.: El Colegio de México.
Levy, Daniel C.
    1980 *University and Government in Mexico: Autonomy in an Authoritarian System.* New York: Praeger.
Lewis, Oscar
    1958 "Mexico desde 1940." *Investigación Económica* 18:185-256.
Lind, Scott
    1987 "Rector Warns Against Political Involvement." *The Mexico City News,* October 27.
Llinas Zárate, Isabel
    1987 "Se Cubrirá en Ciento por Ciento la Demanda de Primaria en el Próximo Ciclo Escolar." *Uno Más Uno,* August 23, p. 3.
Lorey, David
    1988 "Professional Expertise and Mexican Modernization: Sources, Methods, and Preliminary Findings." In James W. Wilkie, David Lorey, and Enrique Ochoa, eds., *Statistical Abstract of Latin America,* volume 26. Los Angeles: UCLA Latin American Center Publications, University of California.
Mabry, Donald J.
    1982 *The Mexican University and the State: Student Conflicts, 1910-1971.* College Station: Texas A&M Press.

Malo, Salvador, Jonathan Garst, and Graciela Garza
    1981 *El Egresado de Posgrado de la UNAM.* México, D.F.: UNAM.
Mosk, Sanford
    1950 *Industrial Revolution in Mexico.* Berkeley and Los Angeles: University of California Press.
Myers, Charles Nash
    1965 *Education and National Development in Mexico.* Princeton, N.J.: Industrial Relations Section, Princeton University.
Reynolds, Clark W.
    1967 *The Mexican Economy: Structure and Growth.* New Haven, Conn.: Yale University Press.
Reynolds, Clark W., and Blanca M. de Petricioli
    1967 *The Teaching of Economics in Mexico.* New York: Education and World Affairs.
Riding, Alan
    1984 *Distant Neighbors.* New York: Vintage Books.
Secretaría de Programación y Presupuesto
    1985 *Antología de la Planeación en México (1917-1985),* 19 volumes. México, D.F.: Fondo de Cultura Económica.
Silva Herzog, Jesús
    1974 *Una Historia de la Universidad de México y Sus Problemas.* México, D.F.: Siglo XXI.
Thomas, Brinley
    1972 *Migration and Urban Development: A Reappraisal of British and American Long Cycles.* London: Methuen and Company.
UNAM
    1986 *Fortaleza y Debilidad de la UNAM: Respuesta de la Comunidad Universitaria; Propuestas y Alternativas.* Suplemento extraordinario No. 16 (August). México, D.F.
Urquidi, Víctor, and Adrián Lajous Vargas
    1967 *Educación Superior, Ciencia y Tecnología en el Desarrollo Económico de México.* México, D.F.: El Colegio de México.
Vernon, Raymond, ed.
    1964 *Public Policy and Private Enterprise in Mexico.* Cambridge, Mass.: Harvard University Press.
Wichtrich, A. R.
    1979 "Manpower Planning—A Business Perspective." In Daniel Heyduk, ed., *Education and Work: A Symposium.* New York: Institute of International Education.
Wilkie, James W.
    1978 *La Revolución Mexicana: Gasto Federal y Cambio Social.* México, D.F.: Fondo de Cultura Económica.

3

The Class Structure of Mexico, 1895–1980

STEPHANIE GRANATO and AÍDA MOSTKOFF

Social change in Mexico since the 1910 Revolution has been of great interest to students of contemporary Mexico. Measuring the Mexican class structure over time provides one important way to understand the degree and nature of change that has occurred since the Revolution: a system of social stratification tells much about the progress and problems of a country. Since the Revolution, many changes have affected occupational stratification and income distribution in Mexican society, which in turn has altered Mexico's class structure.

Until Wilkie and Wilkins developed their time series on Mexico's class structure (1981), hereafter identified as the SALA series, there had been little attempt to formulate a comprehensive long-term measure of Mexico's class structure that could be systematically carried forward with data obtained at regular intervals. In their study, titled "Quantifying the Class Structure of Mexico, 1895–1970," Wilkie and Wilkins furnish a measure of class structure over an 85-year period that reveals considerable and continuous alterations in Mexico's underlying social fabric. Because of their work, it is now possible to apply census data to a structured methodology to obtain quantitative estimates for Mexico's class structure.

Our purpose here is threefold: to update the existing series; to examine, reevaluate, and more fully explain the methodology applied by Wilkie and Wilkins; and to examine the trends, patterns, and implications of the new updated series in the context of 1980 Mexico.

History of the Series

A brief summary of the development of the baseline data series provides the necessary background to discuss the present class structure series. In 1951 José Iturriaga developed baseline statistical estimates of Mexican class structure for 1895 and 1940. His series used occupation and standard of living as the indicators for class rank.

In 1963 Howard F. Cline constructed methodology that allowed him to build on Iturriaga's work and to estimate the Mexican class structure for 1940, 1950, and 1956. For 1940 Cline determined class structure according to language use and consumption patterns. Cline's 1950 and 1956 indicators used occupation and income. Thus data on standard of living and occupation in the Iturriaga estimates for 1895 and 1940 were linked by Wilkie and Wilkins to the Cline figures for 1950 and were then carried forward to 1960 and 1970. Wilkie and Wilkins's SALA series showed that Cline's 1940 and 1956 estimates were flawed because the latter used debatable criteria (e.g., language usage), and the estimate for 1956 was not based on population census material.

Although other class structure estimates have been made, such as those of John J. Johnson (1958) and Robert E. Scott (1959), the Cline-Iturriaga work represented the most logical and comprehensive estimates to build upon. The overlapping Cline-Iturriaga series provide both the database and the methodology for estimating class structure from pre-Revolu-

AUTHORS' NOTE: This essay is based on a paper presented at El Tercer Encuentro del Programa Linkages, UNAM-UCLA-UABC, "Estudios cuantitativos sobre la historia de México," Mexico City, August 8–9, 1986, and published as "The SALA Series on Class Structure in Mexico (1895–1970) Examined and Carried Forward to 1980," in Samuel Schmidt, James W. Wilkie, Manuel Esparza, eds., *Estudios Cuantitativos sobre la Historia de México* (México, D.F.: Universidad Nacional Autónoma de México, published jointly with UCLA and Universidad Autónoma de Baja California, 1988), pp. 103–128. We would like to thank Dr. Andrés Larraza for his valuable advice and suggestions on the arrangement of the statistical data.

tionary times to the present. According to Wilkie and Wilkins (1981:578):

Overlapping statistics for some of the same years by decade allow us to test the "reliability" of the estimates through an examination of the "logic" in the trajectory of the data. . . . The purpose here is to follow baseline methodology with adjustments, in order to carry combined analysis of occupations and incomes through 1960 and 1970.

Thus placing the Cline and Iturriaga estimates in the context of Mexican history showed the Iturriaga estimate for 1940 to be more logical than Cline's estimate (ibid.).

The SALA Series Concept of Class Structure

The class concept used in the SALA series combines elements of the methods used by Cline and Iturriaga. For example, Iturriaga used a standard three-class definition (upper, middle, lower) of class structure while Cline saw the lower group as two distinct classes (Cline 1963*b*:113–114):

. . . the opening up of society [since the Revolution] has created a stratum of people who do not fit neatly into any of the orthodox three main social classes. A new upper class, different in origins and functions from its pre-Revolutionary counterpart, has come into being; and at the base of the social pyramid there is still a large mass which is now, more politely, labelled 'popular' rather than 'lower class'. Between these two extremes, however, there is an important stratum whose class status is ambiguous. A large portion of this segment is, by generally accepted Western standards, unequivocally 'middle class', but there is also a substantial group remaining who do not quite fit this category, although economically and socially they have gone beyond the upper limits usually set for the 'lower class'. [I] propose therefore to call them collectively 'the transitional class'.

For the SALA series, Cline's popular and transitional classes became subclasses of the lower class.

To calculate the actual dimensions of class structure, the SALA series measures income distribution and occupational structure for the economically active population. This definition of class as a combination of occupation and income indicators is central to the SALA class structure series. The definition works for four reasons. First, in order to assure continuity of the baseline data series it is necessary to use the same indicators initially used to establish the class size estimates. Second, occupation and income figures for the Mexican population are readily available in current census data. Third, since we do not focus on the so-called subjective variables of social stratification, such as class consciousness, value orientation, life-

style, and peer perception, income and occupation indicators best show the trends and patterns that have characterized the Mexican class structure through time. Fourth, these criteria are based on a historical precedent of class concept: social theorists from Marx to Weber have defined class according to socioeconomic criteria. In a discussion of class concept Werner Slandecker (1981:29) writes that:

Like Marx, Weber stipulates a minimal requirement for a class system; without it classes cannot exist, but its presence alone is not sufficient basis for a high degree of class formation. Furthermore, both place this prerequisite within the economic realm, so that for Weber as for Marx, class stratification is basically economic stratification.

Combining the two factors of income and occupation essentially creates a socioeconomic index. Such an index measures the inequity or differences among the classes.

As Max Weber has shown, social stratification is not cut from a single piece of cloth. In any stratified population one finds that its members are unequal to one another not just in one respect, but in various ways. A stratification system must be viewed therefore, as a composite of several qualitatively different kinds of inequity. They will be designated as rank systems to distinguish them from the total stratification system of which they are components. Basic to the concept of stratification as consisting of a number of rank systems is the view that stratified society occupies a number of positions in that society. These positions, not their occupant per se, carry a given amount of status in a particular rank system. Positions may include occupational roles, education, ancestry, (and) material objects acquired. [Ibid., p. 18]

Although there are several possible variables for measuring class structure, such as consumption patterns, education, and place of residence, income and occupation still seem to be the most valid. In a discussion of changing class structure Cline acknowledges the increased importance of economic status in the Mexican social system since the Revolution (1963*a*:84–85):

[Upper class status] is now something that can be achieved; once upon a time the only way to get [into the upper class was] by birth . . . but now [status is] derived from attainable position bestowed by political power, economic wealth, and sometimes intellectual talents. Abundant leisure, a high standard of living, and a general air of "refinement" are also usually present. Normally, pride in lineage and consciousness of who is "in" and who is "out" of class are strong, but in Mexico the Revolution has damped down much talk of that, though some of the older families are still avid genealogists. Political conservatism, the tendency to look abroad for social and economic models, and incomes drawn from large investments, could be joined to these other items to complete a profile of the upper class. Recruits come from rising middle-class families; occasionally a successful Indian leader, like Juan Amaro, rises up into this stratosphere. It is a very small group, probably composed of no more than from 10,000 to 30,000 individuals in contemporary Mexico, though this is but a guess. No one has ever counted this group, which now includes a handful of large property owners, industrialists, large merchants, private bankers, successful national politicians, and large-scale entrepreneurs. In Mexico, as elsewhere, "upper class" is a shadowy matter.

Lines between the middle and the upper class are thin. Mainly the middle class is defined by its economic dependence on personal work which requires education, technical training, or administrative abilities, equipment the individual has developed for himself. Middle-class or "white-collar" standards of living ape the upper class on a little lower scale. A middle-class trait is the urge to keep up the appearances of gentility and to observe proper social forms, even at considerable economic sacrifice. Traditionally the components of the class have been bureaucrats, teachers, small businessmen, storekeepers, skilled laborers, small industrialists, intellectuals, and members of the professions. In Mexico, recruits to the middle class have come from above and below. Dispossessed *hacendados* and their sons, social victims of radical agrarianism, drop a notch or so, for instance, as do displaced politicians whose influence and income wane when their faction drops from official favor. The expanding business and government bureaucracy, the industrialization and the constant upgrading of labor, the agrarian programs building individual yeoman-size units, the urbanization, and the developing system of technical and higher education, all create routes by which the members of the "popular class" and their children can move up the scale.

Mexican social and political systems are now based on the "popular class," which in any other society would be called an outright "lower class." Like their counterparts all over the globe, these various Mexican groups fall below minimum standards in education, living quarters, furnishings, clothes, diets, even recreational pursuits. Most if not all are manual laborers, dependent on their hands and backs rather than their minds for livelihoods, sweated out in drudgery. Their low economic skills bring them small cash incomes, with the subsequent marginal standards of living.

Income, more than any other factor, facilitates the acquisition of advantages such as education, health care, and material security which in turn creates a secure environment for individual and family life. Income and occupation are closely related because income often depends on the type of occupation a particular worker engages in. Because of its ability to bring a certain level of income, occupation is a means of passing advantages from parents to children. If the head of the household holds a prestigious job and earns a secure income the rest of the family will probably enjoy a comfortable living standard and hence a secure position (upper or middle) in the social strata.

Methodology

An examination of the specific methodology used in the construction of the income, occupation, and combined income-occupation tables illustrates how class dimensions are measured in the SALA series and carried forward to 1980.

Income

Table 1 shows calculations for individual income distribution from 1895 to 1980. As stated above, Iturriaga's estimates for 1895 and 1940 were made on the basis of occupation and standard of living. Calculations for the years from 1950 to 1980 have been made using a series of steps that begins with the division of monthly salaries into upper, middle, and lower class levels of earnings. The wage divisions are measured in pesos according to a scheme devised by Cline. He determined that in 1950 pesos, 300 pesos per month was "the minimum for a reasonably secure but marginal living in Mexico" (Cline 1963a: 116). Cline then developed the remaining income/class divisions. He considered anyone earning from 1 to 299 pesos per month part of the lower class. Those earning from 300 to 999 pesos per month constituted the middle class and those with a minimum monthly salary of 1,000 pesos constituted the upper class.

In order to compare data over time it is necessary to measure income in constant pesos. A deflator is applied to wage data to convert current pesos to their 1950 equivalent. Table 2 shows income distribution measured in 1950 pesos from 1950 to 1970. The index used in this series is the wholesale price index prepared by Mexico's Dirección General de Estadística (DGE). Because of political considerations, however, the DGE wholesale price index ceased publication in 1976. As Wilkie notes (1985:863):

By the early 1970s the DGE wholesale price index was showing inflation to be at an embarrassingly high level compared to the BDM wholesale price index. The issue was resolved in 1975 when the government of President Luis Echeverría Alvarez (1970–76), realizing that it could enjoy better propaganda mileage out of the BDM wholesale price index (and could hold down increases in wage levels if the higher index were dropped), suppressed the DGE wholesale price index.

An alternative to the DGE index was to use the Banco de México (BDM) wholesale price index, which carries forward to 1982. Compared with other measures, however, the BDM appears to significantly understate inflation after 1965. A second alternative was to use Wilkie's DGE–BDM composite index of

Table 1

INCOME DISTRIBUTION MEASURED IN 1950 PESOS, 1950–80[a]
(Constant Pesos and %)

Workers by Class and Subclass[b]	Minimum Monthly Income[c]	1950 N	1950 %	1960 N	1960 %	1970 N	1970 %	1980 N	1980 %
Upper	**	148,461	1.8	411,874	5.6	881,010	7.0	1,231,461.0	6.7
Leisure	3,000.0	20,068	.2	72,566	1.0	194,089	1.5	451,217.0	2.5
Semi-leisure	1,000.0	128,393	1.6	339,308	4.6	686,921	5.5	780,244.0	4.2
Middle	**	1,602,546	19.4	1,597,803	21.8	4,406,548	32.5	6,684,982.0	36.3
Stable	600.0	267,567	3.2	352,334	4.8	980,870	7.9	2,050,498.0	11.1
Marginal	300.0	1,334,979	16.2	1,245,469	17.0	3,065,678	24.6	4,634,484.0	25.2
Lower	**	6,521,081	18.8	5,306,692	72.6	7,539,078	60.5	10,481,192.0	57.0
Transitional	200.0	2,097,934	25.4	1,154,035	15.8	1,542,960	12.4	2,208,240.0	12.0
Popular	0.0	4,423,147	53.4	4,152,607	56.8	5,996,118	98.1	8,272,952.0	45.0
Total	**	8,272,093	100.0	7,316,321	100.0	12,466,636	100.0	18,397,635.0	100.0

a. For figures on class structure for 1895 and 1940, see Wilkie and Wilkins (1981).

b. The highest income category for the 1980 census actually translates into 1,675.5 pesos of 1950. The 3,000+ minimum could not be calculated with the present methodology due to the change in census income categories. The highest income category for the 1980 census (22,171+ pesos) may serve as a rough estimate (probably overstated) of the size of the leisure class. Class totals are more likely to be accurate than smaller subclass totals.

c. The total economically active population surveyed.

SOURCE: Income categories follow Cline (1963b) except for the popular class which was expanded to include unpaid workers. Income figures for 1980 are deflated using the DGE-EPI (see Appendix A). Revised data on income by class are calculated from Mexico, DGE (1953b:42, 66; 1964b, table 1; 1964c:53; 1972:285, 288; 1984:191).

Table 2

INCOME DISTRIBUTION MEASURED IN 1950 PESOS, 1950–70
(Constant Pesos and %)

Workers by Class and Subclass[b]	Minimum Monthly Income[c]	1950 N	1950 %	1960 N	1960 %	1970 N	1970 %
Upper	**	148,461	2.0	411,874	5.7	881,010	7.6
Leisure	3,000.0	20,068	.3	72,566	1.0	194,089	1.7
Semi-leisure	1,000.0	128,393	1.7	339,308	4.7	686,921	5.9
Middle	**	1,602,546	22.0	1,597,803	22.2	4,046,548	34.8
Stable	600.0	267,567	3.7	352,334	4.9	980,870	8.4
Marginal	300.0	1,334,979	18.3	1,245,469	17.3	3,065,678	26.4
Lower	**	5,547,038	76.0	5,185,469	72.1	6,692,911	57.6
Transitional	200.0	2,097,934	28.7	1,154,035	16.1	1,542,960	13.3
Popular	1.0	3,449,104	47.3	4,031,432	56.0	5,149,951	44.3
Total	**	7,298,050	100.0	7,195,146	100.0	11,620,469	100.0

SOURCE: Wilkie and Wilkins (1981:581).

prices which links the DGE wholesale price index and the BDM GDP deflator at 1965. This DGE–BDM composite index of prices provides a more liberal estimate of inflation than the BDM wholesale index. The DGE–BDM is essentially a GDP deflator after 1965.

Since the BDM is the only existing wholesale price index that extends forward to 1980, the third choice for the SALA series was to calculate an alternative wholesale price index. Using the DGE's 1976 inflation figure as a base and the percentage change in inflation from 1976 to 1980 as measured by the BDM wholesale price index, we calculated a new wholesale price index for 1980. We call this the DGE estimated price index, or DGE-EPI. Calculations yielded a 1980 inflation index equal to 1323.5 with 1950 as a base year. (See Appendix A.) The DGE-EPI lies between the conservative BDM wholesale price index and Wilkie's DGE-BDM composite price index.

Once income figures have been deflated, the wage earners in each income group are divided according to the income distribution schema used in the SALA series. The series uses the following Income Proportion Equation (IPE) to divide wage earners in the census categories into the schema:

    a. Proportion of lower income group $= (P/R)$ $(D - r_1)$

    b. Proportion of upper income group $= (P/R)$ $(r_2 - D)$

Where P = persons within a stated income range; R = range of income distribution given by census figures (i.e., upper minus lower limit of the range); r_1 = lower limit of the income range; r_2 = upper limit of the income range; D^* = the peso value of the dividing line between subclasses in the SALA income schema; and D = the peso value of the dividing line (D^*) in current terms (Wilkie and Wilkins 1981:581).

A three-step example illustrates the application of the IPE to 1980 census data.

Step 1.—Deflate current census income figures to 1950 terms using the DGE-EPI. When deflated to 1950 pesos the first three income ranges for the 1980 census fall below the 200-peso boundary which separates the popular and transitional subclasses. The fourth monthly income category records 2,828,538 workers with a monthly salary of 1,971 to 3,610 pesos. These income figures are converted to 1950 pesos which gives a range of 148.9 to 272.7 pesos. Therefore this category overlaps the 200-pesos dividing line between the popular and transitional classes.

Step 2.—Calculate the value of the dividing line in current terms. The dividing line of 200 must be

"inflated" using the DGE-EPI = 1323.5. $D = 200 \times$ $1323.5 = 2647$.

Step 3.—Apply the IPE. For this example, then, $P = 2,828,538$ workers; $R = 3610 - 1971 = 1639$; $r_1 = 1971$; $r_2 = 3610$; $D^* = 200$; $D = 2647$.

Because formulas *a* and *b* are mathematical equivalents they will yield the same division and become a useful means of checking calculations. The IPE, then, yields, 1,166,776 or the original 2,828,538 below the 200-peso dividing line (popular category) and 1,661,762 above the 200-peso dividing line (transitional category).

Occupation

Like income, occupation relies on a proportional distribution formula for assigning workers to upper, middle, and lower classes. Table 3 places workers in eight occupational categories according to principal position (managerial, professional, office workers, tradesmen, artisans, services, agricultural workers, and an unspecified category). The occupations are arranged to reflect their relative prestige. According to Donald J. Treiman (1977:5) this hierarchy is helpful for measuring the Mexican class structure because:

> Specialization of function carries with it important differences in the control over scarce resources which is the primary basis of stratification. These resources include skill, authority, and property each of which functions in a somewhat different way. Together they create differential power in the most general sense of the term.

Further, Treiman (ibid., p. 17) argues that within the same occupation substantial differences in income and prestige may be found.

> In fact occupations perhaps more than any other social roles are multifaceted. They vary in terms of the tasks they entail, the setting in which they are performed, the relations of authority they imply.

The occupations in Table 3 are therefore divided among six social subclasses according to a scheme that reflects both the implicit occupational hierarchy and the variance within any given occupation. At the extremes the SALA series places all workers with managerial positions in the leisure subclass and all agricultural workers in the popular subclass. The remaining groups are fractionally divided among upper, middle, and lower classes in the following manner (Wilkie and Wilkins 1981:582):

> Professionals and technicians are also usually well trained, but some distinction must be drawn, for example, between technicians in high government positions and primary

Table 3

OCCUPATIONAL STRATIFICATION IN MEXICO, 1950–80

Workers by Class and Subclass[b]	Share of Workers[a]	1950 N	1950 %	1960 N	1960 %	1970 N	1970 %	1980 N	1980 %
Upper	**	134,087	1.6	231,834	2.0	564,231	4.4	788,252	3.6
Managerial	All	65,108	.8	95,132	.8	319,828	2.5	260,834	1.2
Professional	1/3	68,979	.8	136,702	1.2	244,403	1.9	527,418	2.4
Middle/Stable	**	546,088	6.6	961,421	8.5	1,299,817	10.0	2,581,101	11.7
Professional	2/3	137,960	1.7	273,405	2.4	488,806	3.8	1,054,836	4.8
Office Workers	1/2	192,407	2.3	346,570	3.1	488,589	3.8	991,604	4.5
Tradesmen	1/3	215,721	2.6	341,446	3.0	322,422	2.4	534,661	2.4
Middle/Marginal	**	823,176	10.0	1,324,911	11.7	1,728,938	13.4	3,130,770	14.2
Office Workers	1/2	192,407	2.3	346,571	3.1	483,590	3.8	991,604	4.5
Tradesmen	1/3	215,722	2.6	341,446	3.0	322,422	2.4	534,662	2.4
Artisans[b]	1/3	415,047	5.1	636,894	5.0	922,926	7.2	1,604,504	7.3
Lower/Transitional	**	1,653,292	20.0	2,370,898	20.9	3,208,686	24.8	5,461,774	24.7
Tradesmen	1/3	215,722	2.6	341,446	3.0	322,423	2.4	534,662	2.4
Artisans	2/3	830,094	10.1	1,273,788	11.2	1,845,854	14.4	3,209,009	14.5
Services	2/3	607,476	7.3	755,664	6.7	1,040,409	8.0	1,718,103	7.8
Lower/Popular	**	5,115,450	61.8	6,442,952	56.9	6,148,385	47.4	10,104,187	45.8
Services	1/3	303,740	3.6	377,832	3.4	520,205	4.0	859,051	3.9
Agriculture	All	4,811,710	58.2	6,065,120	53.5	4,952,200	38.2	5,511,763	25.0
Unspecified	All					675,980	5.2	3,733,373[c]	16.9
Total	**	8,272,093	100.0	11,332,016	100.0	12,955,057	100.0	22,066,084[d]	100.0

a. Estimates from Cline (1963b:121)
b. Includes semi-skilled workers.
c. Includes 124,391 in a category labelled "nunca ha trabajado."
d. Includes the total economically active population.

SOURCE: 1950–1970: Wilkie and Wilkins (1981:582).
1980: Mexico, DGE (1984:table 10).

school teachers who, too, are professionals. Therefore, one-third of the professionals are classified as upper class, the other two-thirds are classified as stable middle class. Office workers vary greatly between public and private enterprise, and between local and international levels of operation. Office workers are thus evenly divided between the stable and marginal middle class. Also, differences apply to tradesmen and artisans, whose career will differ according to education or skills, background, connections, or locale. Tradesmen are split with one-third each allocated to the stable and marginal middle class, and the final third counted with the transitional class. One-third of the artisans belong to the marginal middle class; two-thirds belong to the transitional sector. Service workers are generally unskilled urban migrants or poorer urban born. The distribution of service workers has two parts counted as transitional, with one part added to the total group of agriculturalists to form the popular sector.

The unspecified occupation category has been included in census data only since 1970. All of the workers in this category are included in the popular class for reasons discussed in the methodological explanation.

Because the categories are fairly general they remain valid over time even though the relative importance of specific occupations such as taxi drivers and sales clerks may shift. The hierarchy of the general categories remains a "realistic" appraisal of reality. The more specialized and developed a society becomes, the more defined and stable the occupational hierarchy becomes.

Synthesis of Data

Utilization of statistics from Mexico's decennial population census imposes certain restrictions on the type and quality of data available. The organization of the census data and terminology employed have changed from period to period requiring slight adjustments in both income and occupation calculations used to measure class structure. Before we can discuss the occupation and income data it is necessary to examine the changes in the 1980 census that resulted in modifications in the methodology used to calculate the SALA series. The most significant change occurred in the income tables: the explicit inclusion of categories for unpaid workers and workers with unspecified income in the census income figures required a recalculation of income distribution for the years 1950 through 1970. Although figures for unpaid workers and workers with unspecified income were implicitly available for 1950, 1960, and 1970, they were not included in the census income tables until 1980 and were therefore not included in the original SALA calculations. The original SALA series calculations showed a discrepancy between the total economically active population and the number of workers with declared income for 1950, 1960, and 1970.

The following adjustments for 1950, 1960, and 1970 resolve possible differences in the totals of the economically active population given in the SALA income distribution and occupational stratification tables. Though not explicitly stated in the 1950 income table, a figure for unpaid workers for that year can be found with occupational data in the category titled "ayudan a la familia sin retribución." Adding the total number of workers in this category, 974,043, to the total workers with declared incomes, 7,298,050, gives the total economically active population, 8,272,093 (the figure given in the occupation table). Thus there are no workers with unspecified income for 1950.

Similar calculations for 1960 yield a group with indeterminate income. The total economically active population is given as 11,332,106. The number of workers with declared incomes is 7,195,146 and the number of unpaid workers (again found with occupational data) is 121,171. Subtracting the workers with declared incomes and the unpaid workers from the total economically active population yields a discrepancy of 4,015,695 workers with indeterminate income. Like those for 1960, figures for 1970 yield numbers for unpaid and unspecified workers. Figures for workers with zero or unspecified income are given in Table 4.

Table 1, showing income distribution, has been revised to include figures for unpaid workers. Workers with unspecified income are excluded. Why include unpaid workers but not workers with unspecified income? According to income standards, workers without pay share approximately the same purchasing power as those earning one peso. Therefore they fit into our classification scheme in the lowest (popular) subclass. Unlike workers with zero earning power, workers in the unspecified income category may have several reasons for not revealing their earnings: fear of taxation, desire to keep their economic standard hidden, workers with irregular jobs may not know their average monthly salary, and therefore cannot report it, and so on.

Workers with unspecified occupations, unlike those with indeterminate income, are included in the calculations for occupational stratification for several reasons. Most importantly, the structure of the census facilitates reporting of upper- and middle-class occupations because it lists broad but specific categories for these types of occupations, such as professional and technical jobs. However, many workers in the economically active lower classes hold a variety of temporary jobs that are not specifically listed, making reporting such a job more difficult if not impossible. It is more likely that these individuals will report their occupations as unspecified. Therefore, we include workers with unspecified employment in the popular subclass.

Changing occupational definitions and categories is another difficulty posed by census data. As shown by the changes in income categories, working with census data can be confusing. From 1960 to 1970, occupational categories showed minor shifts. The 1980 census expanded the eight occupational categories of 1970 to 22 separate categories. Figure 1 shows how 1980 categories were distributed among 1970 groupings. Because of slight changes in definitions for some types of occupations, the 1980 groupings fit closely but not exactly into the 1970 categories.

Table 4

WORKERS WITH UNSPECIFIED INCOME OR OCCUPATION AND UNPAID WORKERS,[a] 1950–80

(N and %)

Workers	1950 N	1950 %	1960 N	1960 %	1970 N	1970 %	1980 N	1980 %
Unpaid	974,043	11.8	121,175	1.1	488,421	3.7	4,334,008	19.6
Unspecified Income	**	**	4,015,695	35.4	488,167	6.5	3,688,449	16.7
Unspecified Occupation	**	**	**	**	675,980	5.2	3,733,373	16.9

a. Changes in the means of asking census questions and organizing data may account in part for the large percentage fluctuation in unpaid workers with unspecified occupation.

SOURCE: Mexico, DGE (1953b:66; 1964b:table 1; 1964c:53; 1972:285, 288; 1984:191).

Figure 1

**CHANGES IN OCCUPATIONAL CATEGORIES
OF THE MEXICAN CENSUS, 1970 to 1980[a]**

Categories in the SALA Series	DGE 1970 Census	DGE 1980 Census
1. Managerial	a. Public and Private Managers	a. Managers in the Private Sector b. Public Functionaries c. Agriculture and Fishing Administrators
2. Professional	a. Professionals and Technicians	a. Teachers b. Professionals c. Technicians and Specialized Personnel d. Arts Personnel
3. Office Workers	a. Administrative Personnel	a. Office Workers
4. Tradesmen	a. Merchants, Vendors, etc.	a. Shop Workers b. Street Vendors
5. Artisans	a. Nonagricultural Workers	a. Artisans and Factory Workers b. Assistants to Factory Workers c. Factory Workers' Supervisors
6. Services	a. Workers in Diverse Services and Vehicle Drivers	a. Domestic Workers b. Transportation Operators c. Security Personnel d. Service Personnel
7. Agriculture	a. Workers in the Agriculture and Fishing Sectors	a. Agricultural Workers b. Agriculture and Fishing Supervisors c. Agriculture and Fishing Machine Operators
8. Unspecified	a. Insufficiently Specified	a. Not specified

a. Categories from the 1970 and 1980 Mexican censuses are placed in the eight categories used in the SALA series.

SOURCE: Mexico, DGE (1972:table 30; 1984:table 10).

In addition to incorporating modified definitions, the Mexican census uses three terms to identify occupation: principal occupation, occupational position, and branch of economic activity. The principal occupation categories are really subcategories of the more general occupational position categories: both reflect a specific occupational hierarchy. The principal occupation figures are the basis for the SALA occupational stratification data. The third category, branch of economic activity, gives a breakdown of workers according to the sector of the economy they are employed in, such as industry or mining.

Although they are qualitatively different, the terms branch of economic activity and principal occupation have often been understood to represent the same concept. On the contrary, whereas principal occupation (such as manager or office worker) necessarily represents a hierarchical ranking, branch of economic activity does not. To add to the confusion, though most categories in the branch of economic activity data are not associated with a specific degree of

prestige, a few, such as agriculture, represent both an economic sector and a specific (low) prestige rank among occupations. Although the agriculture category transcends the boundaries of an economic sector to become a category of the principal occupation, other branches of economic activity do not cross this boundary. Therefore, principal occupation figures rather than economic sector data must be used to measure occupational stratification. Occupational stratification figures for 1950–80 are given in Table 3.

Recently, Mexican academic lore has tried with some reason to discredit the 1980 population census by claiming that it is not a valid source for analyzing the employment situation in Mexico. The lore notes, rightly, that 30 percent of Mexico's economically active persons in 1980 did not indicate the *branch* of economic activity in which they worked, thus compromising historical series on occupation by branch. However, the lore uses, wrongly, the same "30 Percent Factor" to try to discredit interpretation about the history of employment by *principal occupation*. In reality, the share of persons not specifying their prin-

Table 5

MEXICO CLASS STRUCTURE: REVISED

(%)

Class and Subclass	1950			1960			1970			1980		
	Income[a]	Occupation	Combined[a]	Income[a]	Occupation	Combined[a]	Income	Occupation	Combined[a]	Income	Occupation	Combined[a]
Upper	1.8	1.6	1.7	5.6	2.0	3.8	7.0	4.4	5.7	6.7	3.6	6.2
Leisure	.2	.8	.5	1.0	.8	.9	1.5	2.5	2.0	2.4	1.2	1.8
Semi-leisure	1.6	.8	1.2	4.6	1.2	2.9	5.9	1.9	3.7	4.3	2.4	3.4
Middle	19.4	16.6	18.0	21.8	20.2	21.0	32.5	23.4	27.9	36.3	25.9	31.1
Stable	3.2	6.6	4.9	4.8	8.5	6.6	7.9	10.0	8.9	11.1	11.7	11.4
Marginal	16.2	10.0	13.1	17.0	11.7	14.4	24.6	13.4	19.0	25.2	14.2	19.7
Lower	78.8	81.8	80.3	72.6	77.8	75.2	60.5	72.2	66.4	67.0	70.5	63.7
Transitional	25.4	20.0	22.7	15.8	20.9	18.4	12.4	24.8	18.6	12.0	24.7	18.3
Popular	53.4	61.8	57.6	56.8	56.9	56.8	48.1	47.4	47.8	45.0	45.8	45.4
Total	100.0	100.0	100.0	100.0	100.0	100.0	100.0	100.0	100.0	100.0	100.0	100.0

a. Arithmetic average of the data for income and occupation.

SOURCE: Tables 1 and 3, above.

Table 6

MEXICO CLASS STRUCTURE

(%)

Class and Subclass	1950			1960			1970		
	Income[a]	Occupation	Combined[a]	Income[a]	Occupation	Combined[a]	Income	Occupation	Combined[a]
Upper	3.0	1.6	2.3	6.5	2.0	4.3	7.6	4.4	6.0
Leisure	.4	.8	.6	1.1	.8	1.0	1.7	2.5	2.1
Semi-leisure	2.6	.8	1.7	5.4	1.2	3.3	5.9	1.9	3.9
Middle	23.6	16.6	20.1	23.4	20.2	21.8	34.8	23.4	29.1
Stable	5.3	6.6	6.0	5.4	8.5	6.9	8.4	10.0	9.2
Marginal	18.3	10.0	14.1	18.0	11.7	14.9	26.4	13.4	19.9
Lower	73.4	81.8	77.6	70.1	77.8	73.9	57.6	72.2	64.9
Transitional	22.2	20.0	21.1	16.0	20.9	18.4	13.3	24.8	19.0
Popular	51.2	61.8	56.5	54.1	56.9	55.5	44.3	47.4	45.9
Total	100.0	100.0	100.0	100.0	100.0	100.0	100.0	100.0	100.0

a. Arithmetic average of the data for income and occupation.

SOURCE: Wilkie and Wilkins (1981:581).

cipal occupation was 16–17 percent for 1980 and 5 percent for 1970. (See Table 4 and Appendix B.) For 1950 and 1960, 100 percent of the workers gave their principal occupation. (See Appendix B.) Hence the data on principal occupation, used here in our occupational stratification analysis, are relatively reliable for interpretation across time.

Criticism of census data shortcomings (especially in Mexico) can be a useful tool for analysis and revision. In this case, however, the stratification data cannot be discredited on the basis of concept. The figure for unspecified workers in the principal occupation table (the table used in our occupational stratification analysis) is approximately one-half the figure given for unspecified workers in the branch of economic activity table (see Appendix B).

One final qualification with respect to census figures must be made before class structure estimates can be understood: the current form of the census measures only the economically active population. Therefore class structure estimates for the economically active population must serve as a proxy for the living standards of the entire population. Even so, the census is still the most complete and regular source available.

Arithmetically averaging the corresponding class and subclass percentage figures for income (Table 1 revised figures) and occupation (Table 3) yields revised class structure dimensions for 1950 to 1970 and new estimates for 1980 (Table 5). Thus, the original SALA series is revised and carried forward to 1980. Tables 2 and 6 show original SALA income and class structure estimates.

Trends, Patterns, and Implications

Despite difficulties posed by working with categories that shift definition over time, sufficient adjustments can be made to ensure the consistency of the Mexican class structure estimates. The SALA series is not a final measure of class structure, but it does provide a foundation for further refinement. The intent has not been to produce definitive answers, but rather to identify trends in class change over time. An examination of the updated series shows that this class structure measure provides logical and useful estimates of the direction of class change.

Income Distribution

From 1970 to 1980 the middle class made the largest percentage gain for any ten-year period since the Revolution, reflecting an increased rate of change in the second half of the twentieth century. In terms of income, the stable middle subclass increased from 7.9 percent in 1970 to 11.1 percent in 1980, representing an increase of approximately 28 percent in the size of this subclass. The marginal middle subclass increased in size at a somewhat slower rate, from 24.6 percent in 1970 to 25.2 percent in 1980. Perhaps the slower rate of growth represents upward movement toward the stable middle subclass. Whatever the reason, the upward trend reveals that a growing percentage of the population enjoyed a fairly secure existence according to 1980 living standards. The lower class declined from 60.5 percent in 1970 to 57.0 percent in 1980 with most of the decrease falling in the popular (lowest) subclass, further illustrating upward mobility in Mexican society.

Occupational Stratification

The slow, steady increase in the number of workers holding middle-class occupations from 1970 to 1980 and the steady decrease in those with lower class occupations (as shown in Table 3) continue a trend begun in 1950. The upper class shows a slight decline in terms of occupational position for the same period. The most noticeable change in occupational

stratification comes in the agricultural sector which has declined from more than 50 percent of the work force in 1960 to 25 percent in 1980. The percentage decline in agricultural workers is also reflected in trends such as the rural to urban shift in Mexico, a further indication of a shifting social structure.

Class Structure

Table 5 shows figures for Mexico's class structure calculated from combined income and occupational data. Not surprisingly, the middle class made the largest overall gain, from 27.9 percent in 1970 to 31.1 percent in 1980. The upper class remained approximately stable from 1970 to 1980, while the lower class declined from 66.4 percent to 63.7 percent.

The Post-1980 Era

Figure 2 illustrates changes in class structure, giving the revised series from 1895 to 1980. Let us project two class structure scenarios for the post-1980 era in Mexico, one positive and one negative. In the positive case, if class structure changes were to follow the 1960–80 trend, one would expect the lower class to fall below 50 percent of the population by around the year 2010 and the middle class to reach 50 percent of the population toward the year 2015.

Special factors that have positively affected the quantity and quality of Mexico's economic opportunities may not exist in 1990 when the next census is taken. Specifically, the oil boom that brought billions of dollars and many jobs to Mexico peaked around 1981 and the Mexican economy has fluctuated through various states of crisis ever since. In the negative case, the 1990 census may show that the growth rate of the middle class has declined since 1980; hence the lower class could account for more than 40 percent of Mexico's population until after the year 2025.

Regardless of future scenarios, however, the period from 1895 to 1980 shows substantial progress toward a socially balanced society.

Conclusion

Class structure estimates are useful tools for helping to explain Mexico's complex and turbulent history. They indicate where and when change has taken place, and may serve to clarify misunderstandings about Mexican society since the Revolution. For example, a recent California newspaper article (*San Francisco Chronicle*, June 3, 1986) refers to Mexico as

Figure 2

**CHANGES IN MEXICAN CLASS STRUCTURE SINCE 1895,
AND POSITIVE PROJECTION TO 2000**

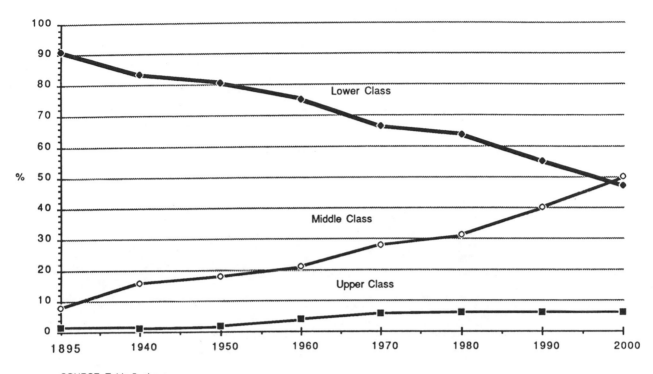

SOURCE: Table 5, above.

one of four remaining dictatorships in Latin America, leading readers to believe that little social change has occurred since the Revolution. As demonstrated here, however, considerable and continuous social change has occurred. In fact, from the series they constructed, Wilkie and Wilkins (1981:584) were able to conclude that:

> It is not the political but the social system that is in transition, as evidenced in the growth of the middle class in Mexico. Social change . . . need not mean concomitant political change because Mexico's political system takes credit for social change that many Mexicans know is taking place.

Moreover, rapid social change will eventually place stress on the political system, which indeed appears to act as a dictatorship while it tries to protect its privileged position.

Like the initial work of Wilkie and Wilkins, the series developed here does "not claim to present de-

finitive answers but rather to try to estimate the trend of class change over time." By explaining the methodology and the difficulties posed in working with census data, we hope to have provided a foundation for further refinement and for the development of even more precise measures for class structure. Varying definitions of class structure such as that based on self-identification with a particular class of consumption patterns will yield different estimates. Once the basic indicators are established, however, the value of time series lies in the consistency of data and methods over time. By using occupation and income, the present series adopts a common historical, socioeconomic definition of class structure. These estimates can help place current economic events in perspective. Only by explaining the many dimensions of society can we understand the complexity of the changing social structure.

APPENDIX A

DGE Estimated Price Index for 1980 and Percentage Differences between DGE and BDM Price Indexes, 1965–80[a]

Year	DGE Price Index	BDM Price Index	Percentage[b] Difference
1965	237.3	208.0	14.1
1966	239.6	210.4	13.9
1967	239.7	216.0	11.0
1968	243.9	220.8	10.5
1969	246.8	226.4	9.0
1970	258.2	240.0	7.6
1971	265.3	248.8	6.5
1972	276.5	255.2	8.3
1973	332.9	296.0	12.5
1974	418.9	362.4	15.6
1975	475.9	400.0	19.0
1976	550.3	489.6	12.4
1977	**[c]	691.2	——
1978	**[c]	800.2	——
1979	**[c]	946.4	——
1980	1,323.5[d]	1,177.5	12.4

a. BDM understated inflation after 1965.
b. Percent difference = $\frac{DGE-BDM}{BDM}$.
c. DGE ceased publication in 1976.
d. Estimated Price Index = (1177.5) × (0.124) + 117.5 = 1323.5.

SOURCE: Wilkie (1985).

APPENDIX B

Unspecified Workers in the Principal Occupation and Branch of Economic Activity Tables as Percentage of the Economically Active Population, Mexican Population Census of 1980[a]

Economically Active Population		Principal[b] Occupation		Branch of Economic[c] Activity	
N	%	N	%	N	%
22,066,084	100.0	3,608,982	16.0	6,552,037	30.0[d]

a. The table illustrates the "30 Percent Factor." For measuring changes in occupational stratification we based our analysis on the figures given in the Principal Occupation table (table 10) in the 1980 Mexican Population Census. The "30 Percent Factor" is based on the figure given in table 9 of the 1980 census.
b. Corresponds to unspecified workers in the Principal Occupation table (table 10).
c. Corresponds to unspecified workers in the Branch of Economic Activity table (table 9).
d. The exact figure is 29.69 percent.

SOURCE: Mexico, DGE (1984: tables 9, 10).

REFERENCES

Cline, Howard F.
1963a *The United States and Mexico*. Revised edition. New York: Atheneum.
1963b *Mexico, Revolution to Evolution: 1940–1960*. New York: Oxford.

Franco, Roland, and Jorge Graciarena
1981 *Formaciones sociales y estructuras de poder en América latina*. Madrid: Centro de Investigaciones Sociológicas.

Iturriaga, José F.
1951 *La estructura social y cultural de México*. México, D.F.: Fondo de Cultura Económica.

Johnson, John J.
1958 *Political Change in Latin America: The Emergence of the Middle Sectors*. Stanford: Stanford University Press.

Kraus, Elliot A.
1971 *The Sociology of Occupation*. Boston: Little Brown.

Mexico, DGE (Dirección General de Estadística)
1934 *Quinto Censo General de Población, Resumen General*.
1943 *Sexto Censo General de Población, Resumen General*.
1953a *Séptimo Censo General de Población, Resumen General*.
1953b *Séptimo Censo General de Población, Parte Especial*.
1964a *Octavo Censo General de Población, Resumen General*.
1964b *Ingresos por Trabajo de la Población Económicamente Activa y Jefes de Familia*.
1964c *Ingresos por Trabajo de la Población Económicamente Activa y Jefes de Familia, Rectificación a los Cuadros 25, 26 y 27 del Resumen General ya Publicado*.
1972 *Noveno Censo General de Población, Resumen Abreviado*.
1984 *X Censo General de Población, Resumen Abreviado*.

Scott, Robert E.
1959 *Mexican Government in Transition*. Urbana: University of Illinois Press.

Slandecker, Werner
1981 *Class Crystalization*. New Brunswick, N.J.: Rutgers University Press.

Treiman, Donald J.
1977 *Occupational Prestige in Comparative Perspective*. New York: Academic Press.

Wilkie, James W.
1985 "Changes in Mexico since 1895: Central Government Revenue, Public Sector Expenditure, and National Economic Growth." In James W. Wilkie and Adam Perkal, eds., *Statistical Abstract of Latin America*, volume 24, pp. 861–880. Los Angeles: UCLA Latin American Center Publications, University of California.

Wilkie, James W., and Peter Reich, eds.
1980 *Statistical Abstract of Latin America*, volume 20. Los Angeles: UCLA Latin American Center Publications, University of California.

Wilkie, James W., and Paul D. Wilkins
1981 "Quantifying the Class Structure of Mexico, 1895–1970." In James W. Wilkie and Stephen Haber, eds., *Statistical Abstract of Latin America*, volume 21, pp. 577–590. Los Angeles: UCLA Latin American Center Publications, University of California.

4

Complexities of Measuring the Food Situation in Mexico: Supply versus Self-Sufficiency of Basic Grains, 1925–86

AÍDA MOSTKOFF AND ENRIQUE C. OCHOA

Much of the recent literature on Mexico's agriculture focuses primarily on the "Mexican food crisis" which seems to have begun in the late 1960s. The crisis centers mainly on Mexico's lack of self-sufficiency in basic grains. Works focusing on the crisis study food imports, rather than food supply, and the majority of them assume that a nation should produce, not import, its own basic foods.[1]

Concerned with Mexico's position as a net importer of basic grains over the past twenty years, analysts tend to see Mexico as a victim of the changing world economic system in which food is produced for export.[2] Mexico has come to cater to the whims of the world capitalist market, by shifting crop production from subsistence crops to crops that are exported to the U.S. market. Traditional producers are now forced to produce food for export, thus being incorporated into the world economy. This restructuring of the world economy to include new segments of the population is called the internationalization of labor. Hence the theorists of self-sufficiency emphasize the international structure.[3]

Utilizing the internationalization of labor theory, Steven Sanderson and David Barkin are the most prominent in explaining Mexico's loss of self-sufficiency. Barkin (in several works) and Sanderson (in

The Transformation of Mexican Agriculture) argue that the agricultural arena is one example of the impact of capitalist expansion on Mexico.[4] Market forces accompanied by the aid of Mexico's food marketing agency, CONASUPO, have compelled Mexico to shift from producing basic goods for internal consumption to producing more lucrative export crops. According to Sanderson, this transformation in the role of Mexican agriculture occurred during the period 1940–80. Both Sanderson and Barkin urge the Mexican government to intervene to rectify the loss of self-sufficiency. Barkin suggests that the state impose quotas on farmers in the irrigation districts to produce basic grains.[5]

Other scholars who have stressed self-sufficiency tend to concentrate on the food policy of the Mexican government under President José López Portillo (1976–1982), who developed the Mexican Food System (Sistema Alimentario Mexicano, SAM). Many of the authors of works on SAM were connected to the project.[6] In a recent example of the SAM literature, *Food Policy in Mexico: The Search for Self-Sufficiency*, the authors cite the reasons for SAM's implementation, describe how SAM cooperated with other gov-

[1] For theory articulating the importance of self-sufficiency in food, see Francis Moore Lappé and Joseph Collins, *Food First: Beyond the Myth of Scarcity* (Boston: Houghton Mifflin, 1977).

[2] For theory about Mexico's failure to maintain food self-sufficiency, see David Barkin and Blanca Suárez, *El Fin de la Autosuficiencia Alimentaria* (México: Ediciones Océano, 1985); Steven E. Sanderson, *The Transformation of Mexican Agriculture: International Structure and the Politics of Rural Change* (Princeton: Princeton University Press, 1986); and James E. Austin and Gustavo Esteva, eds., *Food Policy in Mexico: The Search for Self-Sufficiency* (Ithaca: Cornell University Press, 1987).

[3] For theory about the internationalization of labor, see Steven E. Sanderson, ed., *The Americas in the New International Division of Labor* (New York: Holmes and Meier, 1985).

[4] Barkin and Suárez, *El Fin*; David Barkin, "The End to Food Self-Sufficiency in Mexico," *Latin American Perspectives* 14:3 (Summer 1987), 271–297; David Barkin and Billy R. DeWalt, "Sorghum and the Mexican Food Crisis," in *Latin American Research Review* 23:3 (1988), 30–59; Sanderson, *Transformation*, pp. 38–39.

[5] Barkin, "End to Self-Sufficiency," pp. 289–290.

[6] See, for example, Cassio Luiselli, *El Sistema Alimentario Mexicano (SAM): Elements of a Program of Accelerated Production of Basic Foodstuffs in Mexico*, Research Report 22 (La Jolla: Center for U.S.-Mexican Studies, University of California, San Diego, 1982); Celso Cartas Contreras and Luz María Bassoco, "The Mexican Food System (SAM): An Agricultural Production Strategy," in Bruce F. Johnston, Cassio Luiselli, Celso Cartas Contreras, and Roger D. Norton, eds., *U.S.-Mexico Relations: Agriculture and Rural Development* (Stanford: Stanford University Press, 1987). Cassio Luiselli was General Coordinator for the SAM from 1980 to 1982, and Celso Cartas Contreras was Director General of Macroeconomic Analysis for SAM.

ernment agencies, and analyze the results of the policy. They provide constructive criticism of this major government attempt to reverse the self-sufficiency crisis.[7]

Some recent works on Mexican agriculture are more comprehensive. They focus more on the evolution of Mexican agriculture and on land reform policies.[8] In general these studies do not analyze or present data on food supply. An exception is Cynthia Hewitt de Alcántara's *La Modernización de la Agricultura Mexicana, 1940–70*. Although she does provide data on food supply for wheat and corn up to 1970, she does not do so for other grains, nor does she analyze the data in depth.[9]

Because the existing work focuses on short-term analysis and lacks long-term data analysis, new research on the Mexican food situation is needed. We here examine food supply, defined as food that is actually in the country. We analyze historical time series which are crucial for understanding the variations in agricultural trends; we move beyond data offered in short-term, periodic averages to present long-term yearly series.[10] Thus, we hope to overcome the deficiencies in policy-oriented studies which obscure the larger scope of Mexico's agricultural scene.

Our study adds a new dimension to the understanding of the food situation in Mexico by focusing on supply. We develop long-term data in four series.

1. Consistent per capita data on supply.
2. Per capita data on production, based on explicit population series.
3. Real guaranteed price series for the four basic crops from 1953 to 1985.

In the sections that follow, we discuss the methodology and the sources we have utilized in aggregating the data, and we discuss the implications of our findings. Our purpose is to illustrate the complexities of measuring the food situation in Mexico and to provide consistent historical data for further research.

Sources and Methodology

The Mexican government publishes a vast array of unanalyzed quantitative data on agriculture. The most consistent and complete series of data on agricultural products are *Consumos Aparentes de Productos Agrícolas, 1925–1982* and *Consumos Aparentes de Productos Agrícolas, 1980–1985*, published by the Secretaría de Agricultura y Recursos Hidráulicos (SARH), Subsecretaría de Agricultura y Operación, Dirección General de Economía Agrícola (DGEA), hereafter referred to as SARH data. The SARH data provide information on the production, trade, national supply, and per capita national supply. We update the data in the SARH publication using production and trade data from *Las Razones y las Obras, Gobierno de Miguel de la Madrid: Crónica del Sexenio, 1982–1988*,[11] published each presidential year by the Presidencia de la República, Unidad de la Crónica Presidencial, for the period ending 1988.

Some scholars, such as Paul Lamartine Yates in his *Mexico's Agricultural Dilemma*, suggest that the production data are too favorable. While this might be so, it demonstrates the need for scrutinizing the data and for independent estimates or recalculations. Because SARH data provide the only consistent data for various crops over the long term, we used them for analyzing trends, bearing in mind the limitations of the data.

We focus on national supply, or food availability.[12] To provide data for four basic grains (corn, beans, rice, and wheat) for 1925–86, national supply is calculated by adding the amount produced to the amount imported and then subtracting the amount exported. National supply indicates the amount of food in the country; this is the approach used in the SARH data.

To determine the extent to which supply is keeping pace with Mexico's rapid population growth

---

[7] Austin and Esteva, *Food Policy*.

[8] See, for example, Cynthia Hewitt de Alcántara, *La Modernización de la Agricultura Mexicana, 1940–1970* (Mexico: Siglo Veintiuno Editores, 1978); Susan Walsh Sanderson, *Land Reform in Mexico, 1910–1980* (Orlando: Academic Press, 1984); Paul Lamartine Yates, *Mexico's Agricultural Dilemma* (Tucson: University of Arizona Press, 1981); and Jeffery Brannon and Eric N. Baklanoff, *Agrarian Reform and Public Enterprise in Mexico: The Political Economy of Yucatán's Henequen Industry* (Tuscaloosa: The University of Alabama Press, 1987).

[9] Hewitt de Alcántara, *Modernización*, charts 18 and 19.

[10] Cartas Contreras compares production of twenty-five agricultural products with eight basic products by looking at sexenio averages. The problem with this approach is that he lumps all the products together as if they were equally important, and ignores the yearly variations. See Celso Cartas Contreras, "Policy Choices in Agricultural Trade between Mexico and the United States," in Johnston et al., eds., *U.S.-Mexico Relations*, p. 113.

[11] Mexico: Fondo de Cultura Económica, 1986 and 1987.

[12] For an example of a work that emphasizes agricultural production for all of Latin America, see James W. Wilkie and Manuel Moreno-Ibáñez, "New Research on Food Production in Latin America, since 1952," in James W. Wilkie and Adam Perkal, eds., *Statistical Abstract of Latin America* (SALA), vol. 23 (Los Angeles: UCLA Latin American Center, University of California, 1984), chapter 35, pp. 733–781; also see their "Latin America Food Production and Population in the Era of Land Reform since the 1950s," in John C. Super and Thomas C. Wright, eds., *Food, Politics, and Society in Latin America* (Lincoln: University of Nebraska Press, 1985), pp. 65–105.

we look at per capita food supply (Figs. 1–4). The SARH data on per capita supply do not give a population series; however, we found that by using the population series from SALA (Table 5) the calculations for per capita food supply nearly match those of SARH.[13]

We do not attempt to show whether or not grain supply is sufficient to feed each individual, but we can show the basic per capita trend. One also must bear in mind that other factors limit the interpretation of per capita figures, such as the lack of equity in food distribution, food wastage, food fed to animals, subsistence grains not calculated by the government, and food in storage.

Using per capita national supply figures and per capita production figures (Table 6), we create indexes for each of the four basic grains in terms of production and supply (Figs. 5–8). We designate 1966 as the base year of our index, a year when per capita food availability, production, and exports were high, and imports were low. The year 1966, then, represents a healthy (if not extraordinary) year for basic grain supply in Mexico. Thus, by comparing grain production and supply to a healthy year, we can see how the other years fared. We have chosen our index base for yet another reason: 1966 is heralded as one of the years in which the so-called food crisis began.

To identify the patterns of the total food availability in Mexico, we average the indexes of the four basic grains. This unweighted average index can be taken as a rough summary of the other four indexes because it measures change in supply and production of basic grains over time. Although we realize that corn and rice, for example, do not have the same nutritional value and are not consumed in equal quantities, nevertheless, averaging the four basic crops allows us to indicate and then analyze the general patterns of food availability in Mexico over time (Fig. 9).

We also calculate the percentage of each basic grain supply produced in Mexico in order to analyze grain production patterns. These series provide a better idea of how much food Mexico has been importing as opposed to producing in the period 1925–86 (Figs. 10–13).

Further, to discuss the internal policy toward agriculture, we present data on the guaranteed prices of four basic grains from 1953 to 1985 (Figs. 14–17). Guaranteed prices are the prices at which the govern-

ment's Compañía Nacional de Subsistencias Populares (CONASUPO) buys the agricultural product. Guaranteed prices serve as relative incentives for the producers to grow crops. This kind of data allows for an examination of the relationship between internal government policy toward agriculture and food production in Mexico.

The data on guaranteed prices were compiled from Cynthia Hewitt de Alcántara's *La Modernización de la Agricultura Mexicana, 1940–1970*, Oscar H. Vera Ferrer's *El Caso CONASUPO: Una Evaluación*,[14] and from the third and the fourth year of *Las Razones y las Obras*.

In order to account for inflation we deflate the prices using the combined Dirección General de Estadística (DGE) and Banco de México (BDM) Wholesale Price Index (composite DGE-BDM). The composite DGE-BDM Wholesale Price Index was developed and updated by James W. Wilkie.[15] The DGE-BDM index combines the Dirección General de Estadística Wholesale Price Index which ceased publication in 1976 and the Banco de México index. The link of the two series is made in the year 1965—the last point when the two series were close. Thus the linkage provides a consistent long-term series. (We do not use the BDM wholesale price index, which began in 1939, because it understates inflation.)

We deflate the guaranteed prices with the Wholesale Price Index, not the Consumer Price Index, because guaranteed prices are paid to the producer who in turn purchases an array of goods, including imported goods such as machinery, which are not included in the Consumer Price Index. The real guaranteed prices indicate the relative incentive for producers to grow basic grains.

Implications

Let us now discuss the data on the supply of basic grains in Mexico. We have chosen to analyze the supply of beans, corn, rice, and wheat because traditionally these have been the staples of the rural and urban population. To take a more comprehensive view of the food situation in Mexico, we analyze the trends in supply, addressing these questions: Has Mexico's basic grain supply (corn, beans, rice, and

[13] James W. Wilkie, David E. Lorey, and Enrique Ochoa, eds., *Statistical Abstract of Latin America* (SALA), vol. 26 (Los Angeles: UCLA Latin American Center, University of California, 1988), table 614. Hereafter the *Statistical Abstract of Latin America* is cited as SALA, followed by volume number and reference.

[14] Oscar H. Vera Ferrer, *El Caso CONASUPO: Una Evaluación* (Mexico: Centro de Estudios en Economía y Educación, A.C., 1987).

[15] James W. Wilkie, "Changes in Mexico since 1895: Central Government Revenue, Public Sector Expenditure, and National Economic Growth," in SALA, 24, chapter 34; James W. Wilkie, "From Economic Growth to Economic Stagnaton in Mexico," in SALA, 26, chapter 35.

wheat) kept pace with population growth during the twentieth century? How much basic food is there in Mexico? Has grain supply exceeded production?

Tables 1–4 present data on the supply of the four basic grains. In each of the four tables data are given on production, imports, exports, supply, and per capita supply. Column D shows the amount of food that existed in the country by year from 1925 to 1986. Column E gives the per capita figures.

National supply of Mexico's four basic crops more than quintupled from 1925 to the 1980s (Column D, Tables 1–4). Wheat has shown a more dramatic change, double the growth rate, than have beans, corn, and rice. This growth occurred especially after World War II owing to the government's emphasis on increasing the yield of wheat during the period of the "Green Revolution."[16] The "Green Revolution," a plan to import technology to increase agricultural productivity, began in Mexico in the 1950s. With the aid of the Rockefeller Foundation, irrigated lands in Mexico were able to expand their yield of a variety of products, especially wheat. The "Green Revolution" aided the expansion in yield of private irrigated lands as opposed to rainfed peasant holdings, such as the ejido.

In general, after World War II there was a steady rise in the supply of the basic grains, except for a few disparate years which did not affect the basic trend. It is important to examine the data on a yearly basis rather than periodic averages because, although the basic trend may not be affected, yearly data reflect the reality facing policy makers. Analysis of yearly data isolates other variables that affect decision making, such as weather patterns and natural disasters, and aids in examining the reason for certain policy decisions (for example, we can begin to question why certain years have more imports than other years).

By examining per capita food supply (Figs. 1–4), we can see the extent to which food supply has kept pace with population growth. According to the figures, there has been a steady increase in per capita supply. Also, although there has been a decline in per capita food supply in the last five years, even the lowest point in the last five years is better than the years previous to 1950.

By analyzing data on imports and exports for the basic grains we can compare basic food trade to production (Tables 1–4, Columns B and C). This is an important comparison because it allows us to estimate the percentage of the food supply that is actually produced in the country. Also, inclusion of import and export data illustrates the complexity of policy analysis. For example, one would expect that imports rise because production falls; thus the government had to import to feed the urban masses. Yet this is not the case. Column B, Tables 1–4, indicates a contradictory pattern—when imports rise production also rises. This leads us to question why the government imports when production is on the incline.

Mexico has been an importer of basic grains throughout the twentieth century regardless of whether or not production declined (Tables 1–4). This pattern had already been established years before the "food crisis." One explanation is that after 1970 production fell owing partly to the rise in export crops, thus expanding the pattern of importation. Never has the production level fallen to a point where basic crops imported exceeded crops produced.

Of course this analysis does not take into consideration food distribution. Therefore, although food is being produced, supplemented by imports, this does not mean that the masses are benefiting equally. Actually, the so-called food crisis is probably more akin to the situation in the rural areas. There, due to market forces, the peasants are shifting more and more away from producing their own food, and now have to buy it.

Our data on the percentage of grain supply indicated that the majority of food has been produced in Mexico since 1925 (Figs. 10–13). Column C in Tables 9 to 12 confirms that the major part of the food supply is produced in Mexico. Percentages in Column C that reach levels above one hundred indicate that production was greater than supply, that is, exports have been an important factor. Percentages below one hundred indicate that supply exceeded production, that is, that imports provided the difference. One hundred percent means that all supply was produced in Mexico.

With regard to imports, until the 1970s bean and corn production was high enough to stave off large amounts of imports (see Figs. 10 and 11). Although the 1970s was a period of fluctuation in bean and corn supply, only once did the percentage of grain supply produced in Mexico fall below 70 percent. Analysis of the long-term trends shows that during the last decade and a half imports of basic grains have become more prominent, but the picture does not look as bleak as some claim.

The production-supply relationship of rice and wheat differs markedly from that of beans and corn (see Figs. 12 and 13). Until 1984 rice had been pro-

[16] For a discussion of the "Green Revolution" in Mexico, see Cynthia Hewitt de Alcántara, "The 'Green Revolution' as History: The Mexican Experience," *Development and Change* 5:2(1973–74), pp. 25–44; and Hewitt de Alcántara, *Modernización*.

duced in quantities large enough to permit exports and limit imports. In 1984 and 1985 the percentage of the rice supply that was produced in Mexico dropped dramatically, but government estimates predicted a rebound. Wheat supply shows a different trend. Rarely has wheat been produced in surplus so as to allow wheat exports. The trend in the production-supply relationship of wheat, after fluctuations in the 1970s, seems to be steadily moving back to self-sufficiency.

The indexes of basic grain production and supply indicate that since 1966 the grain supply has worsened, with the exception of wheat (Tables 7 and 8). Per capita supply, however, has fared favorably in comparison to production, thus compensating, to some degree, for the fall in production. Although imports have played a role in compensating for the fall in production of basic grains, the rural classes are bearing the brunt of the production decline since benefits have not trickled down to them.

Real guaranteed prices have generally been on the decline since the mid-1950s (Figs. 14–17). Real prices did increase briefly in the early 1970s but then resumed a downward pattern shortly thereafter. The decline in guaranteed prices, especially since the mid-1970s, can be correlated to the decline in basic grain production and to the rise in export agriculture, as Sanderson, Barkin, and Suárez suggest.[17] However, it is not true that the decline in guaranteed prices began in the 1960s, as Sanderson suggests.[18] Had Sanderson's price data gone back before 1960, he would have discovered that price supports in the 1950s were generally higher or the same as the 1960s. Our data show that the decline in guaranteed prices can be traced, at length, back to the 1950s.

Conclusion

We have shown that the standard works analyzing food policy in Mexico are limited by lack of long-term data analysis. By compiling basic series and presenting them with new insights, we reexamine the fundamental assumptions of the recent literature on Mexico's food situation. Whereas the standard works on Mexican food policy attribute the end of self-sufficiency to an increase in imports of basic products during the last twenty years, complicated by an increase in export crops, we argue that self-sufficiency is only part of the problem in understanding Mexican agricultural policy. Thus we move away from the debates about self-sufficiency to provide the grounds for understanding the complexities of the food situation within a larger historical framework.

Our purpose has been to develop data and to provide the framework for further research. We have shown that food supply has generally kept pace with population growth, and that although there has been an increase in imports in the last twenty years, never have imports grown to the point where production and thus supply have fallen to a significant degree.

Further research on internal factors affecting the food situation, such as food distribution, is needed. We also must begin to more adequately define such terms as food shortage and food crisis. Thus far, most of the literature equates lack of self-sufficiency with a food crisis, but lacking a consistent definition, a crisis can be construed different ways, such as a rural crisis, a crisis in balance of food trade, or a distribution crisis. New data should be developed to test the hypothesis of self-sufficiency and comparative advantage approaches.

[17] Sanderson, *Transformation*, p. 223; and Barkin and Suárez, *El Fin*, pp. 165–166.

[18] Sanderson, *Transformation*, pp. 202–203.

Table 1

MEXICO BEAN SUPPLY, 1925–86

Year	A. Production (Tons)	B. Imports (Tons)	C. Exports (Tons)	D. National Supply (Tons)	E. Supply (kg/Pl)
1925	187,629	2,704	9,775	180,558	11.9
1926	199,471	2,798	1,383	200,886	13.0
1927	189,899	2,091	6,213	185,777	11.8
1928	176,134	344	9,749	166,729	10.4
1929	94,971	101	9,127	85,945	5.3
1930	82,577	3,985	767	85,795	5.2
1931	135,960	8,312	5	144,267	8.5
1932	131,840	301	215	131,926	7.7
1933	185,849	35	5,585	180,299	10.3
1934	123,776	32	12,205	111,603	6.3
1935	120,980	160	5,550	115,590	6.4
1936	106,524	44	954	105,614	5.7
1937	103,796	24	1,387	102,433	5.5
1938	105,499	311	30	105,780	5.5
1939	148,162	3,669	30	151,801	7.8
1940	96,752	18	803	95,967	4.9
1941	160,022	167	7,981	152,208	7.5
1942	182,802	184	12,042	170,944	8.3
1943	157,372	45	5,406	152,011	7.2
1944	183,183	17	4,889	178,311	8.2
1945	161,729	220	6,638	155,311	7.0
1946	138,629	14	574	138,069	6.1
1947	198,854	2,065	24	200,895	8.6
1948	209,629	70	80	209,619	8.7
1949	231,122	40	2	231,160	9.3
1950	250,293	48	815	249,526	9.7
1951	240,018	12,373	2	252,389	9.5
1952	244,500	64,574	0	309,074	11.2
1953	298,687	49,793	23	348,457	12.2
1954	399,458	18,683	251	417,890	14.2
1955	448,908	9,277	9,272	448,913	14.7
1956	432,058	10,052	10,851	431,259	13.7
1957	410,439	7,273	5,051	412,661	12.7
1958	509,524	32,061	0	541,585	16.1
1959	581,398	41,240	17	622,621	17.9
1960	528,175	24,864	197	552,842	15.3
1961	723,340	9,764	4	733,100	19.7
1962	655,608	3,267	2,402	656,473	17.0
1963	677,280	8,656	31,638	654,298	16.4
1964	891,526	8,202	20,083	879,645	21.3
1965	859,584	458	16,519	843,523	19.8
1966	1,013,169	583	102,141	911,611	20.7
1967	980,169	409	56,356	924,222	20.2
1968	856,939	303	79,831	777,411	16.4
1969	934,597	381	53,508	781,470	16.0
1970	925,042	8,647	11,331	922,358	18.2
1971	953,785	466	153	954,098	18.2
1972	869,506	2,686	38,557	833,635	15.4
1973	1,008,887	18,088	28,798	998,177	17.8
1974	971,576	39,478	725	1,010,329	17.4

Table 1 (Continued)

Year	A. Production (Tons)	B. Imports (Tons)	C. Exports (Tons)	D. National Supply (Tons)	E. Supply (kg/PI)
1975	1,027,303	104,400	186	1,131,517	18.9
1976	739,812	179	42,201	697,790	11.3
1977	770,093	29,256	130,076	669,273	10.5
1978	948,744	1,238	44,084	905,898	13.8
1979	640,514	6,786	1,391	645,909	9.6
1980	935,174	443,066	2,138	1,376,102	19.8
1981	1,469,021	490,189	1,985	1,957,225	27.5
1982	1,093,079	146,952	35,539	1,204,492	16.5
1983	1,281,706	1,433	40,903	1,242,236	16.5
1984	930,692	119,125	130,277	919,540	11.8
1985	911,908	144,561	122	1,056,347	13.2
1986†	1,083,000	2,000	0	1,085,000	16.0

SOURCE: 1925–85, from Dirección General de Estadísticas Agrícolas, *Consumos Aparentes de Productos Agrícolas, 1925–1982* (México, D.F.: Secretaría de Agricultura y Recursos Hidráulicos, Subsecretaría de Agricultura y Operación, 1982); and *Consumos Aparentes de Productos Agrícolas*, 1980, 1985 (mimeo); 1983–86, from Presidencia de la República, Unidad de la Crónica Presidencial, *Las Razones y las Obras: Gobierno de Miguel de la Madrid, Cronica del Sexenio 1982–88, Tercer Año* (México, D.F.: Fondo de Cultura Económica, 1986), Vol. 4 (hereafter PRUCP).

Figure 1

MEXICO BEAN SUPPLY PER CAPITA, 1925–86

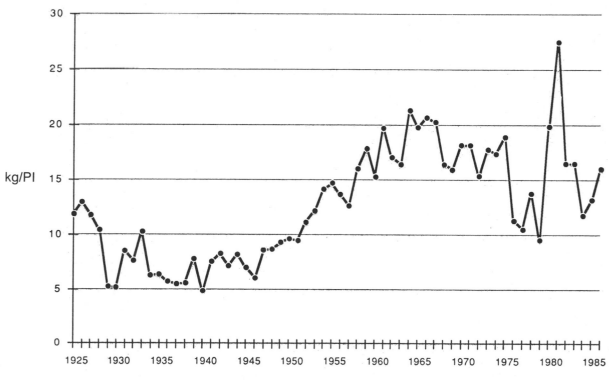

SOURCE: Table 1, Column E.

Table 2

MEXICO CORN SUPPLY, 1925–86

Year	A. Production (Tons)	B. Imports (Tons)	C. Exports (Tons)	D. National Supply (Tons)	E. Supply (kg/PI)
1925	1,968,732	66,432	197	2,034,967	133.8
1926	2,134,842	109,300	62	2,244,080	145.1
1927	2,058,934	28,423	2	2,087,355	132.6
1928	2,172,845	9,941	3	2,182,783	136.3
1929	1,468,805	7,898	1	1,476,702	90.6
1930	1,376,763	79,315	1	1,456,077	87.8
1931	2,138,677	18,731	0	2,157,408	127.8
1932	1,973,469	37	4	1,973,502	114.9
1933	1,923,865	117	0	1,923,982	110.1
1934	1,723,477	16	71,079	1,652,414	93.0
1935	1,674,566	19	81,015	1,593,570	88.1
1936	1,597,203	10	4,452	1,592,761	86.5
1937	1,634,730	3,663	1	1,638,392	87.4
1938	1,692,666	22,062	0	1,714,728	89.9
1939	1,976,731	53,899	2	2,030,628	104.6
1940	1,639,687	8,271	0	1,647,958	83.4
1941	2,124,085	318	2	2,114,401	105.1
1942	2,363,223	1,014	1	2,364,236	114.5
1943	1,808,093	751	15	1,808,829	85.5
1944	2,316,186	163,658	2	2,479,842	114.4
1945	2,186,194	48,586	0	2,234,780	100.5
1946	2,284,000	9,745	914	2,292,831	100.6
1947	2,517,593	695	106	2,518,182	107.4
1948	2,831,937	305	273	2,831,969	117.4
1949	2,870,639	310	14,924	2,856,025	115.0
1950	3,122,042	363	0	3,122,405	120.9
1951	3,424,122	50,735	0	3,474,857	130.1
1952	3,201,890	24,820	0	3,226,710	116.9
1953	3,721,835	376,788	0	4,098,623	143.6
1954	4,487,637	146,716	2	4,634,351	157.0
1955	4,490,080	993	58,629	4,432,444	145.3
1956	4,381,776	119,011	534	4,500,253	142.7
1957	4,499,998	819,084	6,798	5,312,284	162.9
1958	5,276,749	810,436	0	6,087,185	180.5
1959	5,563,254	49,236	1,424	5,611,066	160.9
1960	5,419,782	28,484	457,450	4,990,816	138.5
1961	6,246,106	34,060	78	6,280,088	168.5
1962	6,337,359	17,902	3,829	6,351,432	164.8
1963	6,870,201	475,833	411	7,345,623	184.2
1964	8,454,046	46,496	282,811	8,217,731	199.2
1965	8,936,381	12,033	1,347,189	7,601,225	178.1
1966	9,271,485	4,502	851,865	8,424,122	190.8
1967	8,603,279	5,080	1,253,963	7,354,396	161.0
1968	9,061,823	5,500	896,607	8,170,716	172.9
1969	8,410,894	8,442	789,063	7,630,273	155.9
1970	8,879,384	761,791	2,594	9,638,581	190.1
1971	9,785,734	18,308	274,411	9,529,631	181.6
1972	9,222,838	204,213	425,896	9,001,155	165.7
1973	8,609,132	1,145,184	31,589	9,722,727	173.1
1974	7,847,763	1,282,132	1,603	9,128,292	157.3

Table 2 (Continued)

Year	A. Production (Tons)	B. Imports (Tons)	C. Exports (Tons)	D. National Supply (Tons)	E. Supply (kg/PI)
1975	8,448,708	2,660,839	6,289	11,103,258	185.3
1976	8,017,294	913,786	4,151	8,926,929	144.4
1977	10,137,914	1,985,619	1,383	12,122,150	190.3
1978	10,930,077	1,418,523	1,702	12,346,898	188.2
1979	8,457,899	746,278	1,497	9,202,630	136.4
1980	12,374,400	4,187,072	429	16,561,043	238.8
1981	14,765,760	2,954,574	1,024	17,719,310	248.8
1982	10,147,167	252,784	1,205	10,398,746	142.2
1983	13,061,208	4,632,448	1,300	17,692,356	236.0
1984	12,788,809	2,444,756	352	15,233,213	198.0
1985	14,103,454	1,724,221	9,111	15,818,564	196.0
1986†	13,600,000	2,600,000	0	16,200,000	196.0

SOURCE: 1925–82 from SARH; 1986 from PRUCP, 4.

Figure 2

MEXICO CORN SUPPLY PER CAPITA, 1925–86

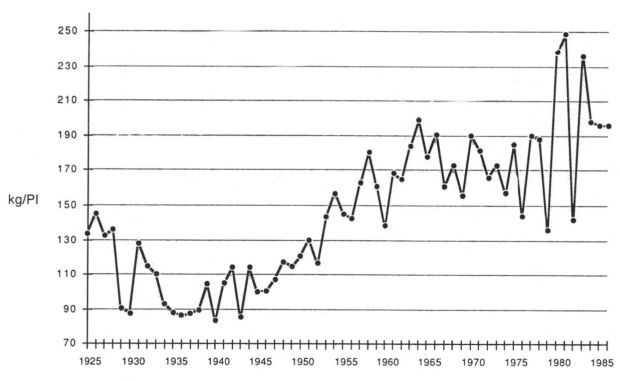

SOURCE: Table 2, Column E.

Table 3

MEXICO RICE SUPPLY, 1925–86

Year	A. Production (Tons)	B. Production Clean Rice[1] (Tons)	C. Imports (Tons)	D. Exports (Tons)	E. National Consumption (Tons)	F. Supply (kg/Pl)
1925	86,126	56,843	1,630	4,066	54,407	3.6
1926	91,356	60,295	1,486	9,950	51,831	3.4
1927	82,909	54,720	1,210	11,058	44,872	2.9
1928	83,153	54,881	1,580	7,298	49,163	3.1
1929	67,280	44,405	1,015	7,838	37,582	2.3
1930	74,793	49,363	986	90	50,259	3.0
1931	72,150	47,619	469	4,156	43,932	2.6
1932	72,382	47,772	143	951	46,964	2.7
1933	66,950	44,187	22	5,819	38,390	2.2
1934	68,729	45,361	19	8,142	37,238	2.1
1935	70,549	46,562	167	18,497	28,232	1.6
1936	86,227	56,910	24	13,459	43,475	2.4
1937	74,560	49,210	10	19,944	29,276	1.6
1938	80,119	52,879	719	6,332	47,266	2.5
1939	103,078	68,031	5	2,201	65,885	3.4
1940	107,713	71,091	43	1	71,133	3.6
1941	109,355	72,174	167	7,306	65,035	3.2
1942	108,177	71,397	48	23,241	48,204	2.3
1943	114,487	75,561	543	3,172	72,932	3.4
1944	104,195	68,769	1	0	68,770	3.2
1945	121,108	79,931	311	0	80,242	3.6
1946	139,465	92,047	1,494	1	93,539	4.1
1947	137,821	90,962	2,023	10,020	82,965	3.5
1948	162,893	107,509	19	28,599	78,929	3.3
1949	184,640	121,862	3	41,218	80,647	3.2
1950	186,589	123,149	5	0	123,154	4.8
1951	179,767	118,646	5	0	118,651	4.4
1952	151,001	99,661	468	0	100,129	3.6
1953	151,732	100,143	421	1	100,563	3.5
1954	169,903	112,136	239	1	112,374	3.8
1955	209,744	138,431	249	0	138,680	4.5
1956	235,067	155,144	70	1,407	153,807	4.9
1957	239,903	158,336	171	5,566	152,941	4.7
1958	252,490	166,643	503	7,782	159,364	4.7
1959	261,017	172,271	748	11,563	161,456	4.6
1960	327,512	216,158	22,304	2,015	236,447	6.6
1961	332,944	219,743	236	3,026	216,953	5.8
1962	288,973	190,722	100	63,040	127,782	3.3
1963	296,373	195,606	2,065	342	197,329	4.9
1964	274,430	181,124	41	48	181,117	4.4
1965	377,531	249,170	17,834	31	266,973	6.3
1966	372,227	245,670	11,514	0	257,184	5.8
1967	417,888	275,806	28	0	275,834	6.0
1968	347,249	229,184	9,107	45,733	192,558	4.1
1969	394,937	260,658	4,844	0	265,502	5.4
1970	405,385	267,554	16,301	0	283,855	5.6
1971	369,167	243,650	801	1	244,450	4.7
1972	403,192	266,107	662	11,785	254,984	4.7
1973	450,575	297,380	37,866	12,002	323,244	5.8
1974	491,608	324,461	71,274	4,150	391,585	6.7

Table 3 (Continued)

Year	A. Production (Tons)	B. Procution Clean Rice[1] (Tons)	C. Imports (Tons)	D. Exports (Tons)	E. National Consumption (Tons)	F. Supply (kg/PI)
1975	716,628	472,974	9	0	472,983	7.9
1976	463,432	305,865	18	277	305,606	4.9
1977	567,338	374,443	92	3,212	371,323	5.8
1978	401,780	265,175	112	59,631	205,656	3.1
1979	493,794	325,904	35,679	1	361,582	5.4
1980	445,364	293,940	95,002	0	388,942	5.6
1981	643,550	424,743	93,255	0	517,998	7.3
1982	600,071	396,047	21,690	1	417,736	5.7
1983	415,667	274,340	243	0	274,583	3.6
1984	484,014	319,449	170,454	0	489,903	6.3
1985	807,529	532,969	165,172	0	698,141	8.7
1986†	406,000	267,960	0	0	406,000	5.0

1. Clean rice is the rice that is fit for human consumption. It is calculated
   as 66% of total rice production. Columns C, D, E, and F refer to clean
   rice.
SOURCE: 1925–85 from SARH; 1986 from PRUCP, 4.

Figure 3

MEXICO RICE SUPPLY PER CAPITA, 1925–86

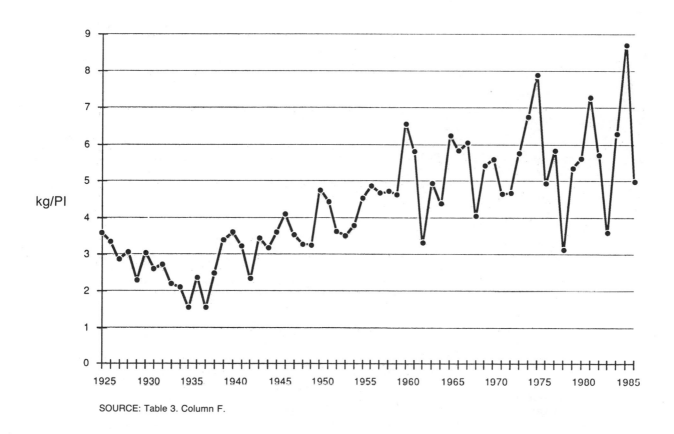

SOURCE: Table 3. Column F.

Table 4

MEXICO WHEAT SUPPLY, 1925–86

	A. Production (Tons)	B. Imports (Tons)	C. Exports (Tons)	D. National Supply (Tons)	E. Supply (kg/PI)
Year					
1925	298,131	43,758	0	341,889	22.5
1926	334,365	84,795	0	419,160	27.1
1927	384,768	37,706	0	422,474	26.8
1928	356,951	47,437	0	404,388	25.3
1929	366,744	96,107	0	462,851	28.4
1930	370,394	69,527	0	439,921	26.5
1931	525,071	30,091	0	555,162	32.9
1932	312,532	67	0	312,599	18.2
1933	392,249	1,648	0	393,897	22.5
1934	354,324	220	0	354,544	19.9
1935	346,630	46	0	346,676	19.2
1936	439,464	95	2	439,557	23.9
1937	342,259	4,932	1	347,190	18.5
1938	386,349	89,684	0	476,033	25.0
1939	428,784	51,086	0	479,870	24.7
1940	463,908	1,225	0	465,133	23.5
1941	434,293	124,117	0	558,410	27.6
1942	489,144	119,646	0	608,790	29.5
1943	364,294	296,891	0	661,185	31.2
1944	374,421	438,845	0	813,266	37.5
1945	346,757	311,873	0	658,630	29.6
1946	340,441	259,655	0	600,096	26.3
1947	421,859	279,023	0	700,882	29.9
1948	477,156	286,965	0	764,121	31.7
1949	503,244	250,927	8,696	745,475	30.0
1950	587,297	427,074	0	1,014,371	39.3
1951	589,898	378,247	0	968,145	36.3
1952	512,212	452,310	0	964,522	34.9
1953	670,629	249,437	0	920,066	32.2
1954	839,466	68,515	0	907,981	30.8
1955	849,988	9,545	23	859,510	28.2
1956	1,242,538	84,886	251	1,327,173	42.1
1957	1,376,502	19,058	55	1,395,505	42.8
1958	1,336,759	431	0	1,337,190	39.7
1959	1,265,526	4,012	12,386	1,257,152	36.1
1960	1,189,979	4,363	125	1,194,217	33.1
1961	1,401,910	7,605	234	1,409,281	37.8
1962	1,455,256	27,127	1,313	1,481,070	38.4
1963	1,702,989	46,163	72,633	1,676,519	42.0
1964	2,203,066	62,411	576,343	1,689,134	40.9
1965	2,150,354	12,535	684,947	1,477,942	34.6
1966	1,647,368	1,122	47,827	1,600,663	36.3
1967	2,122,389	1,172	279,053	1,844,508	40.4
1968	2,080,725	1,599	2,978	2,079,346	44.0
1969	2,326,055	762	252,875	2,073,942	42.4
1970	2,676,451	1,130	41,727	2,635,854	52.0
1971	1,830,880	177,107	85,775	1,922,212	36.6
1972	1,809,018	641,499	16,923	2,433,594	44.8
1973	2,090,844	719,558	12,384	2,798,018	49.8
1974	2,788,577	976,643	20,111	3,745,109	64.5

Table 4 (Continued)

Year	A. Production (Tons)	B. Imports (Tons)	C. Exports (Tons)	D. National Supply (Tons)	E. Supply (kg/PI)
1975	2,798,219	88,526	45,064	2,841,681	47.4
1976	3,363,299	5,331	21,034	3,347,596	54.2
1977	2,455,774	456,373	25,453	2,886,694	45.3
1978	2,784,660	506,062	27,130	3,263,592	49.8
1979	2,286,525	1,169,006	21,871	3,433,660	50.9
1980	2,784,914	923,469	24,469	3,683,914	53.1
1981	3,189,402	1,129,610	6,410	4,312,604	60.6
1982	4,467,647	314,841	1,740	4,780,748	65.4
1983	3,460,242	402,424	8,303	3,854,363	51.1
1984	4,505,245	346,425	11,208	4,840,462	62.3
1985	5,214,315	323,233	13,884	5,523,664	69.1
1986†	4,347,000	0	0	4,347,000	53.0

SOURCE: 1925–85 from SARH; 1986 from PRUCP, 4.

Figure 4

MEXICO WHEAT SUPPLY PER CAPITA, 1925–86

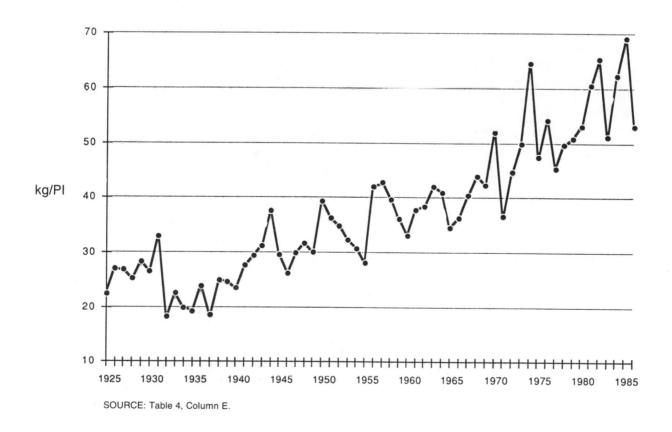

SOURCE: Table 4, Column E.

Table 5

MEXICO POPULATION AND INDEX, 1925–86

Year	Population	Index (1966 = 100)	Year	Population	Index (1966 = 100)
1925	15,200,000	34	1960	36,050,000	82
1926	15,470,000	35	1961	37,270,000	84
1927	15,740,000	36	1962	38,540,000	87
1928	16,010,000	36	1963	39,870,000	90
1929	16,930,000	38	1964	41,250,000	93
1930	16,550,000	37	1965	42,690,000	97
1931	16,880,000	38	1966	44,140,000	100
1932	17,170,000	39	1967	45,670,000	103
1933	17,470,000	40	1968	47,270,000	107
1934	17,780,000	40	1969	48,930,000	111
1935	18,090,000	41	1970	50,690,000	115
1936	18,410,000	42	1971	52,450,000	119
1937	18,760,000	43	1972	54,270,000	123
1938	19,070,000	43	1973	56,160,000	127
1939	19,410,000	44	1974	58,120,000	132
1940	19,650,000	45	1975	60,150,000	136
1941	20,210,000	46	1976	62,330,000	141
1942	20,660,000	47	1977	64,590,000	146
1943	21,170,000	48	1978	65,430,000	148
1944	21,670,000	49	1979	67,420,000	153
1945	22,230,000	50	1980	69,350,000	157
1946	22,780,000	52	1981	71,190,000	161
1947	23,440,000	53	1982	73,010,000	165
1948	24,130,000	55	1983	75,100,000	170
1949	24,830,000	56	1984	76,790,000	174
1950	25,790,000	58	1985	78,520,000	178
1951	25,590,000	58	1986	79,560,000	180
1952	27,850,000	63			
1953	28,700,000	65	SOURCE: SALA, 26–614.		
1954	29,610,000	67			
1955	30,560,000	69			
1956	31,560,000	71			
1957	32,610,000	74			
1958	33,700,000	76			
1959	34,860,000	79			

Table 6

**ABSOLUTE MEXICO BASIC GRAIN PRODUCTION
PER CAPITA, 1925–86
(kg/PI)**

Year	Bean	Corn	Rice	Wheat	Year	Bean	Corn	Rice	Wheat
1925	12.3	129.5	5.7	19.6	1960	14.7	150.3	9.1	33.0
1926	12.9	138.0	5.9	21.6	1961	19.4	167.6	8.9	37.6
1927	12.1	130.8	5.3	24.4	1962	17.0	164.4	7.5	37.8
1928	11.0	135.7	5.2	22.3	1963	17.0	172.3	7.4	42.7
1929	5.6	86.8	4.0	21.7	1964	21.6	204.9	6.7	53.4
1930	5.0	83.2	4.5	22.4	1965	20.1	209.3	8.8	50.4
1931	8.1	126.7	4.3	31.1	1966	23.0	210.0	8.4	37.3
1932	7.7	114.9	4.2	18.2	1967	21.5	188.4	9.2	46.5
1933	10.6	110.1	3.8	22.5	1968	18.1	191.7	7.3	44.0
1934	7.0	96.9	3.9	19.9	1969	19.1	171.9	8.1	47.5
1935	6.7	92.6	3.9	19.2	1970	18.2	175.2	8.0	52.8
1936	5.8	86.8	4.7	23.9	1971	18.2	186.6	7.0	34.9
1937	5.5	87.1	4.0	18.2	1972	16.0	169.9	7.4	33.3
1938	5.5	88.8	4.2	20.3	1973	18.0	153.3	8.0	37.2
1939	7.6	101.8	5.3	22.1	1974	16.7	135.0	8.5	48.0
1940	4.9	83.4	5.5	23.6	1975	17.1	140.5	11.9	46.5
1941	7.9	105.1	5.4	21.5	1976	11.9	128.6	7.4	54.0
1942	8.8	114.4	5.2	23.7	1977	11.9	157.0	8.8	38.0
1943	7.4	85.4	5.4	17.2	1978	14.5	167.0	6.1	42.6
1944	8.5	106.9	4.8	17.3	1979	9.5	125.5	7.3	33.9
1945	7.3	98.3	5.4	15.6	1980	13.5	178.4	6.4	40.2
1946	6.1	100.3	6.1	14.9	1981	20.6	207.4	9.0	44.8
1947	8.5	107.4	5.9	18.0	1982	15.0	139.0	8.2	61.2
1948	8.7	117.4	6.8	19.8	1983	17.1	173.9	5.5	46.1
1949	9.3	115.6	7.4	20.3	1984	12.1	166.5	6.3	58.7
1950	9.7	121.1	7.2	22.8	1985	11.6	179.6	10.3	66.4
1951	9.4	133.8	7.0	23.1	1986†	13.6	170.9	5.1	54.6
1952	8.8	115.0	5.4	18.4					
1953	10.4	129.7	5.3	23.4					
1954	13.5	151.6	5.7	28.4					
1955	14.7	146.9	6.9	27.8					
1956	13.7	138.8	4.9	39.4					
1957	12.6	138.0	7.4	42.2					
1958	15.1	156.6	7.5	39.7					
1959	16.7	159.6	7.5	36.3					

SOURCE: Calculated from Tables 1 4, Column A, using population series from Table 5.

Table 7

INDEX OF MEXICO BASIC GRAIN PRODUCTION
PER CAPITA, 1925–86
(1966 = 100)

Year	A. Bean	B. Corn	C. Rice	D. Wheat	E. Average[1] Index	Year	A. Bean	B. Corn	C. Rice	D. Wheat	E. Average[1] Index
1925	54	62	67	53	59	1960	64	72	107	88	83
1926	56	66	70	58	62	1961	84	80	105	101	93
1927	52	62	62	66	61	1962	74	78	88	101	85
1928	48	65	61	60	58	1963	74	82	88	115	90
1929	24	41	47	58	43	1964	94	98	78	143	103
1930	22	40	53	60	44	1965	88	100	104	135	107
1931	35	60	50	83	57	1966	100	100	100	100	100
1932	33	55	50	49	47	1967	93	90	108	125	104
1933	46	52	45	60	51	1968	79	91	87	118	94
1934	30	46	46	53	44	1969	83	82	95	127	97
1935	29	44	46	51	43	1970	79	83	94	142	100
1936	25	41	55	64	46	1971	79	89	83	94	86
1937	24	41	47	49	40	1972	70	81	88	89	82
1938	24	42	50	54	43	1973	78	73	95	100	86
1939	33	48	63	59	51	1974	73	64	100	129	91
1940	21	40	65	63	47	1975	74	67	140	125	102
1941	34	50	64	58	51	1976	52	61	88	145	86
1942	38	54	62	63	55	1977	52	75	104	102	83
1943	32	41	64	46	46	1978	63	80	72	114	82
1944	37	51	57	46	48	1979	41	60	86	91	70
1945	32	47	64	42	46	1980	59	85	76	108	82
1946	26	48	72	40	47	1981	90	99	107	120	104
1947	37	51	69	48	51	1982	65	66	97	164	98
1948	38	56	80	53	57	1983	74	83	65	124	86
1949	40	55	88	54	59	1984	53	79	74	157	91
1950	42	58	85	61	62	1985	50	86	121	178	109
1951	41	64	83	62	62	1986†	59	81	60	146	87
1952	38	55	64	49	52						
1953	45	62	62	63	58						
1954	59	72	68	76	69						
1955	64	70	81	75	72						
1956	60	66	88	106	80						
1957	55	66	87	113	80						
1958	66	75	88	106	84						
1959	73	76	88	97	84						

1. Unweighted arithmetic average.

SOURCE: A–D, calculated from Table 6.
$$E = A + B + C + D/4.$$

Table 8

**INDEX OF NEW VIEW OF MEXICO BASIC GRAIN
SUPPLY PER CAPITA, 1925–86**
(1966 = 100)

Year	A. Bean	B. Corn	C. Rice	D. Wheat	E. Average[1] Index	Year	A. Bean	B. Corn	C. Rice	D. Wheat	E. Average[1] Index
1925	57	70	62	62	63	1960	74	73	113	91	88
1926	63	76	58	75	68	1961	95	88	100	104	97
1927	57	70	49	74	62	1962	82	86	57	106	83
1928	50	71	53	70	61	1963	79	97	85	116	94
1929	25	47	40	78	48	1964	103	104	76	113	99
1930	25	46	52	73	49	1965	96	93	108	95	98
1931	41	67	45	91	61	1966	100	100	100	100	100
1932	37	60	47	50	49	1967	98	84	104	111	99
1933	50	58	38	62	52	1968	79	91	70	121	90
1934	30	49	36	55	43	1969	77	82	94	117	92
1935	31	46	27	53	39	1970	88	100	97	143	107
1936	28	45	41	66	45	1971	88	95	80	101	91
1937	26	46	27	51	38	1972	74	87	81	123	91
1938	27	47	43	69	46	1973	86	91	99	137	103
1939	38	55	58	68	55	1974	84	82	116	178	115
1940	24	44	62	65	49	1975	91	97	136	131	114
1941	36	55	55	76	56	1976	55	76	85	149	91
1942	40	60	40	81	55	1977	51	100	101	125	94
1943	35	45	59	86	56	1978	67	99	54	137	89
1944	40	60	55	103	64	1979	46	71	92	140	88
1945	34	53	62	82	58	1980	96	125	97	146	116
1946	29	53	71	73	56	1981	133	130	125	167	139
1947	41	56	61	82	60	1982	80	75	98	180	108
1948	42	62	56	87	62	1983	80	124	62	141	102
1949	45	60	56	83	61	1984	57	104	109	172	110
1950	47	63	82	108	75	1985	64	103	150	190	127
1951	46	68	77	100	73	1986†	77	103	86	146	103
1952	54	61	63	96	69						
1953	59	75	61	89	71						
1954	68	82	66	85	75						
1955	71	76	78	78	76						
1956	66	75	84	116	85						
1957	61	85	81	118	86						
1958	78	95	81	109	91						
1959	86	84	80	99	87						

1. Unweighted arithmetic average.

SOURCE: A–D, calculated from Tables 1–4, Column E.

Figure 5

INDEX OF MEXICO BEAN PRODUCTION AND SUPPLY PER CAPITA, 1925–86
(1966 = 100)

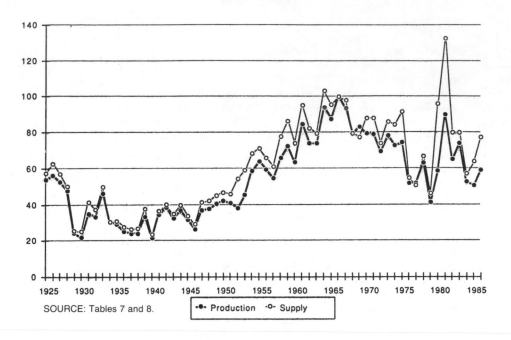

SOURCE: Tables 7 and 8.

Figure 6

INDEX OF MEXICO CORN PRODUCTION AND SUPPLY PER CAPITA, 1925–86
(1966 = 100)

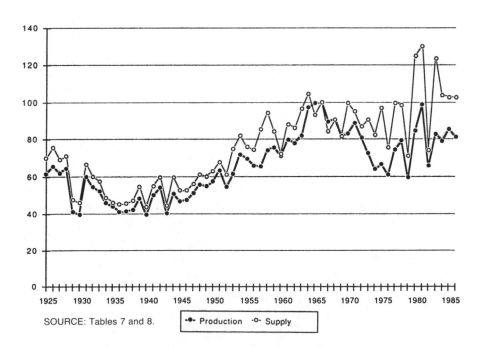

SOURCE: Tables 7 and 8.

Figure 7

INDEX OF MEXICO RICE PRODUCTION AND SUPPLY PER CAPITA, 1925–86
(1966 = 100)

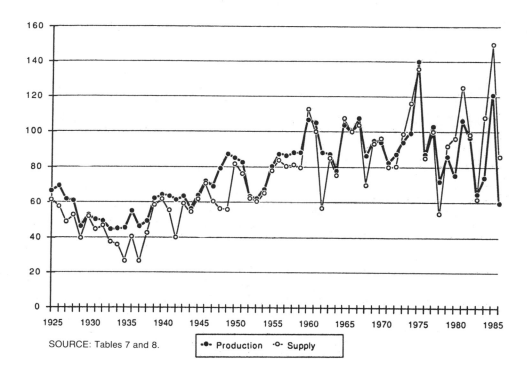

SOURCE: Tables 7 and 8.   -•- Production   -o- Supply

Figure 8

INDEX OF MEXICO WHEAT PRODUCTION AND SUPPLY PER CAPITA, 1925–86
(1966 = 100)

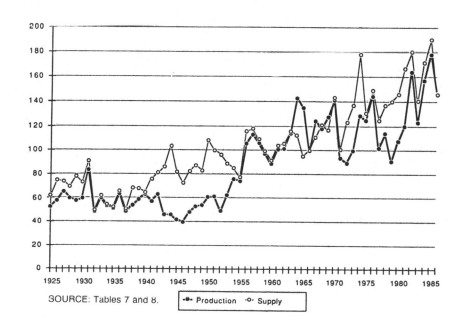

SOURCE: Tables 7 and 8.   -•- Production   -o- Supply

Figure 9

AVERAGE INDEX OF MEXICO BASIC GRAIN SUPPLY AND PRODUCTION, 1925–86

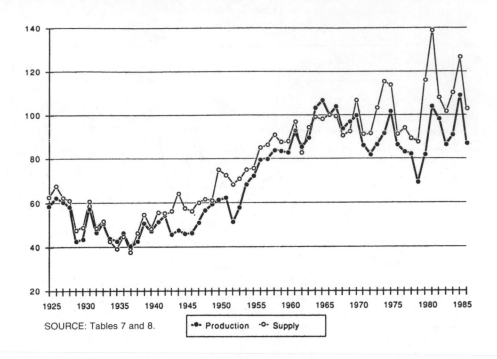

SOURCE: Tables 7 and 8.   -●- Production -○- Supply

Table 9

PERCENTAGE OF BEAN SUPPLY PRODUCED IN MEXICO, 1925–86
(100 = No Imports)

Year	A. Bean Production (Tons)	B. Bean Supply (Tons)	C. (A/B) % Produced in Mexico	Year	A. Bean Production (Tons)	B. Bean Supply (Tons)	C. (A/B) % Produced in Mexico
1925	187,629	180,558	103.9	1945	161,729	155,311	104.1
1926	199,471	200,886	99.3	1946	138,629	138,069	100.4
1927	189,899	185,777	102.2	1947	198,854	200,895	99.0
1928	176,134	166,729	105.6	1948	209,629	209,619	100.0
1929	94,971	85,945	110.5	1949	231,122	231,160	100.0
1930	82,577	85,795	96.2	1950	250,293	249,526	100.3
1931	135,960	144,267	94.2	1951	240,018	252,389	95.1
1932	131,840	131,926	99.9	1952	244,500	309,074	79.1
1933	185,849	180,299	103.1	1953	298,687	348,457	85.7
1934	123,776	111,603	110.9	1954	399,458	417,890	95.6
1935	120,980	115,590	104.7	1955	448,908	448,913	100.0
1936	106,524	105,614	100.9	1956	432,058	431,259	100.2
1937	103,796	102,433	101.3	1957	410,439	412,661	99.5
1938	105,499	105,780	99.7	1958	509,524	541,585	94.1
1939	148,162	151,801	97.6	1959	581,398	622,621	93.4
1940	96,752	95,967	100.8	1960	528,175	552,842	95.5
1941	160,022	152,208	105.1	1961	723,340	733,100	98.7
1942	182,802	170,944	106.9	1962	655,608	656,473	99.9
1943	157,372	152,208	103.4	1963	677,280	654,298	103.5
1944	183,183	178,311	102.7	1964	891,526	879,645	101.4

Table 9 (Continued)

Year	A. Bean Production (Tons)	B. Bean Supply (Tons)	C. (A/B) % Produced in Mexico	Year	A. Bean Production (Tons)	B. Bean Supply (Tons)	C. (A/B) % Produced in Mexico
1965	859,584	843,523	101.9	1977	770,093	669,273	115.1
1966	1,013,169	911,611	111.1	1978	948,744	905,898	104.7
1967	980,169	924,222	106.1	1979	640,514	645,909	99.2
1968	856,939	777,411	110.2				
1969	934,597	781,470	119.6	1980	935,174	1,376,102	68.0
				1981	1,469,021	1,957,225	75.1
1970	925,042	922,358	100.3	1982	1,093,079	1,204,492	90.8
1971	953,785	954,098	100.0	1983	1,282,706	1,242,236	103.3
1972	869,506	833,635	104.3	1984	930,692	919,540	101.2
1973	1,008,887	998,177	101.1				
1974	971,576	1,010,329	96.2	1985	911,908	1,056,347	87.9
				1986†	1,083,000	1,085,000	99.8
1975	1,027,303	1,131,517	90.8				
1976	739,812	697,790	106.0	SOURCE: Calculated from Table 1, Columns A and D.			

Figure 10

PERCENTAGE OF BEAN SUPPLY PRODUCED IN MEXICO, 1925–86

SOURCE: Table 9.

Table 10

PERCENTAGE OF CORN SUPPLY PRODUCED IN MEXICO, 1925–86
(100 = No Imports)

Year	A. Corn Production (Tons)	B. Corn Supply (Tons)	C. (A/B) % Produced in Mexico	Year	A. Corn Production (Tons)	B. Corn Supply (Tons)	C. (A/B) % Produced in Mexico
1925	1,968,732	2,034,967	96.7	1957	4,499,998	5,312,284	84.7
1926	2,134,842	2,244,080	95.1	1958	5,276,749	6,087,185	86.7
1927	2,058,934	2,087,355	98.6	1959	5,563,254	5,611,066	99.1
1928	2,172,845	2,182,783	99.5				
1929	1,468,805	1,476,702	99.5	1960	5,419,782	4,990,816	108.6
				1961	6,246,106	6,280,088	99.5
1930	1,376,763	1,456,077	94.6	1962	6,337,359	6,351,432	99.8
1931	2,138,677	2,157,408	99.1	1963	6,870,201	7,345,623	93.5
1932	1,973,469	1,973,502	100.0	1964	8,454,046	8,217,731	102.9
1933	1,923,865	1,923,982	100.0				
1934	1,723,477	1,652,414	104.3	1965	8,936,381	7,601,225	117.6
				1966	9,271,485	8,424,122	110.1
1935	1,674,566	1,593,570	105.1	1967	8,603,279	7,354,396	117.0
1936	1,597,203	1,592,761	100.3	1968	9,061,823	8,170,716	110.9
1937	1,634,730	1,638,392	99.8	1969	8,410,894	7,630,273	110.2
1938	1,692,666	1,714,728	98.7				
1939	1,976,731	2,030,628	97.3	1970	8,879,384	9,638,581	92.1
				1971	9,785,734	9,529,631	102.7
1940	1,639,687	1,647,958	99.5	1972	9,222,838	9,001,155	102.5
1941	2,124,085	2,114,401	100.5	1973	8,609,132	9,722,727	88.5
1942	2,363,223	2,364,236	100.0	1974	7,847,763	9,128,292	86.0
1943	1,808,093	1,808,829	100.0				
1944	2,316,186	2,479,842	93.4	1975	8,448,708	11,103,258	76.1
				1976	8,017,294	8,926,929	89.8
1945	2,186,194	2,234,780	97.8	1977	10,137,914	12,122,150	83.6
1946	2,284,000	2,292,831	99.6	1978	10,930,077	12,346,898	88.5
1947	2,517,593	2,518,182	100.0	1979	8,457,899	9,202,630	91.9
1948	2,831,937	2,831,969	100.0				
1949	2,870,639	2,856,025	100.5	1980	12,374,400	16,561,043	74.7
				1981	14,765,760	17,719,310	83.3
1950	3,122,042	3,122,405	100.0	1982	10,147,167	10,398,746	97.6
1951	3,424,122	3,474,857	98.5	1983	13,061,000	17,706,000	73.8
1952	3,201,890	3,226,710	99.2	1984	12,932,000	15,360,000	84.2
1953	3,721,835	4,098,623	90.8				
1954	4,487,637	4,634,351	96.8	1985	13,962,000	15,637,000	89.3
				1986†	13,600,000	16,200,000	84.0
1955	4,490,080	4,432,444	101.3				
1956	4,381,776	4,500,253	97.4	SOURCE: Calculated from Table 2, Columns A and D.			

Table 11

PERCENTAGE OF RICE SUPPLY PRODUCED IN MEXICO, 1925–86
(100 = No Imports)

Year	A. Clean Rice Production (Tons)	B. Rice Consumption (Tons)	C. (A/B) % Produced in Mexico	Year	A. Clean Rice Production (Tons)	B. Rice Consumption (Tons)	C. (A/B) % Produced in Mexico
1925	56,843.16	54,407	104.5	1957	158,336	152,941	103.5
1926	60,294.96	51,831	116.3	1958	166,643.40	159,364	104.6
1927	54,719.94	44,872	121.9	1959	172,271.20	161,456	106.7
1928	54,880.98	49,163	111.6				
1929	44,404.80	37,582	118.2	1960	216,157.90	236,447	91.4
				1961	219,743	216,953	101.3
1930	49,363.38	50,259	98.2	1962	190,722.20	127,782	149.3
1931	47,619	43,932	108.4	1963	195,606.20	197,329	99.1
1932	47,772.12	46,964	101.7	1964	181,123.80	181,117	100.0
1933	44,187	38,390	115.1				
1934	45,361.14	37,238	121.8	1965	249,170.50	266,973	93.3
				1966	245,669.80	257,184	95.5
1935	46,562.34	28,232	164.9	1967	275,806.10	275,834	100.0
1936	56,909.82	43,475	130.9	1968	229,184.30	192,558	119.0
1937	49,209.60	29,276	168.1	1969	260,658.40	265,502	98.2
1938	52,878.54	47,266	111.9				
1939	68,031.48	65,885	103.3	1970	267,554.10	283,855	94.3
				1971	243,650.20	244,450	99.7
1940	71,090.58	71,133	99.9	1972	266,106.70	254,984	104.4
1941	72,174.30	65,035	111.0	1973	297,379.50	323,244	92.0
1942	71,396.82	48,204	148.1	1974	324,461.30	391,585	82.9
1943	75,561.42	72,932	103.6				
1944	68,768.70	68,770	100.0	1975	472,974.50	472,983	100.0
				1976	305,865.10	305,606	100.1
1945	79,931.28	80,242	99.6	1977	374,443.10	371,323	100.8
1946	92,046.90	93,539	98.4	1978	265,174.80	205,656	128.9
1947	90,961.86	82,965	109.6	1979	325,904	361,582	90.1
1948	107,509.40	78,929	136.2				
1949	121,862.40	80,647	151.1	1980	293,940.20	388,942	75.6
				1981	424,743	517,998	82.0
1950	123,148.70	123,154	100.0	1982	396,046.90	417,736	94.8
1951	118,646.20	118,651	100.0	1983	274,340	274,583	99.9
1952	99,660.66	100,129	99.5	1984	319,449.20	489,903	65.2
1953	100,143.10	100,563	99.6				
1954	112,136	112,374	99.8	1985	532,969.10	698,141	76.3
				1986†	267,960	406,000	66.0
1955	138,431	138,680	99.8				
1956	155,144	153,807	100.9	SOURCE: Calculated from Table 3, Columns A and E.			

Figure 11

PERCENTAGE OF CORN SUPPLY PRODUCED IN MEXICO, 1925–86

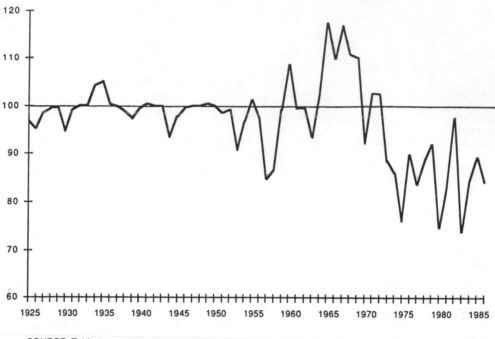

SOURCE: Table 11.

Figure 12

PERCENTAGE OF RICE SUPPLY PRODUCED IN MEXICO, 1925–86

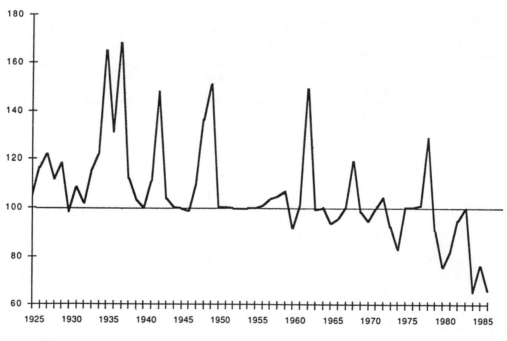

SOURCE: Table 10.

Table 12

PERCENTAGE OF WHEAT SUPPLY PRODUCED IN MEXICO, 1925–86
(100 = No Imports)

Year	A. Wheat Production (Tons)	B. Wheat Supply (Tons)	C. (A/B) % Produced in Mexico	Year	A. Wheat Production (Tons)	B. Wheat Supply (Tons)	C. (A/B) % Produced in Mexico
1925	298,131	341,889	87.2	1957	1,376,502	1,395,505	98.6
1926	334,365	419,160	79.8	1958	1,336,759	1,337,190	100.0
1927	384,768	422,474	91.1	1959	1,265,526	1,257,152	100.7
1928	356,951	404,388	88.3				
1929	366,744	462,851	79.2	1960	1,189,979	1,194,217	99.6
				1961	1,401,910	1,409,281	99.5
1930	370,394	439,921	84.2	1962	1,455,256	1,481,070	98.3
1931	525,071	555,162	94.6	1963	1,702,989	1,676,519	101.6
1932	312,532	312,599	100.0	1964	2,203,066	1,689,134	130.4
1933	392,249	393,897	99.6				
1934	354,324	354,544	99.9	1965	2,150,354	1,477,942	145.5
				1966	1,647,368	1,600,663	102.9
1935	346,630	436,676	79.4	1967	2,122,389	1,844,508	115.1
1936	439,464	439,557	100.0	1968	2,080,725	2,079,346	100.1
1937	342,259	347,190	98.6	1969	2,326,055	2,073,942	112.2
1938	386,349	476,033	81.2				
1939	428,784	479,870	89.4	1970	2,676,451	2,635,854	101.5
				1971	1,830,880	1,922,212	95.2
1940	463,908	465,133	99.7	1972	1,809,018	2,433,594	74.3
1941	434,293	558,410	77.8	1973	2,090,844	2,798,018	74.7
1942	489,144	608,790	80.3	1974	2,788,577	3,745,109	74.5
1943	364,294	661,185	55.1				
1944	374,421	813,266	46.0	1975	2,798,219	2,841,681	98.5
				1976	3,363,299	3,347,596	100.5
1945	346,757	658,630	52.6	1977	2,455,774	2,886,694	85.1
1946	340,441	600,096	56.7	1978	2,784,660	3,263,592	85.3
1947	421,859	700,882	60.2	1979	2,286,525	3,433,660	66.6
1948	477,156	764,121	62.4				
1949	503,244	745,475	67.5	1980	2,784,914	3,683,914	75.6
				1981	3,189,402	4,312,604	74.0
1950	587,297	1,014,371	57.9	1982	4,467,647	4,780,748	93.5
1951	589,898	968,145	60.9	1983	3,460,242	3,854,363	89.8
1952	512,212	964,522	53.1	1984	4,505,245	4,840,462	93.1
1953	670,629	920,066	72.9				
1954	839,466	907,981	92.5	1985	5,214,315	5,523,664	94.4
				1986†	4,347,000	4,347,000	100.0
1955	849,988	859,510	98.9				
1956	1,242,538	1,327,173	93.6				

SOURCE: Calculated from Table 4, Columns A and D.

Figure 13

PERCENTAGE OF WHEAT SUPPLY PRODUCED IN MEXICO, 1925–86

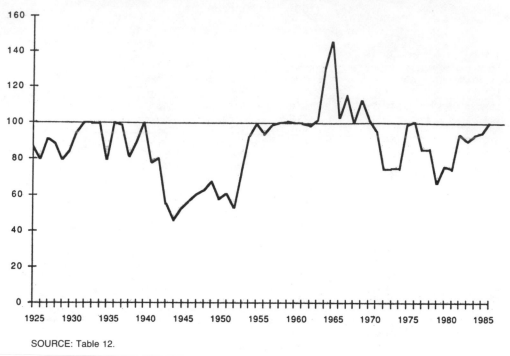

SOURCE: Table 12.

Table 13

MEXICO REAL GUARANTEED BEAN PRICES, 1953–85

Year	A. Nominal Price (Pesos/Ton)	B. DGE-BDM WPI (1950 = 100)	C. (A/B) Real Price (Pesos/Ton)	Year	A. Nominal Price (Pesos/Ton)	B. DGE-BDM WPI (1950 = 100)	C. (A/B) Real Price (Pesos/Ton)
1953	1,250	135.2	925	1970	1,750	303.1	577
1954	1,500	145.6	1,030	1971	1,750	320.0	547
				1972	1,750	340.0	515
1955	1,500	168.0	893	1973	5,000	384.6	1,300
1956	1,500	178.3	841	1974	6,000	472.3	1,270
1957	1,500	189.3	792				
1958	1,500	198.0	758	1975	6,000	546.2	1,098
1959	1,500	200.8	747	1976	5,000	652.3	767
				1977	5,000	850.8	588
1960	1,500	212.3	707	1978	6,250	993.8	629
1961	1,750	214.2	817	1979	7,750	1,195.4	648
1962	1,750	217.2	806				
1963	1,750	221.2	791	1980	12,000	1,538.5	780
1964	1,750	228.4	766	1981	16,000	1,956.9	818
				1982	21,100	3,155.4	669
1965	1,750	244.6	715	1983	31,250	6,063.1	515
1966	1,750	255.4	685	1984	29,225	9,809.2	298
1967	1,750	256.9	681				
1968	1,750	263.1	665	1985	46,025	15,147.7	304
1969	1,750	273.8	639				

SOURCE: A, Hewitt de Alcántara, *Modernización*; Vera, *El Caso
CONASUPO*; PRUCP.
B, Wilkie, "Changes in Mexico"; Wilkie, "From Economic
Growth."

Figure 14

MEXICO REAL GUARANTEED BEAN PRICES, 1953–85

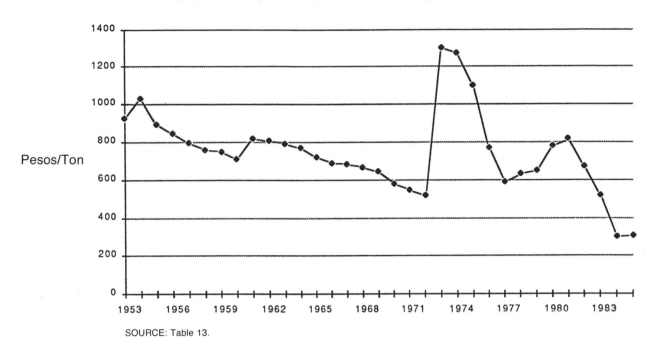

SOURCE: Table 13.

Table 14

MEXICO REAL GUARANTEED CORN PRICES, 1953–85

Year	A. Nominal Price (Pesos/Ton)	B. DGE-BDM WPI (1950 = 100)	C. (A/B) Real Price (Pesos/Ton)	Year	A. Nominal Price (Pesos/Ton)	B. DGE-BDM WPI (1950 = 100)	C. (A/B) Real Price (Pesos/Ton)
1953	500	135.2	370	1970	940	303.1	310
1954	550	145.6	378	1971	940	320.0	294
				1972	940	340.0	276
1955	550	168.0	327	1973	1,200	384.6	312
1956	562	178.3	315	1974	1,500	472.3	318
1957	680	189.3	359				
1958	800	198.0	404	1975	1,900	546.2	348
1959	800	200.8	398	1976	2,340	652.3	359
				1977	2,900	850.8	341
1960	800	212.3	377	1978	2,900	993.8	292
1961	800	214.2	373	1979	3,480	1,195.4	291
1962	800	217.2	368				
1963	940	221.2	425	1980	4,450	1,538.5	289
1964	940	228.4	412	1981	6,550	1,956.9	335
				1982	8,850	3,155.4	280
1965	940	244.6	384	1983	17,600	6,063.1	290
1966	940	255.4	368	1984	29,475	9,809.2	300
1967	940	256.9	366				
1968	940	263.1	357	1985	48,400	15,147.7	320
1969	940	273.8	343				

SOURCE: A, Hewitt de Alcántara, *Modernización*; Vera, *El Caso CONASUPO*; PRUCP.

B, Wilkie, "Changes in Mexico"; Wilkie, "From Economic Growth."

Figure 15

MEXICO REAL GUARANTEED CORN PRICES, 1953–85

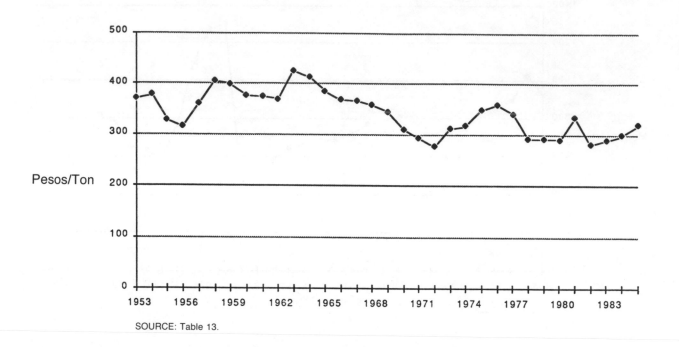

SOURCE: Table 13.

Table 15

MEXICO REAL GUARANTEED RICE PRICES, 1960–85

Year	A. Nominal Price (Pesos/Ton)	B. DGE-BDM WPI (1950 = 100)	C. (A/B) Real Price (Pesos/Ton)	Year	A. Nominal Price (Pesos/Ton)	B. DGE-BDM WPI (1950 = 100)	C. (A/B) Real Price (Pesos/Ton)
1960	891	212.3	420	1975	2,820	546.2	516
1961	928	214.2	433	1976	3,026	652.3	464
1962	1,008	217.2	464	1977	3,012	850.8	354
1963	1,056	221.2	477	1978	3,458	993.8	348
1964	1,077	228.4	472	1979	4,090	1,195.4	342
1965	1,137	244.6	465	1980	5,879	1,538.5	382
1966	1,125	255.4	440	1981	6,828	1,956.9	349
1967	1.098	256.9	427	1982	9,242	3,155.4	293
1968	1,145	263.1	435	1983	20,967	6,063.1	346
1969	1,187	273.8	434	1984	27,550	9,809.2	281
1970	1,190	303.1	393	1985	43,550	15,147.7	288
1971	1,226	320.0	383				
1972	1,127	340.0	331				
1973	1,608	384.6	418				
1974	2,691	472.3	570				

SOURCE: A, Hewitt de Alcántara, *Modernización*; Vera, *El Caso CONASUPO*; PRUCP.

B, Wilkie, "Changes in Mexico"; Wilkie, "From Economic Growth."

Figure 16

MEXICO REAL GUARANTEED RICE PRICES, 1960–85

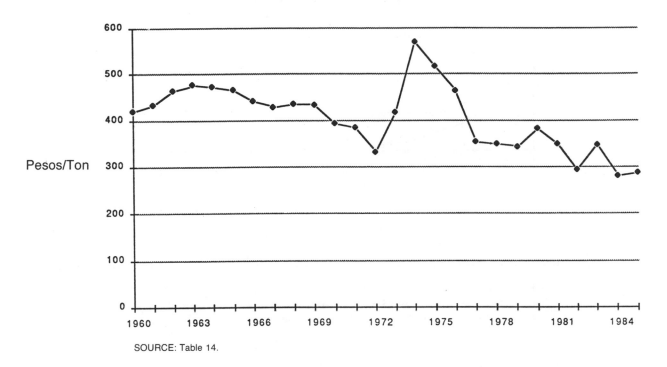

SOURCE: Table 14.

Table 16

MEXICO REAL GUARANTEED WHEAT PRICES, 1953–85

Year	A. Nominal Price (Pesos/Ton)	B. DGE-BDM WPI (1950 = 100)	C. (A/B) Real Price (Pesos/Ton)	Year	A. Nominal Price (Pesos/Ton)	B. DGE-BDM WPI (1950 = 100)	C. (A/B) Real Price (Pesos/Ton)
1953	830	135.2	614	1970	913	303.1	301
1954	913	145.6	627	1971	913	320.0	285
				1972	870	340.0	256
1955	913	168.0	543	1973	1,200	384.6	312
1956	913	178.3	512	1974	1,300	472.3	275
1957	913	189.3	482				
1958	913	198.0	461	1975	1,750	546.2	320
1959	913	200.8	455	1976	1,750	652.3	268
				1977	2,050	850.8	241
1960	913	212.3	430	1978	2,600	993.8	262
1961	913	214.2	426	1979	3,000	1,195.4	251
1962	913	217.2	420				
1963	913	221.2	413	1980	3,550	1,538.5	231
1964	913	228.4	400	1981	4,600	1,956.9	235
				1982	6,930	3,155.4	220
1965	840	244.6	343	1983	16,100	6,063.1	266
1966	913	255.4	357	1984	26,150	9,809.2	267
1967	913	256.9	355				
1968	913	263.1	347	1985	33,500	15,147.7	221
1969	913	273.8	333				

SOURCE: A, Hewitt de Alcántara, *Modernización*; Vera, *El Caso CONASUPO*; PRUCP.
B, Wilkie, "Changes in Mexico"; Wilkie, "From Economic Growth."

Figure 17

MEXICO REAL GUARANTEED WHEAT PRICES, 1953–85

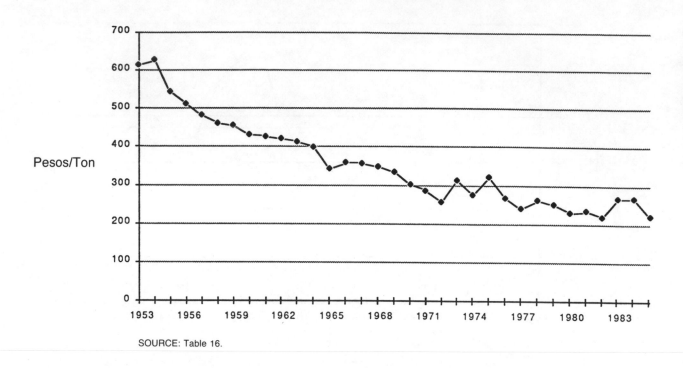

SOURCE: Table 16.

5

Borrowing as Revenue: The Case of Mexico, 1935–82

JAMES W. WILKIE

My purpose here is to suggest a revised theoretical basis for clearly charting patterns in the long-term generation of revenues by central governments. Further, I wish to analyze those patterns in a Mexican case study. That I should return to examine matters of government finance has been urged on me by others for some time,[1] and the problem of Mexico's development since the post-1974 new Mexican petroleum era along with the post-1982 "debt crisis" have engendered much renewed discussion of Mexican finances.[2]

In this study, I shall examine the results of revenue policy and I use a method differing in two ways from that used by most other scholars. First, I do not focus on the public sector,[3] but on one of its components—the central government.[4] Second, I include borrowings in my analysis to show the real share of income taxes in total revenues generated by central government.

Theory

Whereas most other analysts are interested in calculating the total impact of the public sector (excluding its borrowing) on gross domestic product, my concern is with assessing the role of the central government (including its borrowing), because the central government is the one subsector of the public sector over which the chief executives of nations have real discretionary power. Although since 1977 the Mexican parastate subsector theoretically has been divided up under the control of the most relevant secretariats within the central government subsector (for example, Petróleos Mexicanos falls under the jurisdiction of the Secretaría de Patrimonio y Fomento Industrial),[5] such a system is hardly workable because many of the "controlled" enterprises are much more powerful than the ministry under which they fall. Too, some of the nearly 700 parastate enterprises in Mexico do not neatly fall under any one secretariat; subsequently at least 100 have been transferred into a grouping of agencies beyond ministerial

AUTHOR'S NOTE: This essay was first published in *The Mexican Forum/El Foro Mexicano*, vol. 5, no. 2 (April 1985), pp. 3–7, and is reprinted with permission from the University of Texas at Austin.

[1] Francisco Solana, president of the Banco Nacional de México, urged during a visit to Los Angeles, 3 February 1984, that I follow up on my book *La revolución mexicana (1910–1976): gasto federal y cambio social* (México, D.F.: Fondo de Cultura Económica, 1978), which includes a special study of Mexico from 1963 to 1976, and on my article "Recentralization: The Budgetary Dilemma in the Economic Development of Mexico, Bolivia, and Costa Rica." The latter article was originally published in David T. Geithman, ed., *Fiscal Policy for Industrialization and Development in Latin America* (Gainesville: University of Florida Press, 1974), pp. 200–247.

[2] Notable studies, which build on my work and examine the total of (rather than the functional analysis of) expenditure, include the following: Arthur J. Mann, "The Evolution of Mexico's Public Expenditure Structure, 1895–1975," *Bulletin for International Fiscal Documentation* 33:11 (1979), pp. 514–523; and E. V. K. Fitz-Gerald, "Patterns of Public Sector Income and Expenditure in Mexico," Technical Papers Series, 17 (1978), published by the Office for Public Sector Studies, Institute of Latin American Studies, Uni-

versity of Texas. For discussion of other works on expenditure, see the introduction to James W. Wilkie, ed., *Money and Politics in Latin America* (Los Angeles: UCLA Latin American Center Publications, 1977).

[3] The public sector is defined as having 4 subsectors: (*a*) central government; (*b*) state government; (*c*) local government; and (*d*) parastate or decentralized government, including autonomous agencies, government-owned and majority-share-owned enterprises, and trust funds. The parastate subsector receives most of its funds by charging the populace served for its services (for example, the national airline sells tickets), by receiving subsidies from the central government, or by borrowing funds.

[4] The central government is defined as the executive, legislative, and judicial branches of government, which are allotted all of their funds from the Treasury. The executive branch includes all of the secretariats (for example, education, public health, defense, transportation, irrigation, land reform) as well as funds allocated to subsidize noncentral government programs.

[5] See *El Mercado de Valores*, 20 July 1981, pp. 757–767.

control.[6] Whereas central government secretariats do not have their own income, parastate enterprises collect most of their own revenue and thus are relatively free to go about their own business.

Standard theory about the proper method of analyzing government finances argues that borrowing and repayments should not be included as part of total income and expenditure for many reasons. The first is that borrowing and repayment are nonrecurrent items and outside of the normal revenue base. The second is that, if included in income and expenditure totals, borrowing and repayment subtotals would overstate government activity (for example, repayments eventually would be double-counted if included as amortization of the debt when earlier they were counted in the budget category where the borrowed funds were expended). The third reason claims that government borrowing's impact on the nation is no different than private borrowing's. The fourth is that the use of borrowing is cost free, except for payment of interest, which is indeed included in expenditure totals.

Other arguments for excluding borrowings and repayments from analysis of government finance are also influential. One is that debts incurred on behalf of the nation only mean that the nation's people owe themselves money. A variation of that argument says that, contrary to the case of the private sector, borrowing by the government is irrelevant, as is the size of the national debt, because governments cannot "go broke." Yet another argument claims that borrowings involve an exchange of assets and hence are neither receipts nor expenditures. Last, but not least, the 1985 U.S. budget gives one reason that it sees as predominant: if borrowing were counted in revenues, the budget would be balanced simply by borrowing,[7] thus hiding deficits.

As a result of accepting standard theory on the basis of one or more of the above reasons, governments publish net revenues and implicitly hide the pattern in gross revenue collections—and it is the latter factor that we need to know. Ironically, the Third World has tended to accept standard theory worked out for the developed world, yet, although the theory

was never applicable to developing areas, in my view it appears that neither is it applicable to the developed world. We now know that for most countries domestic and foreign borrowing have long since become a form of recurrent revenue, especially in such countries as Mexico and the United States. In the meantime, the possibility of governments "going broke" has indeed become a possibility that frightens the international banking community and influences the availability of loan funds available to countries developing with or without large debts.

To show the problem with standard theory, let us take the case of Mexico. For example, to analyze the revenue of Mexico's central government without relating it to borrowings is to ignore the extent to which revenue stability (or instability) has been built into the Mexican system. Central government borrowing competes with the private sector for credit, thus forcing up the interest rate. (A rise in interest rates because of competition between government and private sectors is not always the case, as in the United States, where under President Reagan a continued influx of foreign deposits, seeking political stability or relatively high U.S. interest rates, is credited with helping to reduce the impact of U.S. government borrowing, which otherwise would have crowded private credit needs out of money markets.)[8]

Further, the idea is naive that national debts anywhere can be justified by presidents when they claim that "we only owe the money to ourselves." Borrowing and repayments show how national and international obligations relate to other recurrent income and outlay as well as the extent to which government fund-raising activity is required for repayment of previously expended loans—these are hardly matters limited to an unimportant exchange of assets.[9] Central governments use funds very differently than does the private sector in any country. Finally, to revise the standard view by including borrowings in total revenues does not mean that we are double counting funds or hiding deficits, if we keep in mind the purpose of adding analysis rather than trying to find only one form of analytical category.

[6] Compare ibid. and *El Mercado de Valores*, 12 April 1984, pp. 377–384.

[7] On this last point, see Executive Office of the President, Office of Management and Budget, *Budget of the United States Government, FY 1985* (Washington, D.C.: 98th Congress, 2d Session. House Document No. 98–138, 1984), pp. 7–14. Such a justification is rare; compare Arthur J. Mann, who, like most analysts, simply assumes that borrowings should be excluded, and he does not offer any rationale for doing so in his otherwise valuable study: "The Evolution of Mexico's Public Revenue Structure, 1877–1977," *Bulletin for International Fiscal Documentation* 32:7 (1978), pp. 294–300.

[8] Foreign loans to Mexico and foreign investment in Mexico may have somewhat the same effect as foreign deposits in the United States, that is, relief of the credit shortage caused by government borrowings.

[9] For arguments against the idea that borrowing and repayment only involve exchange of assets and hence should not be included either in receipts or expenditures, see James W. Wilkie, *Statistics and National Policy* (Los Angeles: UCLA Latin American Center Publications, 1974), p. 104.

The Mexican Case

Heavy parastate borrowings have long required Mexico's central government to finance the deficits of those agencies that operate inefficiently or with public-interest limits on what they can charge for services rendered. Because the parastate enterprises operate autonomously (so that, theoretically, businesses such as the National Railways of Mexico can collect revenues and balance expenditures to produce a profit that can be used to develop the nation), the central government does not have direct leverage unless the enterprises have a deficit that needs subsidy (which, in reality, has been the case for most of the enterprises). Although since the mid-1970s the central government theoretically has had the power to veto proposed parastate borrowings, in practice such vetos have been used sparingly (notable in the immediate aftermath of the 1982 "debt crisis"); were the central government to veto too many decentral borrowings, that would only increase pressures on the central government to cover deficits or face damaging cutbacks in national enterprises.

Because I am here interested in tracing patterns in revenue generation, that is, in the results of policy, I am not concerned with the causes of revenue policy, which are indeed complicated. Causes of the patterns developed here can be traced to an ever-shifting number of single, multiple, or interrelated factors, including (among others):

1. Intended or unintended consequences of changing Mexican revenue and nonrevenue laws, especially as new laws revise or layer on old legislation that is often unrepealed in whole or part.

2. Irregular or selective enforcement of Mexico's laws or emphasis on portions of the law or means of collection that yield quickest results.

3. The Central Bank's placing of money in circulation and the availability of funds borrowable in national and international money markets by competing public- and private-sector sources.

4. Mexican government valuation of Mexico's peso,[10] for various reasons such as to support goals other than maximization of exports or, at times, imports.

5. Possibilities in Mexico's foreign trade; and reserve and balance of payments policy.

6. Health of national economic production, including expansion or contraction of Mexico's private and public sectors.

7. Shifts in public-sector expenditure policy by Mexico's central government and parastate subsectors.

8. Increased share of public-sector activity in Mexico's total activity.

9. Public sector investment in the economic infrastructure and subsidies and loans to the private sector.

10. Attempts by the Mexican central government since 1965 to control parastate revenue and expenditure policies.

11. Changes in availability of development loans and grants from bilateral and multilateral sources.

12. Conscious shifts in Mexico's theory of government, revenue collection, or subconscious or reflexive adaptation to changing economic realities and political needs.

14. Changing climates of world and regional political opinion about "solutions" to economic fluctuations.

15. Shifting national and international pricing structures.

16. Speculative policies by nationally and internationally oriented private and official investors and money and commodity dealers.

17. Other factors, including "excessive" Mexican corruption.

Many of these topics have been studied for Mexico by a number of authors,[11] but none have traced

---

[10] On valuation of the peso and on the size of Mexican borrowings as well as on fluctuations in foreign trade, see James W. Wilkie, "Mexico's 'New' Financial Crisis of 1982 in Historical Perspective," in Wilkie and Adam Perkal, eds., *Statistical Abstract of Latin America*, vol. 22 (1983), pp. vii–xvii. See also René Villarreal, *El desequilibrio externo en la industrialización de México (1929–1975)* (México, D.F.: Fondo de Cultura Económica, 1976).

[11] For example, on the general economy, see Clark W. Reynolds, *The Mexican Economy: Twentieth-Century Structure and Growth* (New Haven: Yale University Press, 1970); and Leopoldo Solís, *La realidad económica mexicana: retrovisión y perspectivas*, rev. ed. (México, D.F.: Siglo XXI Editores, 1981).

On public finance, see Roberto Santillán López and Aniceto Rosas Figueroa, *Teoría general de las finanzas públicas y el caso de México* (México, D.F.: Escuela Nacional de Economía, Universidad Nacional Autónoma de México, 1962); and Roberto Anguiano Equihua, *Las finanzas del sector público en México* (México, D.F.: Escuela Nacional de Economía, Universidad Nacional Autónoma de México, 1968).

On revenue policy, see John S. Evans, "The Evolution of the Mexican Tax System, with Special Reference to Developments ... [1957–1965]" (Ph.D. dissertation, University of Wisconsin, 1970). Evans admits the case for including foreign borrowings in analysis of government revenues (p. 112), but he concludes wrongly that "more is gained by excluding debt amortization than by including it," because amortization outlays "have almost always been offset by new borrowings."

On the size of revenues from recurrent categories by public-sector level (central, decentral, state, local), see Mann, "The Evolution of Mexico's Public Revenue Structure."

On monetary policy, see B. Griffiths, *Mexican Monetary Policy and Economic Development* (New York: Praeger, 1972); John K. Thompson, *Inflation, Financial Markets, and Economic Development: The Mexican Experience* (Greenwich, Conn.: JAI Press, 1979); Antonio Gómez Oliver, *Política monetaria y fiscal de México* (México, D.F.: Fondo de Cultura Económica, 1981).

Table 1
APPARENT AND TRUE SHARE OF INCOME TAX COMPARED
TO BORROWING AS SHARE OF MEXICAN
CENTRAL GOVERNMENT REVENUES,
1935–82
(%)

Period	President	A. Apparent Income Tax (In Net Total Revenue[a])	B. True Income Tax	C. Borrowing
			(In Gross Total Revenue[b])	
1935–40	Lázaro Cárdenas	9.3	8.9	4.5
1941–46	Manuel Avila Camacho	16.9	15.2	12.0
1947–52	Miguel Alemán	22.3	20.3	9.8
1953–58	Adolfo Ruiz Cortines	24.8	22.2	10.8
1959–64	Adolfo López Mateos	32.9	22.8	30.8
1965–70	Gustavo Díaz Ordaz	35.7	25.7	28.2
1971–76	Luis Echeverría Alvarez	38.4	25.9	32.0
1977–82	José López Portillo	37.7	23.0	39.7

a. Net excludes borrowing.
b. Gross includes borrowing.

SOURCE: James W. Wilkie, "Changes in Mexico since 1895: Central Government Revenue, Public Sector Expenditure, and National Economic Growth," SALA, 24, p. 879.

the patterns in revenues generated as presented here. The problem is that it is necessary to reorganize and adjust official categories to arrive at a series of data that is internally consistent and meaningful through time.

The Mexican government itself is confused about its own time-series data on revenues. Although the raw data presented by Mexico's Treasury Department in its yearly summaries of projected and actual income and expenditure have ignored standard theory to include borrowings, Nacional Financiera, one of the major parastate agencies and the major source for published Mexican longitudinal statistics, claims that it does not include borrowings in its time-series data on revenues (that is, it gives net totals), but it does so only for 1935 and 1938–48. In fact, Nacional Financiera gives revenues in gross terms (including borrowing) for 1936 and 1937 and for years beginning in 1949.[12] To end this confusion and to revise the standard analysis of data on revenues, I developed a consistent series presented in gross terms.

[12] Nacional Financiera, *La economía mexicana en cifras* (México, D.F., 1981), pp. 307–310. Nacional Financiera mistakenly claims in note 1 that data after 1949 are for net revenue. However, it is important to say here that the figures are really in gross terms. Further, it should be pointed out for comparative purposes that in the U.S. definition, "gross" includes borrowings, subsidies, and virtual revenue whereas "net" does not. In Mexico, the concept of "gross" is the same as in the United States; but Mexico's "net" (which is not used here) excludes subsidies and virtual revenue and includes borrowings, whereas its "effective income" (not used here) excludes borrowings as well as subsidies and virtual income.

The Standard Analysis

Table 1 shows the standard analysis of Mexico's income tax as a share of net revenue. With borrowing excluded from the total central government income, income tax constitutes the single most important share of revenue. The share of tax on income apparently rose in dramatic fashion from about 9 percent under Cárdenas to about 38 percent under Echeverría and López Portillo. Such a view leads to the impression that Mexico has had a consistently increasing and important income tax base, especially since the 1960s. Because tax on income presumably falls on the middle sectors, implicitly, then it seems that the middle class has been either growing in size and economic strength, it has been effectively taxed, or a combination of these factors.

Revised Analysis

Table 1, however, also reveals that since the period of López Mateos it is borrowing that has become the most important source of central government revenue, rising dramatically from less than 5 percent under Cárdenas to nearly 40 percent under López Portillo. By taking into account borrowing, we can also see the revised long-term trend of Mexico's income-tax share (see Table 1 and Figure 1). The true share of tax on income is revealed to have gone from

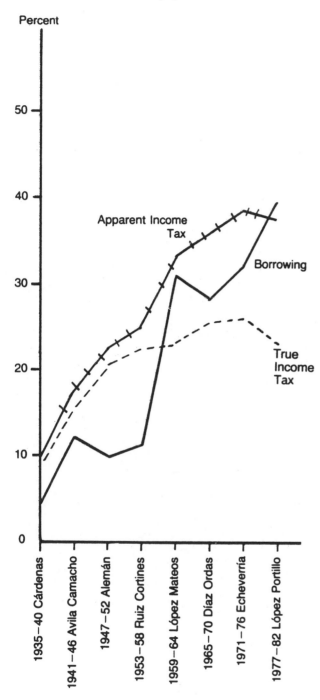

Figure 1
MEXICAN CENTRAL GOVERNMENT
REVENUE SHARES, 1935–82
(%)

SOURCE: Table 1.

9 percent under Cárdenas (the same as the unrevised figure) to only 26 percent or less since the late 1940s. (This true figure reached into the twentieth percentile under Alemán and subsequently has remained rather constant.) In the revised view, then, the midsector tax base has not grown, and if indeed income taxes fall disproportionately on that base, implicitly the importance of the middle class in financing the central government has declined when compared to the importance of domestic and foreign moneylenders. In any case, it is evident that borrowing became much more important than tax on income between 1959 and 1982.

Conclusion

I have shown here that if borrowing is omitted from analysis of central government income, we cannot comprehend the relative importance of income taxes over time, let alone the contribution of borrowing as a form of revenue. Unfortunately, the exclusion of borrowing in examining the case of Mexico has clouded interpretation by analysts inside and outside of Mexico.

Although Mexico's "debt crisis" after 1982 did not necessarily come as a surprise to a few observers who had cautioned, beginning in 1976, that Mexico was borrowing too much to be justified by the oil boom income, from data developed here, it can be seen that the caution came fifteen years too late. The real shift in revenue patterns came not during the period of López Portillo but 3 presidents earlier, under López Mateos. Prior to 1959, borrowing did not constitute on the average more than 12 percent of central government revenues. Under López Mateos it reached about 30 percent and remained there under 2 presidents who also helped to lay the basis for López Portillo's financial disaster of 1982. The López Portillo average was almost 40 percent.

Borrowing may be financially "cost free" except for interest payments, as some economists claim, but there are serious costs to planning if borrowing is not included in analysis: exclusion of borrowing, which is *a* (if not *the*) major source of revenue for most governments, distorts our views of revenue shares. Inclusion of borrowing in analysis is required if state planning is to be meaningful.

6

The Dramatic Growth of Mexico's Economy and the Rise of Statist Government Budgetary Power, 1910–82

JAMES W. WILKIE

Although most observers are aware that the petroleum boom of the middle and late 1970s caused a strong expansion in Mexico's gross domestic product (GDP) and that the nationalization of the banking system in 1982 by one leader of the Official Party of Permanent Revolution (now called "PRI") gave the state broad new power over the economy,[1] few analysts are aware of the magnitude of these actions and how they fit into the historical trajectory of government budgetary activity. It is my intention to suggest here that the rise in Mexico's GDP and statist government budgetary expenditure has been a long-term process that began in the 1920s, gained impetus in the period from 1934 to 1970, and came to fruition after 1970.

In the meantime, the official party, exercising power through the Mexican government since 1929, seemingly has come to believe that it has been responsible for the dramatic economic growth that has seen GDP increase more than fourteen times in the real terms developed in this study.[2] Ironically, the official party always takes credit for expansion of the economy but argues that it is not responsible for economic stagnation or decline.

My approach is to test across time the growth of GDP and budgetary power over national actions to change the government to statist operations wherein

AUTHOR'S NOTE: This essay was first published in *The Mexican Forum/El Foro Mexicano*, vol. 5, no. 4 (October 1985), pp. 33–41, and is reprinted with permission from the University of Texas at Austin.

[1] On the theory of permanent revolution under the official party (from 1929 to 1938 called the PNR, or Party of National Revolution, and from 1938 to 1945 called the PRM, or Party of the Mexican Revolution), see Wilkie (1976).

[2] "Real GDP" has been adjusted for inflation, with data here computed in standard pesos of 1950. The methodology needed to calculate data in real pesos involved the development of a composite price index from 1895 to 1982 (no single index being available for the entire period), and is explained in Wilkie (1985b).

the private sector plays an ever smaller role. What began with Mexico's Constitution of 1917 as a plan for intervention in the country's affairs by an active state has become since 1970 a policy of statism: the state sector, with its extensive attempts to "control" the economic and social life of Mexico, has become much more important than the private sector.

Mexico's GDP and State Policy

The total production of economic goods and services (GDP) in Mexico during the last sixteen years of the Porfirio Díaz regime (1895–1910) was quite low compared to Mexico's subsequent growth of GDP, especially beginning with the Cárdenas period up through 1952. Utilizing the index of real GDP developed in Table 1 and Figure 1, wherein data for the year 1950 equal 100, we can see that during the Díaz "glory years" the level of economic output only averaged 31.1, reflecting the small size of the country's economic wealth.

Growth of real GDP started slowly once the violent years from 1911 to 1920 passed. President Alvaro Obregón would initiate recovery and would watch real GDP rise to a score of 41.8 on the index in Table 1. Under presidents Plutarco Elías Calles and Emilio Portes Gil, the economy would make slight gains, to reach an average of about 45 on the index of real GDP. But gains to that level were offset by the World Depression of the 1930s, when presidents Pascual Ortiz Rubio and Abelardo Rodríguez presided during an economic situation that fell below the real GDP index's average level of even the Obregón years.

Impetus for the new growth of Mexico's economy came during the years from 1935 to 1952. Real GDP finally recovered during Lázaro Cárdenas's six-

Table 1
MEXICO'S REAL GDP, AVERAGE BY PRESIDENTIAL PERIOD,
1895–1982
(Pesos of 1970 and Index for 1950)

Year	Total		Per Capita		
	Pesos of 1970 (Million)	Index (1950 = 100)[a]	Pesos of 1970 GDP/C	Index (1950 = 100)[b]	President
1895–1910	38,845.3	31.1	2,763.8	60.6	Díaz
1911–1920[c]	—	—	—	—	—[d]
1921–1924	52,217.5	41.8	3,527.4	77.4	Obregón
1925–1928	57,326.5	45.9	3,633.8	79.7	Calles
1929	54,915.3	44.0	3,344.2	73.4	Portes Gil
1930–1932	49,966.3	40.0	2,944.1	65.0	Ortiz Rubio
1933–1934	52,058.1	41.7	2,935.3	64.4	Rodríguez
1935–1940	64,821.3	51.9	3,407.8	74.8	Cárdenas
1941–1946	87,769.5	70.3	3,992.8	87.6	Avila Camacho
1947–1952	120,592.4	96.6	4,543.6	99.7	Alemán
1953–1958	172,501.9	138.2	5,333.0	117.0	Ruiz Cortines
1959–1964	247,367.5	198.2	6,330.5	138.9	López Mateos
1965–1970	378,397.2	303.3	7,980.6	175.1	Díaz Ordaz
1971–1976	555,428.6	445.1	9,646.1	211.6	Echeverría
1977–1982	800,220.7	641.3	11,651.4	255.6	López Portillo

a. GDP Index of 100 for 1950 equals 124,779.4 million pesos of 1970.
b. GDP/C Index of 100 equals, 4,558 pesos of 1970.
c. No data for civil-war period.
d. Competing leaders, for whom no GDP data available.

SOURCE: Wilkie (1985*b*).

year presidency (*sexenio*), 1935–1940,[3] the index averaging 51.9, or 1.7 times the Díaz average. As evidence of Mexico's economic strength, it was under President Manuel Avila Camacho (1940–1946) that Mexico's real GDP grew to an average level of 70.3, or more than double the Díaz average. During the term of President Miguel Alemán (1946–1952) Mexico's real GDP reached 96.6, triple the Díaz average.

With such growth in real GDP, comparisons of the official party's performance to that of Díaz no longer seemed very interesting, and by the late 1960s the increases began to be measured by comparison to gains made under the various presidents who have led the official party's "permanent revolution." When Adolfo López Mateos left office in 1964, real GDP had more than doubled (the six-year average reaching 198.2 on the index) compared to the Alemán term that ended in 1952. The size of the economy would again more than double during the twelve years under presidents Gustavo Díaz Ordaz (1964–1970) and Luis Echeverría (1970–1976)—the latter's average reaching 445.1 on the index of real GDP. During the presidency of José López Portillo (1976–1982), Mexico's oil boom helped real GDP to increase an average index figure of 641.3 or 1.4 times the figure of his predecessor. If that López Portillo rate had continued

[3] Since Cárdenas, Mexican presidents have been inaugurated every six years on December 1—meaning that effectively the record of each presidency begins January 1 of the following year.

for the present term (1982–1988), by 1988 the two terms since 1976 would have seen the economy triple rather than double in size!

Because in 1982 the world economic recession hurt Mexico's oil exports and the price that Mexico could charge for its oil, and in this manner helped to cause the first decline in Mexico's real GDP since 1932, three important questions arise:

1. Should the Mexican government have realized that the country's economic growth was based on a fragile boom of oil?

2. To what extent is the Mexican government responsible for Mexico's economic change, either positively or negatively?

3. What would have happened to Mexico in the face of its population explosion had it not "enjoyed" the bonanza of an oil boom while it lasted?

Let us take up the last question first.

GDP Per Capita and Mexico's Oil Boom of the Late 1970s

If Mexico's population had not been increasing so rapidly between 1940 and 1980, the country's real GDP would have gone much farther on a per capita basis, as can be seen in Table 1 and Figure 1. Although the GDP is never divided equally among all the inhabitants of a country (be it communistic or

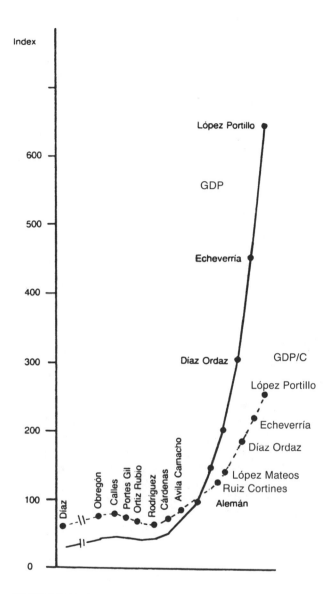

Figure 1
REAL GDP AND GDP/C IN MEXICO,
BY PRESIDENTIAL PERIOD, 1895–1982
(1950 = 100)

SOURCE: Table 1.

index of real GDP.[4] Contrariwise, under López Portillo (when the population had reached high levels) the real GDP index (641.3) was more than halved (real GDP/C index equals 255.6). Over time, the growth of Mexico's population has in effect "eaten up" the dramatic growth in the country's real GDP. If Mexico had begun to slow its population growth years earlier, it would be a much richer country today.

Although Figure 1 reveals starkly the growing disparity between real GDP and real GDP/C, nevertheless, it does show some marked gains. The per capita average under López Portillo was four times greater than under Díaz. The real GDP/C figure of 1929 had almost doubled by the time of López Mateos. The average almost doubled again between the term of López Mateos and that of López Portillo.

Given the population pressures on the Mexican system, which have generated a need to supply from five hundred thousand to one million new jobs each year, it is clear that had Mexico's economy not expanded as rapidly as it did, the crisis at present faced by Mexico would have been faced several decades earlier and at a time when the country did not have the edge in cheap energy that could fuel its industrial plant. Mexico has the gold (albeit black) necessary to finance industry capable of competing in the international market.

The first step in shifting Mexico from an industrial producer for the domestic market to one producing for the international sphere involves changing Mexico from the dollar to the peso standard, as I suggest elsewhere (1983). Given this need, the economic crisis since 1982 has been salubrious in that the Mexican government has been able to convince the Mexican middle class that the crisis is genuine and that it has been generated by the international economic recession.

That Mexico's middle class would have to accept the "belt-tightening" needed to solve the crisis since 1982 can be seen as necessary from the point of view of the PRI for at least two reasons:

A. The PRI's economic technicians had undervalued the peso in relation to the dollar for so long that after about 1975 the middle class became accustomed to being one of the richest middle classes in world history. Favored by raises in income that outpaced inflation, a significant sector of the middle class could afford to buy Mexican property and pay it off in three to five years rather than the twenty-five to thirty years of payment common in such countries

capitalistic), for the purposes of understanding how much economic output is available in relation to population, it is convenient to divide real GDP by the number of persons to obtain the real GDP per capita (GDP/C),

Once real GDP is converted to real GDP/C in Table 1, we can see important relationships. Under Díaz (when population was low) there was twice as much national economic wealth measurable on the

---

[4] Thus, for the period from 1895 to 1910, the economy (total GDP) registered 31.1 on the index wherein data for 1950 equal 100. Once we divide the 31.1 by the average population for those years, the per capita GDP (GDP/C) increases to 60.6 on the index, or almost double.

as the United States, where the middle class is strong in number. Too, the Mexican middle class had become accustomed to traveling abroad for vacation as well as for purchase of goods at the expense of Mexican industry.

B. If the PRI had tried to value the dollar correctly without the rationale of crisis, the middle class would have rebelled against further PRI rule. The fact that to date Mexico has remained relatively peaceful in spite of the economic stagnation since 1982 shows the extent to which the Mexican population does not blame the government (read PRI) for Mexico's current difficulties.

The problem is that if the Mexican government tightens its belt too severely, Mexico's populace will not have the funds necessary to help Mexico's industry sell domestically and thereby provide the national base needed for expansion into international markets. Concomitantly, industrial problems will slow the transition of lower-class persons into middle-class participants in the national economic life of Mexico, and the rise of the middle class has been an important factor in Mexico's economic growth.[5]

The complexity behind economic growth and GDP/C leads us to the second question raised earlier about the extent to which the government is responsible for economic change in Mexico.

Measuring National Government Expenditure "Power"

Because we are here interested in expenditure power of the government in relation to Mexico's GDP, we need to know the total amount of government funds spent (including transfer payments and debt rescheduling over which the government makes decisions). To overcome standard economic theory for developed areas, which omits amortization of the debt from analysis, amortization must be included because, as the debt rises, payments on amortization (as well as payments of interest) distort the national budgetary priorities—factors now finally understood as important even for the United States.[6]

In reality Mexico does not have one national government, but two, so we need to know not only the sum but the relative power of each. One, the central government sector, deals with the traditional functions of administering national legislative, judicial, and executive affairs, including defense, police, mails, and transportation. The other national government, the decentralized (or parastate) sector of state enterprises, involves administering (1) the activities of nationalized companies such as PEMEX (the National Oil Company) and Ferrocarriles Nacionales (the National Railway System), often formerly owned by foreign interests; (2) companies owned wholly or jointly with minority private shareholders (such as Ferrocarril Chihuahua al Pacífico, S.A. de C.V.); (3) the national trust funds such as IMSS, the Mexican Social Security Institute; (4) trust funds administered jointly with state and local governments (such as the Junta Federal de Mejoras Materiales de Acapulco); (5) other autonomous activities, such as funding programs to stimulate agriculture (e.g., Fideicomiso Relativo a las Siembras de Maíz, Frijol y Cacahuate) and export development (e.g., Impulsora de Empresas Turísticas, S.A. de C.V.). In effect the decentralized government reaches into every corner of the country and into places the central government does not touch.

When constituents in Mexico seek redress from the government, they must turn to the decentralized sector rather than to their congressional representatives because the Mexican Congress is really "selected" by the president of the country. Selection is made according to "occupational" origins and secret political machinations between wings of the official party rather than members being elected to represent states (as ostensibly is the case).[7] Congressmen do not represent their "home districts" but represent their party and the PRI members rubber-stamp the president's plans.[8]

---

[5] On the rise of the middle class and methodology for measuring the size of classes in Mexico according to occupation and income, see Wilkie and Wilkins (1981).

[6] The majority of Mexican government presentations include amortization of the debt. One wonders if the standard analysis as developed, for example, in the United States is not intended to protect both major political parties and their "academic" advisers by hiding the fact that huge amounts of income are beyond the discretionary power of the president to spend because the amounts go to cover amortization of the debt—if amortization were included in the U.S. budgetary analysis, the public would soon become aware of how small are the percentages of outlay really spent on present national social and economic needs.

Certainly the U.S. budgetary picture is almost impossible to penetrate even for experts; and from my analysis of the way assistance has been budgeted in Bolivia by the U.S. Agency for International Development, I can say with understatement that the Latin American budgets are paragons of clarity in comparison to the U.S. approach.

For a further discussion of why borrowing should be included in analysis of public financial matters, see Wilkie (1985a).

[7] The corporatist nature of the official party has included representation in Congress from the following groups: the labor sector, the peasant sector, the popular sector (bureaucrats, unaffiliated persons, etc.), and until 1940 the military sector (which since then is divided into individuals who can join the popular sector). (Priests are precluded, in theory, from participation in politics.)

[8] Since the electoral reform of 1963, the PRI has permitted an increasing number of opposition-party representatives to join the Chamber of Deputies but not the Senate. Such representatives do not win in any district; rather, their party wins enough votes nationwide so that the party's top vote getters win a position in the

Table 2
GROSS INCOME IN MEXICO:
CENTRAL, STATE, AND LOCAL GOVERNMENT
SHARES IN SELECTED YEARS

Year	Total Pesos per Capita of 1950	Percent			
		Total	Central	State[a]	Municipio[a]
1900	63	100.0	63.0	24.1	12.9
1923	84	100.0	72.6	14.5	12.9
1929	101	100.0	71.1	21.2	7.7
1932	86	100.0	64.0	27.1	8.9
1940	122	100.0	71.4	23.3	5.3
1950	180	100.0	78.3	18.4	3.3
1960	369	100.0	71.1	26.3	2.6
1970	480	100.0	72.6	24.4	3.0
1976	945	100.0	77.5	20.5	2.0
1981	1,546	100.0	76.7	21.3	2.0

a. Includes subsidies from the central government.

SOURCE: Wilkie (1985*b*).

Likewise, when constituents seek assistance from the government, generally it does little good to apply to the central government's representatives (who are located throughout the republic to enforce regulations) and it is necessary to turn to the decentralized agencies, which have competing networks throughout the country and often compete for "clients." Those citizens who become clients of the decentralized government often have a way to resolve problems without going through traditional, central government—for example, a client who wishes to resolve a matter or even to borrow funds may apply to the regional offices of competing agencies, each of which may respond favorably.

Beyond the national government there are state and *municipio* (county) governments in Mexico, but most are so poverty stricken that they are unimportant in the scheme of governance. The relative state and local power is revealed in Table 2, which shows that the *municipios* have declined in the share of gross income received by the central, state, and *municipio* sectors. In 1900 and 1923 the *municipios* received about 13 percent of the combined gross income. This figure declined to less than 10 percent by the late 1920s and to less than 4 percent by the 1950s. It is now about 2 percent, but the De la Madrid administration has promised since 1983 to raise the *municipios'* share.

If the *municipios* have declined in power, the state governments have usually received an average of 22 percent of gross income for the 10 years sampled in Table 2. State shares have ranged from a low of 14.5 percent in 1923 to a high of 27.1 in 1932. Much of the state's income is derived from federal subsidies, further weakening Mexico's historical goal of assuring that regions have some autonomy.

With no real tax base of their own, the states, and to an even greater extent the *municipios*, have no way to be autonomous, and they must look to the central or decentralized governments for assistance, hence the need to measure the power of both of the national governments.

To relate actual gross expenditures to GDP, data are presented in Table 3 for the centralized sector by period since 1900 and in Table 4 for the decentralized sector since 1940, when data are available. (Data in Table 4 are incomplete for all years prior to implementation of budgetary reform to audit and compile analysis on the parastate sector beginning in 1965 and subsequently are increasingly complete for the number of decentralized agencies and trust funds audited as more have been brought under direct budgetary control over time.) The trends in both tables are compared in Figure 2. As given here, central government and parastate expenditures include transfer payments, especially central government subsidies to the emerging decentralized government sector and decentralized sector subsidies to the private sector.[9]

Central government expenditures were low in the time of Díaz but then grew steadily as a share of GDP. Whereas the Díaz figure averaged only 3.9 percent, beginning with Obregón's average of 5.0 percent the growth in share of GDP has been uninterrupted except for the small downturn during the World Depression when Ortiz Rubio was in office. For each *sexenio*, the share usually added about 1.0 percent between presidents Rodríguez and Díaz Ordaz—except for Alemán, under whom the increase was only .6 percent. It was under Echeverría that the average leaped to 15.9 percent and then accelerated at a dizzying pace to reach 26.9 under López Portillo. In 1981 the percent reached a high of 42.7!

When the central and parastatte average expenditures are consolidated by adding them together, as in Figure 2, the result is revealing. Consolidated figures show that under López Mateos the two sectors stood at about 24 percent in relation to GDP. By the

Chamber of Deputies. This system further weakens the concept that congressmen in Mexico are in any way beholden to the electorate in a particular region, and it means that the PRI permits opposition without losing many district seats. On these points, see Wilkie (1978).

[9] For an analyst of the "standard" school who disagrees with my methodology of examining expenditures, see Arthur Mann (1979). Mann argues (with no explicit theoretical basis) that net rather than gross figures should be used and he deducts for transfers as well as amortization of the debt. My implicit response is in Wilkie (1985*a*).

Table 3
CENTRAL GOVERNMENT ACTUAL GROSS
EXPENDITURE AS SHARE OF GDP, BY PRESIDENT

Year	President	Percent[1]
1900–1911[a]	Díaz	3.9
1912–1920	Era of Turmoil	_ [b]
1921–1924	Obregón	5.0
1925–1928	Calles	5.9
1929	Portes Gil	5.7
1930–1932	Ortiz Rubio	6.0
1933–1934	Rodríguez	6.5
1935–1940	Cárdenas	7.4
1941–1946	Avila Camacho	8.3
1947–1952	Alemán	8.9
1953–1958	Ruiz Cortines	9.9
1959–1964	López Mateos	11.1
1965–1970	Díaz Ordaz	12.2
1971–1976	Echeverría	15.9
1976–1982	López Portillo	26.5[c]

1. Average.
a. 1900–1901 and 1910–1911.
b. No data for expenditure or GDP or both.
c. In 1981, the share reached 42.7 percent.

SOURCE: Wilkie (1985*b*).

Table 4
PARASTATE ACTUAL GROSS EXPENDITURE
AS SHARE OF GDP, BY PRESIDENT

Years	President	Percent
1940[a]	Cárdenas	7.2
1946[a]	Avila Camacho	4.7
1952[a]	Alemán	6.0
1958[a]	Ruiz Cortines	7.6
1965–1970[b]	Díaz Ordaz	11.7[d]
1971–1976[b]	Echeverría	15.4[d]
1977–1982[b,c]	López Portillo	21.4[d]

a. Data available only for one year and may be in net terms that exclude dozens of agencies or trust funds.
b. Data have been increasing in coverage since the budgetary reform of 1965 began to bring the decentralized sector under direct central government control—control that is by no means complete by the mid-1980s.
c. Data for 1982 do not include the nationalized banking sector, which has not yet been brought under budgetary control.
d. Six-year average.

SOURCE: Wilkie (1985*b*).

sexenio of Echeverría, they reached over 31 percent. Under López Portillo the average reached 48 percent in relation to GDP.

Over time, then, through increasingly statist philosophy reflected in budgetary power, the stage had been set to justify the idea that the state could solve all of Mexico's problems. Exponents of this theory, such as Carlos Tello Macías (1979 and 1984; also see Ramírez 1985), could argue implicitly that, if the state had failed in implementing any of its policies of expanded state power, those failures came from the fact that the state did not yet have *enough* power. Ironi-

cally, these exponents ignored the fact that failures in policy might have to do with the state's having too much power already.

The appropriate end of state policy, Tello had long suggested, is control of the private banking network in order to coordinate that aspect of the Mexican financial system with state planning over the central and parastate budgetary systems (including publicly owned banks). Thus, on September 1, 1982, Tello and others convined President López Portillo to nationalize the private banking system and to incorporate it into the parastate sector of government.

This nationalization of Mexico's private banks in 1982, of course, involved the expropriation of investments owned by those fifty-three banks, and in this manner the government saw its statist activity expanded greatly. Although exact figures are difficult to know,[10] it is possible to estimate tentatively the extent of state gains through the nationalization process.

If the assets managed by the entire banking system (both private and public) amounted to 36.7 percent of GDP,[11] and if the state acquired control over 55.6 percent of that system,[12] then with one stroke of López Portillo's pen he created for the state a "new financial sector" to control wealth equal to 20.4 percent of GDP.

Taking into account the statist roles of the centralized sector, the decentralized sector and the new financial sector, the Mexican government found itself increasingly powerful. Huge amounts of funds were being controlled by each government sector and many policymakers therein came to believe that they had real authority (including the authority to decide upon the amount of transfers to which sector)—certainly they had more faith in their own power than they could possibly exercise meaningfully.

When President De la Madrid took office in December 1982, however, he worked out a plan to reduce state control over the new financial sector (which eventually is to be incorporated into the decentralized sector of government). In 1984, the government offered for sale 34 percent of the banking shares and 339 of the 467 nonbanking companies (thus retaining under government control 34 percent of the banking system and 128 expropriated companies related to banking and credit services).[13] The

[10] Not only has the government released sparse data in order to avoid political problems on the extreme left and the right, but valuation differs according to methodology and accounting adjustments.
[11] The assets share of GDP is calculated from Mexico, INEGI (1984:15, 141).
[12] Murphy (1985:17). López Portillo had exempted two private banks from the 1982 nationalization: the Banco Obrero and the Mexican branch of City Bank.
[13] Murphy (1985:17).

Figure 2
CENTRAL AND PARASTATE "POWER" IN MEXICO:
AVERAGE REAL GROSS EXPENDITURE AS SHARE OF GDP
(%)

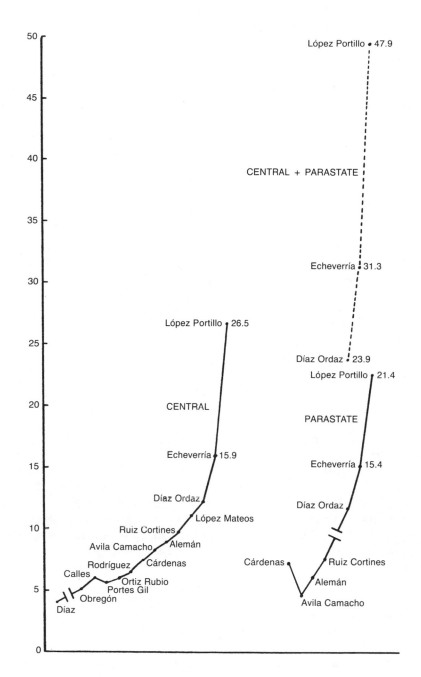

SOURCE: Tables 3 and 4.

value of assets retained by the Mexican government, then, perhaps exceeds an amount equal to 10 percent of GDP.

When we combine the Mexican government's budgetary power with its control of banking and take into account its ever increasing regulatory power, it is clear that Mexican government leaders have enormous power over the GDP. Whether or not the actual impact of the government funds discussed is lower after deduction for transfers or amortization of the debt,[14] and whether or not the government is actually able to fully coordinate its new banking sector, the image of power has increased for the Mexican government and that very image will slow private reinvestment and foreign investment, which Mexico must have to forge to higher levels of GDP and GDP/C.

In spite of such a bleak picture of a long period of slow growth (portrayed even by the Mexican government), there are some important qualifications:

A. The present world oil "glut" may once again turn into a shortage if one of the major OPEC countries (such as Iran or Iraq, which are at war since 1980) should be taken out of the world production picture.

B. In any case, as the world depression of the early and mid-1980s passes and the industrial world regains its level of activity, Mexico's oil will stand it in good stead on the export market, meanwhile also fueling the country's possibility to develop a price-competitive international industry for export.

C. Beyond oil and beyond the new financial sector, Mexico's government is not monolithic, and competition between the central and parastate sectors may help to resolve the lack of private confidence in Mexico's "government activity." In reality, the parastate sector has a direct interest in the economic well-being of its clients as does the central government, which only appears to be more interested in itself.

If the Mexican system that emerged with the Constitution of 1917 created an implicit pact between the private and government sectors because it allowed for both, the pact has been threatened by the steady growth of state activity, which seems to have reached the point beyond which, since 1970, statism is assured.

Yet the meaning of statism is itself complex and does not necessarily foreclose a major role for the private sector. On the one hand, the nationalization of the private banks has seemed to many observers to mark a breakdown of the implicit pact that dates from 1917 (see Newell and Rubio 1984). On the other hand, in my view the bank nationalization probably "saved" Mexican capitalism from complete liquidation—most of Mexico's capitalists simply could not make payments (of interest or principal) on the large foreign debts they had assumed.

If López Portillo had great faith in the idea of government planning (stimulated no doubt by his private desire to save his public image, which had collapsed along with the peso in early 1982), De la Madrid (the chief planner for López Portillo) seems to have realized that the government cannot plan the future so much as try to coordinate the present. Whereas under López Portillo the state plan was developed in such detail and in so many volumes that it could not be understood let alone implemented, under De la Madrid at least it has become much shorter and easier to comprehend.

In recognizing some of the limits of state power and operating in a time of little or no economic growth for Mexico, De la Madrid has moved to restore confidence in the pact between the private and state sectors by, for example, restructuring the new banking system. Although it is doubtful that the country needed all of the fifty-three banks that it had before the nationalization, it is doubtful that the structure as set forth in 1985 can provide the diversity to solve the country's peculiar regional problems. Mexico now has six national banks (with 77.4 percent of total bank capital), thirteen multiregional banks (with 13.7 percent), and ten regional banks (with 8.9 percent).[15]

Personally I can attest to the extreme shortage of pesos allocated to Chiapas, where in the summer of 1984 the local banks of San Cristóbal de las Casas frequently went without currency with which to keep the regional economy functioning on a day-to-day basis. Such a liquidity problem was an unanticipated consequence of bank nationalization—Mexico City's bureaucrats do not and cannot keep up with the changing needs of a Mexico that is famous for its hundreds of unique regions.

Beyond the problems of a government under which the sectors are too complicated to be planned in a unified way (as Tello thought possible), the first question raised at the outset of this study remains to be answered: should the Mexican government have realized that the economic growth of the late 1970s was based upon a fragile oil boom? In light of the interpretation developed in this study, this often-asked question needs to be rephrased. The issue really has been as follows: how can Mexico keep its GDP ahead

---

[14] In their tables on the Mexican budget, Roberto Newell G. and Luis Rubio F. (1984) follow my nonstandard budgetary analysis, which includes amortization. Yet in a personal letter from Newell (July 11, 1985), he accepts standard budgetary analysis of revenues, which excludes borrowings (whereas I do not—see note 9). In my view, Newell's approach to revenue and budgets is inconsistent.

[15] *El Financiero* (1985:4).

of population growth unless it takes every possible avenue to expand its economic base quickly? To put the matter in another way: have not oil exports provided the needed impetus to achieve a stronger GDP and GDP/C that (even with some subsequent stagnation in growth) has forever moved Mexico to a much higher economic base?

Some arguments against Mexico's oil-boom economic growth are naive. The view often advanced that Mexico could have expanded more judiciously (by not overheating its economy with too fast a spurt in growth) overlooks an important fact: Mexico had to get as much foreign capital as it could before the tide of funds to Latin America would again be shifted away by the fickle managers of international funds.

Critics who argue that Mexico will be financially strapped for years to pay off its foreign debt forget an important fact: countries do not pay off debts—they refinance them and in the meantime pay as little interest over as long a time as possible. Mexico must continually renegotiate better terms as other "models" (such as Alan Garcia's Peru of 1985) change the "rules of the game" and make possible new negotiation.

The view that the oil boom has distorted the "real" Mexico (as argued by such an important observer as Alan Riding in his dispatches of the middle and late 1970s to the *New York Times*) assumes wrongly that there is only one reality (and a permanent one). Riding especially misled his readers by arguing that the oil boom would only result in more corruption for Mexico—in fact, a huge new infrastructure was put in place (if at a high cost).

The idea that Mexico lives with a dilemma has finally worn out—all countries live with many dilemmas. The point about the image of Mexico's worn-out "dilemma" is worth comment. Taking a cue from Vernon (1963), who wrote about the dilemma of Mexico's development and the decreasing lack of policy space enjoyed by the Mexican president, Newell and Rubio (1984:4) conclude two decades later that

Mexico's continued stability [since the consensus of the Constitution of 1917] has been a direct function of the government's ability up through the 1970s to organize changing alliances and institutions that could sustain and develop that original consensus. However, as Mexico grew ever more complex as a society, the disparities between its "political relevant forces" grew wider, making it impossible for the contradictory and ambiguous consensus to serve as a viable source of legitimacy for the 1980s. Mexico of 1983 bears no resemblance to Mexico of 1917. Therefore, it requires a new political arrangement to reestablish a viable consensus for its future.

On its face this old view is well stated, but it ignores the power of the Mexican president to coopt new political forces and the complexity of Mexican history —the consensus for an official party was not won until 1929 and had to be revised in 1938 and 1946. I have argued tongue-in-cheek that a new consensus might be won not around Madero-like calls for democracy-as-solution but around an expanded and revised official party (1976), which might well be called the Partido Revolucionario de la Crisis Permanente (PRCP—a wonderfully unpronounceable acronym). The official party uses a series of new "crises" to justify its continued rule.

The long-term crisis facing Mexico is the extent to which the private sector is willing to work under a statist-oriented official party. When the private sector in Mexico loses its confidence in the system, it does not put its money in the banks (be they public or private); it changes the money into dollars. Mexico's bureaucracy could nationalize everything, but given its "track record" at managing the economy, such a "solution" hardly makes any sense, even if it were conceivable that the United States would permit such a solution on its "soft underbelly."

Conclusion

With regard to measuring Mexico's governmental budgetary power, I have attempted to show the extent to which it has become increasingly statist in relation to GDP and GDP/C since 1910. I have not only tried to show where other analysts agree or disagree with my methodology, which itself is subject to ongoing refinement, but also I have discussed limitations in my approach. On the one hand, expenditure data on parastate agencies are incomplete; on the other hand, there is a double-counting of transfer payments between the two sectors, and bank data are not fully comparable. Nevertheless, both sectors are made more powerful because they each have options over how expenditures are to be made and each has grown tremendously in importance when related to GDP. Transfers may be deducted and amortization omitted by some analysts, and if done consistently, that may be a useful methodology of their limited purposes, none of which are mine.

By the *sexenio* of López Portillo, the budgetary power of Mexico's centralized sector had reached an average of about 26 percent of GDP (compared to Díaz's 3.9 percent, with López Portillo's decentralized sector reaching about 23 percent).

With regard to the nationalization of Mexico's private banking system, which has added a dimension beyond budgetary power, when the final value of bank assets retained by the government is seen as equaling about 10 percent of GDP (according to the crude estimate developed here), then it is clear that statist power has gone well beyond 50 percent of GDP. This statement would still be "true" even if transfers and amortization of the debt were to be deducted and bank data were used that are more comparable.

With regard to interpretation, I have sought to suggest some of the complexities in understanding what the data mean. To my way of thinking, most existing interpretations about Mexico are too simple, as in the case of the nationalization of the private banks. The bank expropriation process can be seen both as an attack on the private sector and as a way of saving it from liquidation—through the banks the state has assumed the obligation to pay the loans of the private sector that could not otherwise have been paid. In other words, not only were the private banks nationalized, the private debt was nationalized.

Mexico is now much "richer" in terms of GDP than it has ever been in its national history, and it would be richer in per capita terms if the population had not grown so rapidly that the state was forced in the late 1970s to take a euphoric view on the prospects for world oil prices. If oil had gone from over thirty dollars per barrel to over fifty dollars, instead of falling toward twenty dollars, or if the Iraq-Iran War had taken either one or both countries out of the world oil market by 1982, then the joint optimism of the Mexican state *and* the world's bankers would have continued to coincide—as it yet may coincide again.

BIBLIOGRAPHY

El Financiero
   1985   "Informe financiero trimestral: enero, febrero-marzo." México, D.F., July 12.
Mann, Arthur
   1979   "The Evolution of Mexico's Public Revenue Structure, 1877–1977." *Bulletin for International Documentation* 33(11):515–522.
Mexico, INEGI (Instituto Nacional de Estadística, Geografía e Informática)
   1984   *El sistema bancario y financiero en México, 1970–*

1982. México, D.F.: Secretaría de Programación y Presupuesto.
Murphy, Ewell E., Jr.
   1985   "The Mexican Expropriation in Retrospect." *The Mexican Forum* 5(3):15–19.
Newell G., Roberto, and Luis Rubio F.
   1984   *Mexico's Dilemma: The Political Origins of Economic Crisis.* Boulder, Colo.: Westview Press.
Ramírez, Carlos
   1982   "Tello Macías, avance desde la nacionalización; Silva Herzog, marcha atrás"; and "Hasta el día primero el Banco de México había sido arrebatado al gobierno." *Proceso,* September 13, pp. 6–13.
Tello [Macías], Carlos
   1979   *La política económica en México.* México, D.F.: Siglo XXI.
   1984   *La nacionalización de la banca en México.* México, D.F.: Siglo XXI.
Vernon, Raymond
   1963   *The Dilemma of Mexico's Development: The Roles of the Private and Public Sectors.* Cambridge: Harvard University Press.
Wilkie, James W.
   1976   "Mexico: Permanent 'Revolution,' Permanent 'Crisis,'" *Los Angeles Times,* December 5, pp. viii–17.
   1978   *La revolución mexicana (1910–1976).* México, D.F.: Fondo de Cultura Económica.
   1983   "Mexico's 'New' Financial Crisis of 1982 in Historical Perspective." In Wilkie and Stephen Haber, *Statistical Abstract of Latin America,* vol. 22. Los Angeles: UCLA Latin American Center Publications. Pp. vii–xxviii.
   1985a "Borrowing as Revenue: The Case of Mexico, 1935–1982." *The Mexican Forum* 5(2):3–7.
   1985b "Changes in Mexico since 1895: Central Government Revenue, Public Sector Expenditure, and National Economic Growth." In Wilkie and Adam Perkal, eds., *Statistical Abstract of Latin America,* vol. 24. Los Angeles: UCLA Latin American Center Publications. Chap. 34.
Wilkie, James W., and Paul Wilkens
   1981   "Quantifying the Class Structure of Mexico, 1895–1970." In Wilkie and Stephen Haber, *Statistical Abstract of Latin America,* vol. 21. Los Angeles: UCLA Latin American Center Publications. Chap. 36.

Contributors

Jeffrey Bortz teaches Latin American history at Appalachian State University. He lived in Mexico City for eleven years, where he published *La estructura de los salarios en México* (UAM, 1985), *El salario en México* (El Caballito, 1986), and *Los salarios industriales en la Ciudad de México* (Fondo de Cultura Económica, 1988). He is currently writing a book on industry and labor in postwar Mexico.

Stephanie Granato graduated from UCLA in 1986 with a B.A. in economics and was elected to Phi Beta Kappa. In 1987 she received her M.A. in economics from the London School of Economics. She has also studied at Cambridge University and the Monterey Institute in Monterey, California, and plans to enter law school.

David Lorey is Research Coordinator for the Program on Mexico in the UCLA Latin American Center. He wrote his doctoral dissertation at UCLA on the social economy of the university in Mexico since 1929. He has taught at UCLA and Pomona College in the United States and at the Universidad de las Américas in Mexico. Lorey is editor of *United States–Mexico Border Statistics since 1900*.

Aída Mostkoff, from Mexico, received her B.A., M.A., and C.Phil. degrees in history from UCLA, where she is continuing her studies in the Ph.D. program, specializing in Mexican social and economic history.

Enrique C. Ochoa is a doctoral student in the department of history at UCLA. He has been co-editor of the *Statistical Abstract of Latin America* for three years and has contributed articles on Latin American political and economic history. His doctoral dissertation is titled "Food and Social Welfare in Mexico since the 1930s: CONASUPO and State Policy."

James W. Wilkie is Professor of History at the University of California, Los Angeles. In addition to developing quantitative research on Latin America, he has developed research on the lore of the elite. His book *Elitelore* was published in 1973 and subsequently he has published in the *Journal of Latin America Lore* six articles on this new area of inquiry. Much of the elitelore theory stems from his oral history interviews with Mexican leaders, interviews published in James W. Wilkie y Edna Monzón de Wilkie, *México Visto en el Siglo XX; Entrevistas de Historia Oral: Ramón Beteta, Marte R. Gómez, Manuel Gómez Morín, Vicente Lombardo Toledano, Miguel Palomar y Vizcarra, Emilio Portes Gil, Jesús Silva Herzog* (México, D.F.: Distribuido por el Instituto de Investigaciones Económicas, 1969).

Since 1983 Wilkie has been President of PROF-MEX—The Consortium of U.S. Research Programs for Mexico, the nationwide organization conducting research on Mexican affairs. He was the founding Universitywide Coordinator (1981–83) of the University of California Consortium on Mexico and the United States (UC MEXUS), which represents the nine UC campuses in their focus on Mexico. At UCLA he is Chair of the U.S.-Mexican Social and Economic Relations Project in the Program on Mexico; and he is Coordinator of the Office of Sociopolitical and Economic Studies in the Latin American Center.